LIFELINES

INTERMEDIATE

STUDENT'S BOOK

TOM HUTCHINSON

OXFORD UNIVERSITY PRESS

Contents

Contents

Starting out

Grammar
Introductions; revision

1 Look at the photograph. Who do you think the people are?

2 🔲 *0.1* **Listen and answer the questions.**
1 What are the people going to do?
2 How long will it take?
3 Which of the people do you hear?
4 Who's Bessie?

3 **You heard some of the people introduce themselves.**

a Complete the table.

Name	Nationality	Occupation
1 *Marie Gregg*	*British*	*Expedition guide*
2		
3		
4		
5		

b 🔲 *0.1* Listen again and check your answers.

c What other information does each person give?

d How would you introduce yourself to the group?

4 **Here are some questions for finding out more information about someone.**

a Complete the questions. Can you add any more?
Have you ever … ?
Do you … ?
How long … ?
Who … ?
Did you … ?
Where … ?
What kind of … ?
How many … ?
Have you got … ?
Can you … ?
Why … ?
What are your … ?
Would you … ?

b Work with a partner. Ask and answer the questions.

c Tell your group or the class something you have found out about your partner.

5 **Bill is applying to join the expedition.**

a Complete his letter to Marie with these words.

repairing	while	introduce	at	of	join	for
forward	never	sincerely	sounds	well	from	
people	driving	hope	exams	trip	old	ago
speak	studying	don't	the (x2)	months	several	

5 Sandy Lane
London
SW12 4YJ
17 May

Marie Gregg
Thrillseekers Tours
67 Bromley Way
Oxford
OX3 6TY

Dear Marie
First let me _____ myself. My name's Bill Reynolds and I'm _____ London. I'm 21 years _____ and at the moment I'm still _____ university. I'm _____ Modern Languages. I'm taking my final _____ next month. After that I'll have a few _____ free, so I'm going to look _____ a job to earn a bit of money.

I saw your advertisement in a magazine _____ I was waiting for a dental appointment. The expedition _____ very exciting and I'd really like to _____ the group. I love travelling and I've been to _____ countries in Europe and to _____ United States, too, but I've _____ been to Africa before.

If I was accepted to go on the _____ I'm sure I would be a useful member _____ the group. I can _____ three languages – English, French, and Spanish – and I like meeting other _____. I can cook quite _____ and I can play _____ guitar, too. I passed my _____ test a couple of years _____, but I'm afraid I _____ know very much about cars, so I wouldn't be much help with _____ the car if it broke down.

I _____ you will consider me for a place on the tour and I look _____ to hearing from you.

Yours _____

Bill Reynolds

b Can you find examples of these grammar points in Bill's letter?
- the present simple tense
- the present continuous tense
- the past simple tense
- the past continuous tense
- the present perfect tense
- the past perfect tense
- two negative forms
- three ways of expressing the future
- a passive
- a second conditional sentence

c One of the items in **b** isn't in the letter. Which one?

6 **Write your own letter to apply for the expedition. Your letter should include**
- some facts about you.
- your reasons for wanting to go on the expedition.
- your skills and abilities.

7 **Think about your English learning.**

Answer these questions.
1 How long have you been studying English?
2 Why are you taking this course?
3 What things help you to learn best? Look through the book and find examples of things that you think will be useful for you.
4 What aspects of learning don't you like? Why not?
5 Which of these things do you have? When do you use them and what for?
- an English–English dictionary
- an English–mother-tongue dictionary
- a grammar reference book
- a vocabulary notebook
- a workbook
- a cassette recorder

8 **Look through *Lifelines*.**

a What sections does each unit contain?

b Where will you find
- the contents?
- the Grammar Reference?
- the IPA chart?
- the tapescripts?

Good luck with your new English course!

1 Modern life

Grammar
Talking about the present

Grammar in use

1 Look at the story and answer the questions.
  1 What is happening in each picture?
  2 What things help to create Richard's problem?

2 Have you ever had days like this? Tell your partner or the class.

Richard's bad day

Richard is going to a meeting with Mr Patel, a new customer. Richard has worked hard to get him and doesn't want to lose him. As Richard is leaving the office, the telephone rings.

Rules

1 In the story there are three tenses for talking about the present.

a What are they and how are they formed?

b When do we use each tense? Write the names of the tenses in the table.

Tense	Use
1 _____	regular actions or events general truths
2 _____	things that are happening now unfinished actions or events
3 _____	an action in a time frame that comes up to the present an action that has an effect in the present

c Find examples of each use in the story.

8

2 **Some verbs are not normally used in the continuous form. We call these stative verbs.**

a Complete these sentences from the story.
Mr Patel _____ for you. … and he _____ very pleased.

b Both sentences are talking about what is happening now. What tense would you expect for this use? What tense is the verb *seem* in?

c Find more verbs like this in the story.

➤ Check the rules for the present tenses, stative verbs, and the present perfect tense in **Grammar References 1.1**, **1.2**, **1.3**, and **1.4**.

Practice

1 **Look at the article.**

a Choose the best present tense to complete the text.

Witnessing the event

We all *know / are knowing* the feeling. Something *happens / is happening* to you and then you *don't stop / aren't stopping* thinking about it for the rest of the day. You *lose / are losing* hours of mental time as a result. Next time, try this. It's called 'witnessing the event'. For example, you *wait / are waiting* at some traffic lights and another vehicle *runs / is running* into the back of your car. You start to feel angry.
Stop these thoughts by pretending that you are a witness and you *watch / are watching* the event. Describe your actions like this. 'I am switching off the engine. I *undo / am undoing* my seatbelt. I *get / am getting* out of the car. The other driver *comes / is coming* towards me. I *think / am thinking* he *wants / is wanting* to apologize. Some people *watch / are watching* us.'
Witnessing *takes / is taking* your mind off your feelings. As a result, you *stay / are staying* calm and you *deal / are dealing* with the problem. Then you *forget / are forgetting* about it.

b What do you think of 'witnessing the event'? In what situations could you use it?

2 **Imagine one of these events.**

a Work with a partner. Describe your actions.
1 You lock your keys in your car. Your spare keys are at home.
2 You can't get to sleep because your neighbours are making a lot of noise.
3 You are at a foreign airport. Your luggage doesn't arrive.
4 You miss your train. You will be late for an important meeting.

b Think of an annoying or stressful event that happened to you. Imagine you are in the situation again. Witness the event.

3 **Complete the text.**

a Put the verbs into the present simple, present continuous, or present perfect tense.

The story of Richard's day _____ (show) the stress of modern life, but Richard could do a lot to help himself. In the first picture he _____ (get) ready to go and see Mr Patel. He _____ (have) a busy day so far. He _____ (be) to three meetings and he _____ (make) several phone calls. He _____ (hurry), because he _____ (not want) to be late and he only _____ (have) half an hour to get there. Then, just as he _____ (leave) the office, the Managing Director _____ (call). What _____ Richard _____ (do)? He _____ (take) the call and then he _____ (blame) the Managing Director because he's late. But it isn't the Managing Director's fault. She _____ (not know) that Richard _____ (go) to an important appointment, so she probably _____ (think) that it's a convenient time to talk. Richard's stress comes from the fact that he _____ (not give) himself enough time for the journey. Then, while he _____ (drive) to his appointment, he _____ (become) more and more stressed. He's late and Mr Patel is already waiting. Then an accident _____ (happen), because Richard _____ (not concentrate) on the road.

b 🔊 *1.1* Listen and check your ideas.

4 **Have you done any of these things recently?**
- lost something
- met someone interesting
- missed an appointment
- been to the dentist
- heard some good news
- had a strange dream
- seen a good film
- booked a holiday
- read an interesting book

a Write your answers.

b Talk to other students. Try and find someone who has done each thing.

EXAMPLE
A Have you lost anything recently?
B Yes, I have./No, I haven't.

Vocabulary
Using a dictionary

1 Discuss these questions.
1 What dictionary do you use?
2 What do you use it for?
3 What kind of information does a dictionary give?

2 Look at the dictionary extract and answer these questions.

> ☆**clerk** /klɑːk; US klɜːrk/ noun [C] **1** a person whose job is to do written work or look after records or accounts in an office, bank, court of law, etc **2** (also **sales clerk**) (US) = SHOP ASSISTANT
> ☆**clever** /'klevə(r)/ adj **1** able to learn, understand or do sth quickly and easily; intelligent: a clever student ○ How clever of you to mend my watch! ○ She's so clever with her hands – she makes all her own clothes. **2** (used about things, ideas, etc) showing skill or intelligence: a clever device ○ a clever plan —**cleverly** adv —**cleverness** noun [U]
> **cliché** /'kliːʃeɪ; US kliːˈʃeɪ/ noun [C] a phrase or idea that has been used so many times that it no longer has any real meaning or interest: the usual cliché of the middle-aged businessman leaving his wife for a twenty-year-old girl
> **click**[1] /klɪk/ noun [C] a short sharp sound: I heard the click of a key in the lock. ○ the click of a switch
> **click**[2] /klɪk/ verb **1** [I,T] to make a short sharp sound; to cause sth to do this: The door clicked shut. ○ He clicked the switch. ○ To open a file on the computer, click on the mouse. **2** [I] (Brit informal) (used about two people) to become friendly immediately: We met at a party and just clicked. **3** [I] (informal) (used about a problem, etc) to become suddenly clear or understood: Once I'd found the missing letter, everything clicked into place.
> ☆**client** /'klaɪənt/ noun [C] someone who receives a service from a professional person
> **clientele** /ˌkliːənˈtel; US ˌklaɪənˈtel/ noun [U] the group of people who regularly go to a particular shop, hotel, etc ☛ This word is more formal than alternatives such as **customers** or **guests**.
> ☆**cliff** /klɪf/ noun [C] a high, very steep area of rock, especially one next to the sea: the white cliffs of Dover ☛ picture at **beach**.
> ☆**climate** /'klaɪmɪt/ noun [C] **1** the norma...

1 What is different about the British and American pronunciation of cliché?
2 Which of these is an uncountable noun: client or clientele?
3 What is the difference in use between clientele and customers?
4 Why are there two entries for the word click?
5 Does the verb click need an object?
6 How many meanings are given for the verb click?
7 What does click mean in this sentence?
   I didn't understand the problem and then it suddenly clicked.
8 What is the British equivalent of an American sales clerk?
9 Where should you look if you want to find out more about the word cliff?

Reading
Modern manners

1 Look at the pictures. What are the people doing? Does anything seem wrong, unusual, or impolite to you?

2 Read the introduction to the article.
a Answer these questions.
1 Whose ideas is it about?
2 What does he think about modern society?
3 What examples does he give?
b Do you agree with him?

3 Read the opinions.
a Match them to the correct pictures.
b What do the speakers think about what's happening in the pictures?
c How many of the speakers agree with Dr St George?

4 Read the whole article again.
a Make a list of all the examples of behaviour that are mentioned.
b Discuss these questions.
1 Are these things considered polite, impolite, or unimportant in your society?
2 Give some more examples of acceptable and unacceptable public behaviour in your society.
3 Do you think your society has better or worse manners than it used to? Why? Give examples.

5 What do you think of modern life?
a Work in groups. Choose one of these topics.
 • work • young people • leisure • society
b Discuss the topic and write about it. Follow the format of the article. Give a general introduction and present different opinions.

EXAMPLE
What is work like now?
How have patterns of work changed?
What are the good and bad points about work today?

Vocabulary file: Idiomatic expressions

Match the expressions from the text with the meanings.

these days	et cetera / etc.
I'll give you that.	It's very noisy.
I wouldn't say	I agree.
It was unthinkable.	generally
You can hardly hear yourself think.	You couldn't do it.
or what have you	It's true.
can't keep their hands off	because of
down to	say
It cuts both ways.	now
like to make out	keep touching
I must admit.	I don't think
on the whole	It has good and bad points.

People today are less polite than they used to be. This is the view of Dr Andrew St George of Oxford University, who has just completed a book on modern social behaviour. As the title, *The Descent of Manners* suggests, he believes that manners have deteriorated since Victorian times. For example, people these days eat while they are walking down the street. They kiss and embrace in public. They push on to buses and trains. Men don't open doors for women any more or offer a woman their seat on a crowded train. The Victorians, Dr St George says, would be horrified at modern behaviour. We went out on to the streets to find out what people think about his ideas. Here are some opinions that we heard.

'Life is certainly more informal these days, I'll give you that, but I wouldn't say that's a bad thing. When I first started work I had to wear a suit and a tie, but these days we all wear casual clothes. And everybody was called Mr This and Mrs That, but today it's all first names. In our office everyone even calls the Managing Director 'Bob'. That was unthinkable when I was younger, but I think it's better now. It's friendlier – more relaxed.'

'I don't think it's true. Things are different nowadays, but I wouldn't say they're worse. Life has become much faster and people don't have time for the more formal manners that the Victorians had. I know people eat in the street, but I wouldn't say there's anything wrong with that. It's just easier and faster like that.'

'Things have certainly changed, but it isn't bad manners. It's all down to equality. Why should I give up my seat so that a woman can sit down? If women want equality in jobs and things like that, they can't expect special treatment for other things, can they? I think equality cuts both ways.'

'Well, Dr St George is right, isn't he? I mean, look at those two young people over there. They can hardly keep their hands off each other. They shouldn't kiss and cuddle like that in public. It's embarrassing for other people.'

'Noise. That's what I don't like about things today. Everyone seems to think they can make as much noise as they like without a thought for other people. When you get on a train, some idiot's probably shouting into a mobile phone or you find yourself sitting next to someone with a personal stereo that's turned up too loud. And have you tried having a quiet day in the garden lately? Quiet? You can hardly hear yourself think with all the lawnmowers, hedge trimmers, and what have you.'

'I think people today have good manners. Things aren't as bad as some people like to make out. Most people still queue up for things properly and drivers usually stop for pedestrians at zebra crossings, because I think most people realize that life's nicer that way. I must admit that people are generally more impatient and less considerate on the roads, but on the whole I think things are all right.'

Listening and speaking
Talking about your life

1 **You will hear a conversation between two people who have just met. They are talking about their lives and work.**

a Look at the photographs. What questions do you think they will ask?

b What words or expressions would you expect to hear?

c 📼 *1.2* Listen and check your ideas.

d How does each person feel about their own life?

2 **Look at the table.**

a Work with a partner and try to complete the table.

b 📼 *1.2* Listen and check your answers.

	Sandra	Colin
Where/work?		
What/do?		
Where/live?		
When/start work?		
How/travel?		

Language focus: Present tenses

a Write the questions for these answers.

_____	_____
I'm a computer programmer.	I'm doing an MA in Management.
_____	_____
No, I live near Oxford.	No, I've got a flat in the city.
_____	_____
Yes, it's all right.	Yes, it's great, but it's hard work.

b Why does Colin use the present continuous tense when he talks to Sandra about her studies?

➤ Check in **Grammar Reference 1.2**.

Conversation pieces: Commenting

In the conversation, Colin and Sandra often comment on what the other person says.

EXAMPLES
Oh, yes?
Really?
That sounds very technical.

a Find more examples in tapescript 1.2.

b What purpose do these comments have?

c A lot of the comments use *That sounds* + an adjective or adjective phrase. Comment on the statements below. Use *That sounds* and these words or expressions.

> a bit of a drag   exciting   wonderful   like fun
> interesting   like a good idea

1 Shall we go to the movies?
2 I live on a houseboat.
3 I work for a music company.
4 I have to work most weekends.
5 We're going to Jamaica for our holidays.
6 I went bungee jumping last week.

d Roleplay Colin and Sandra's conversation with a partner, using tapescript 1.2.

3 Look at the table in 2 again.

a Think about your own job or studies (or note down some facts for an imaginary job).

b Work with a partner. Imagine you have just met. Have a conversation about your lives and work.

c Find a new partner and have another conversation.

Pronunciation
IPA; /s/, /z/, /ɪz/

1 The International Phonetic Alphabet (IPA)

a English is not a phonetic language. The same written letters do not always produce the same sound. Look at these examples:

same letters	**different sound**
love	/lʌv/
move	/muːv/
different letters	**same sound**
there	/ðeə/
fair	/feə/

b To help you learn how new words are pronounced, it is a good idea to know the International Phonetic Alphabet (IPA). You will find a chart of the English IPA on the inside back cover.

c Look at the IPA chart. What are these words?

/kʌm/   /gəʊ/   /bluː/
/ðɪs/   /wɒt/   /tʃiːz/

2 /s/, /z/, /ɪz/ endings

The *-s* ending on plural nouns and the third person singular of the present simple tense can be pronounced in three ways.

a 🔲 *1.3* Listen to these words and match the spelling rules to the sounds. Put **1**, **2**, and **3** in the correct columns in the table.

> rats   kicks   lives   runs
> rushes   catches

1 After /p/ /t/ /k/ /f/ /θ/
2 After /b/ /d/ /g/ /v/ /l/ /m/ /n/ /ð/
3 After *-sh, -ch, -z(e), -s(e), -dg(e)*

/ɪz/	/s/	/z/

b Say these words.

> watches   misses   comes   gets
> needs   uses   knives   cups
> picks   faces   knees   takes
> brushes   finds   laughs   breathes

c 🔲 *1.4* Listen, check, and repeat.

Extension: Reading and listening
What job is best for you?

1 What job do you do (or do you want to do)? What kind of personality do you think you need for the job?

2 Look at the questionnaire.

a What is it used for?

b Answer the questionnaire.

c Discuss your answers with a partner.

3 What do your answers mean?

a 🔊 *1.5* Listen and complete the grid.

	A	?	D
Statements 1–3			
Statements 4 and 5			

b Calculate your scores and read the explanations at the bottom of p15. Use a dictionary for any words that you don't know.

c Discuss these questions with a partner.
1 Do the results match your ideas about yourself?
2 Would this kind of test be helpful in choosing a job?

WHAT JOB IS BEST FOR YOU?

Many employers nowadays use psychological tests to select employees. This is called psychometric testing. Getting the right person for the job is obviously good for the employer, but it is also good for employees, because they will be happier in a job that suits their personality.

This psychometric test will suggest the kind of job that is best for your personality. Read each statement. In the box write D if you disagree with it, a question mark if you are not sure, and A if you agree. Don't think too long about each statement. Give your first answer.

Section A
1 I am an outgoing and sociable person. ☐
2 I never feel shy. ☐
3 I am normally optimistic about the future. ☐
4 I usually like to do things on my own. ☐
5 I don't usually enjoy meeting and talking to new people. ☐

Section B
1 I am a pretty nervous person. ☐
2 I don't like working under pressure. ☐
3 My mood often goes up and down. ☐
4 I don't usually worry about things. ☐
5 I hardly ever feel lonely or depressed. ☐

Section C
1 I am a curious person. I like theories and abstract ideas. ☐
2 I like to try new things: food, holidays, hobbies. ☐
3 I am interested in art and poetry. ☐
4 I don't often daydream. ☐
5 I am generally set in my ways. ☐

Section D
1 I always try to be considerate to other people. ☐
2 I would rather co-operate than compete with other people. ☐
3 I believe that most people are basically good. ☐
4 People sometimes think that I am cold and calculating. ☐
5 I frequently argue with my family and friends. ☐

Vocabulary file: Personality adjectives

a Work with a partner. Complete the table with these adjectives from the questionnaire.

considerate	stable	emotional
competitive	warm	sceptical
talkative	lonely	good-natured
practical	depressed	quiet
traditional	calculating	calm
reserved	sad	cold
serious	guilty	shy
trusting	co-operative	nervous
tough	outgoing	curious
hard-headed	optimistic	sociable

Positive	Negative	Both

b Compare your answers with the class.

c Find words that are of similar meaning.

EXAMPLE
sociable   outgoing

d Find words that can be opposites.

EXAMPLE
quiet   talkative

4 What kind of job would suit each personality type?

a 🔲 *1.6* Listen and check your ideas.

b Do you agree with the ideas on the tape?

5 Write a job advertisement.

a Work in a group. Use the information in the questionnaire. Choose a job and write an advert, without saying what the job is.

EXAMPLE
We're looking for a _____ / someone to work in our _____ .
You must be … (Give the qualities needed.)
If you think you have these qualities, write to: …
(Give an address.)

b Give your advert to another group to read and guess the job.

Language focus: Adverbs of frequency

a Put these adverbs in the correct order from the least to the most frequent.

normally   sometimes   always   frequently
hardly ever   never   often   usually

Where do we put adverbs of frequency?

b Complete these sentences from the questionnaire with the correct adverb of frequency.

I am optimistic about the future.
I feel shy.
I don't worry about things.

c Complete the rule.

Adverbs of frequency go _____ a main verb, but _____ an auxiliary verb or the verb *to be*.

▶ Check in **Grammar Reference 1.5**.

d Complete these sentences with appropriate adverbs of frequency.
1 I can get up on time.
2 I'm honest.
3 I like to be on my own.
4 Stress isn't good for you.
5 People telephone at inconvenient times.
6 Introverts don't enjoy parties.

How often do you do things? Write eight sentences about your life. Use each of the adverbs of frequency in **a**.

e Compare your sentences with a partner.

What do the scores mean?

Section A
5–12: You're an introvert – quiet, reserved, serious. You like being on your own.
13–17: You enjoy being with other people but not all the time. You also need your privacy.
18–25: You're an extrovert – outgoing, talkative. You like being with other people.

Section B
5–12: You're very stable, calm, and optimistic. You can deal with stress easily.
13–17: You're fairly calm, but you sometimes feel guilty, angry, or sad.
18–25: You're a worrier – sensitive, emotional, moody.

Section C
5–12: You're practical and traditional. You like things to be clear.
13–17: You like a balance between the old and the new.
18–25: You're an experimenter. You like new ideas and challenges.

Section D
5–12: You're a competitive person – tough, hard-headed, sceptical.
13–17: You're usually warm and trusting, but you can sometimes be very stubborn.
18–25: You're a co-operative person – warm, good-natured. You don't like conflict.

2 Fortune

Grammar
Talking about the past

Grammar in use

1 Look at the photographs and headline of the newspaper article.

a Where does the story take place?

b What do you think the story is about?

c Read the article and check your ideas.

2 What do you think happened?

a Did Chris win? Justify your opinion.

b What do you think the two missing parts of the text are?

c 🔲 *2.1* Listen and check your ideas.

d What do you think of Chris's gamble?

Rules

1 The article contains four tenses for talking about the past.

a Underline positive and negative examples of each of these tenses.
- the past simple
- the past perfect
- the past continuous
- the present perfect

b How do we form each tense? Find examples of regular and irregular verbs.

c Each paragraph of the article describes one of these things. Which tense is used for each one?
- Events before he made his gamble
- The scene in the casino
- The events of the gamble
- Events since the gamble to the present day

WITH £145,000 IN HIS POCKET HE TOOK THE PLANE TO LAS VEGAS

Mr All or Nothing

IT was early afternoon on 14 January in the Las Vegas casino. At one of the tables was Chris Boyd, a computer programmer from London. For three years Chris had saved every penny. He had rarely gone out and he hadn't spent anything on his house. Finally, he had sold the house and with £145,000 in his pocket he had taken the plane to Las Vegas.

Now Chris was sitting in Binion's Horseshoe casino. He was waiting to gamble the whole £145,000 on one spin of the roulette wheel. A few other gamblers were standing around the table. Among them was Chris's friend, Tony Litt. Chris's girlfriend, June Hillhouse, wasn't watching him, however. He hadn't told her anything about his plans.

Chris placed his bet on red. If the ball landed on a red number, he would double his money. If it

From PETER SHERIDAN in Los Angeles

landed on black, he would lose everything. 'I'm ready to play,' he said. The wheel spun. The small white ball rolled and bounced around the wheel and finally landed on number _____ . The onlookers waited. What would Chris do? 'He didn't do anything really,' said one of the other gamblers. 'He just smiled. Then he stood up from the table, _____ and left.' The next day he returned to London. Since his all-or-nothing gamble, Chris has moved into a one-bedroomed flat. 'The experience hasn't changed my life,' he told reporters, 'but I've given up gambling. It was something that I wanted to do and now I've done it. So that's it.'

The bright lights and roulette wheels of Vegas

2 How do we make questions in these tenses?

a Turn these statements into questions.

1 He had sold his house.
2 His friend was watching.
3 The ball landed on red.
4 He has given up gambling.

b Explain the rules for making questions in each tense.

➤ Check the rules for past tenses in **Grammar References 2.1**, **2.2**, and **2.3**.

Practice

1 Choose the correct form for each sentence.

1 When Chris *landed* / *has landed* at London airport, some reporters *waited* / *were waiting* for him, because his friend *has telephoned* / *had telephoned* them about what Chris *had done* / *did*.
2 Chris's girlfriend *was* / *has been* angry with him, because he *hasn't told* / *hadn't told* her about it.
3 When he *got back* / *has got back* to London, he *moved* / *has moved* into a small flat, because he *had sold* / *sold* his house.
4 Chris *didn't gamble* / *hasn't gambled* again since he *has left* / *left* Las Vegas.

2 Here is part of an interview with Chris Boyd. Write the questions, using the information in brackets.

Interviewer	_____?
	(How/ feel/ while/ sit/ at the table)
Chris Boyd	I felt quite calm.
Interviewer	_____?
	(anyone/ watch/ you)
Chris Boyd	Yes, my friend, Tony Litt, was watching and there were a few other gamblers there, too.
Interviewer	_____?
	(tell/ anyone else/ about your plans)
Chris Boyd	No, I hadn't even told my girlfriend.
Interviewer	_____?
	(How/ save/ the money)
Chris Boyd	I just hadn't spent anything for three years and then I sold the house.
Interviewer	_____?
	(What/ do/ when/ win)
Chris Boyd	I can't remember. I didn't do anything really.
Interviewer	_____?
	(Why/ do/ it)
Chris Boyd	It was something I had always wanted to do and now I've done it.
Interviewer	_____?
	(the experience/ change/ your life)
Chris Boyd	No, it hasn't, although I've decided to take a long holiday.
Interviewer	_____?
	(gamble/ again/ since then)
Chris Boyd	No, I haven't. I've given up gambling forever.

3 Simon is talking about a risk he once took.

a Put the verbs in the box into the past simple, past perfect, or past continuous to complete the text.

pull	stand	go out	risk	run
realize	go	hold	lie	hear
burn	come	hit	look after	say

It happened three years ago while I was staying at my sister's house. She and her husband _____ on holiday and I _____ the house for them. One night I _____ a lot of noise outside and I _____ to see what was wrong. The house next door was on fire. Smoke and flames _____ out of the upstairs windows. A woman shouted, 'Help, help. Tommy's still inside.' Without thinking I _____ into the house, but it was no good. Everything _____ and it was terribly hot. Then, while I _____ there, something _____ me on the back of the head. The next thing that I remember I _____ on the grass in front of the house. The fire brigade _____ me out of the house. The woman was there and she _____, 'It's all right. Tommy's safe.' Then I _____ that she _____ a cat. I _____ my life for a cat!

b 🎧 *2.2* Listen and check your ideas.

4 Can you remember the last time you took a risk?

a Tell your partner and answer any questions that your partner asks.

b Work with a partner. Have you ever done any of these things?

- gamble a lot of money
- win a prize
- be in an accident
- risk your life
- do anything dangerous
- lose anything
- have an exciting experience

Vocabulary
Dealing with new words

1 **Here are a few tips for dealing with unknown vocabulary.**

- Try not to use a dictionary *while* you are reading or listening. It makes things very slow.

- Always try to guess the meaning of a new word first. You often can't use a dictionary when you meet English outside the classroom, so it's a good idea to practise this.

- Only look up a word immediately if the word is vital to understanding the text.

- You can use a dictionary afterwards to check your guesses.

2 **In the reading text you will need to work out the meanings of new words. Here are some words that you might not know. How should you deal with them?**

- *soggy* and *squeeze*

  You can probably guess the meanings from the context. The woman put a piece of cloth in some water and it became *soggy*. So what do you think *soggy* means? Then she *squeezed* the cloth to get the water out. So what do you think *squeeze* means? You can use the dictionary afterwards just to check your guess.

- *lung, jaw,* and *pelvis*

  The context tells you that they are parts of the body, but there are no clues to their exact meaning. However, you don't need the exact meaning to understand the text. So for the moment accept the approximate meaning (parts of the body) and look up the exact meaning afterwards, if you want to.

- *survive*

  This word is important to understanding the text. Look it up before reading further.

- *aisle* and *fuselage*

  You may work out the meanings of these words (parts of a plane), but perhaps you don't know how they are pronounced. Look up the phonetic transcription afterwards if you want to.

3 **While you are reading the magazine article, try to use these strategies. Then discuss how you got on with your partner or the class.**

Reading
I survived!

1 **Look quickly at the magazine article and answer these questions.**
  1 Who is the story about?
  2 What nationality is she?
  3 What happened to her?
  4 Where did it happen?

2 **Read the article. Mark the sentences *True* (✓) or *False* (✗).**
  1 Monika and Johan were married.
  2 They lived in Burma.
  3 They were going to the beach for the weekend.
  4 They almost missed the plane.
  5 The plane crashed at night time.
  6 Only Monika and Johan survived the crash.
  7 The rain helped Monika to survive.
  8 She was able to walk around the plane.

3 **Look at the story again.**

a Make notes under these headings:
  - things that make the story particularly tragic
  - problems that Monika faced in the wreckage
  - things that helped her to survive
  - problems that she faces now

b Discuss your ideas with a partner or the class.

4 **A reporter interviewed Monika to write the article.**

a Work with a partner. Write a list of the reporter's questions.

b One student is a reporter. One is Monika. Roleplay the interview.

5 **Discuss these questions.**
  1 How did you feel when you read Monika's story?
  2 Why are we interested in stories like this?
  3 Air travel is one of the safest forms of travel. It's much safer than going by car, for example. So why do people worry more about air travel? Why do plane crashes get so much publicity?

Vocabulary file: Synonyms

Match the words from the text to the meanings.

bounce	broken
shudder	move slowly
fractured	wet land
soggy	very wet
creep	leave
work out	shake
set off	calculate
swamp	move up and down

I survived nine days alone in plane of death

Strength – Monika's will to live helped her pull through

When the small plane crashed in the Burmese jungle, Monika Kamphuis, 31, from the Netherlands was the only survivor. This is her amazing story.

Three months ago I flew to Myanmar (Burma) to be with my boyfriend, Johan. He worked for an international bank and he was helping to set up a branch of the bank in Rangoon. Johan wanted to go for the weekend to the beautiful old city of Mandalay. I was very excited. I had a feeling that he would ask me to marry him and I knew that I would say yes. I loved him very much. We had got the last two seats on the flight to Mandalay and on Friday afternoon we set off for the airport in a taxi. We were the very last passengers to check in, but we made it with only five minutes to spare.

Our seats were near the back of the small plane and I was next to the window. There were about 25 other passengers. The sky looked very black as we took off, and throughout the flight, we kept our seatbelts fastened. Twenty minutes later we flew into a terrible storm. The plane rolled, bounced, and shuddered in the violent turbulence. We were both very scared.

I can't remember anything after that until I opened my eyes. I didn't know where I was. Slowly I realized that the plane had crashed. I was in terrible pain and I couldn't move. 'Johan,' I called, but he didn't reply. It was dark, but I knew that he wasn't in his seat.

I heard groans and I worked out that possibly six other people were still alive. When daylight came, I could see all the bodies around me in the wreckage. Johan was on the other side of the aisle, but I knew that he was dead.

After a day or two the other voices stopped and I was alone. But the rescuers didn't come. 'They must be on their way,' I told myself. I didn't know that we were in a swamp in the middle of a jungle and that the helicopters couldn't fly in the heavy rain. Outside the window the flood water was creeping slowly up the side of the fuselage.

But that water saved my life. I knew that dehydration was a great danger. I tore a piece of cloth from my clothes and I pushed it through the broken window into the water. Then I pulled the soggy cloth back in and squeezed the dirty water into my mouth. That whole operation took twelve hours. Later I found a piece of metal and I used it to scoop up water.

At night the mosquitoes came. I was terribly hungry and I slipped in and out of consciousness. Then I heard voices. I pushed my hand out of the window and amazingly someone grabbed it.

The rescue team had arrived … nine days after the crash. They took me to a clinic in Rangoon and from there to a hospital in Singapore.

I had a collapsed lung, a fractured jaw, and my pelvis, my left leg, and all the toes on my left foot were broken.

I still dream that I'm in the wreckage with the insects and the snakes. I can't accept Johan's death. I like to believe that he survived through me. I want to forget everything about his death and remember everything about his life.

Listening and speaking
Catching up on news

1 You're going to hear a conversation between two old friends who haven't seen each other for a long time. What do you think they will talk about?

2 ▣ *2.3* Listen and answer the questions.
   1 Who are the two people?
   2 Where did they last meet?
   3 How long ago was it?
   4 What job does each person do?
   5 Who are John and Clara?
   6 Who is Harry Clarkson?

3 What has happened to the two people since they last met?

a Write their names in the table.

b Tick (✓) the things they have done.

c ▣ *2.3* Listen again and check your ideas.

Name		
put on weight		
work in the same place		
have several jobs		
get married		
make a lot of money		
work abroad		
have children		
be promoted		
be a teacher		
be divorced		
buy a house		
stop smoking		
become famous		
move to London		

4 Discuss these questions.
   1 What do you think that each person envies or admires in the other person's life?
   2 What wouldn't they envy or admire?
   3 Whose life do you find more attractive?

Conversation pieces: Responding to news

a Work in pairs. Complete these expressions.

Well, _____ , well!

_____ heavens!

I _____ believe it!

You know _____ it is.

That's the _____ it goes.

These things _____ .

It was just one of those _____ .

Wow! That _____ exciting.

Good _____ you!

Oh, how _____ !

I'm _____ to hear that.

Sounds _____ .

Yes, I _____ you must be.

b 🔊 *2.3* Listen again and check your ideas.

c Write these headings above the correct set of expressions:

Saying: 'That's life.'
Responding to news or information
Expressing surprise

d Find expressions in tapescript 2.3 which mean the same as:
- *I'm really pleased to see you again.*
- *The time has gone very quickly.*
- *What are you doing now?*
- *I'm really going to try it.*
- *We had children.*
- *My wife is expecting another baby.*
- *It went wrong.*

e Roleplay the conversation, using tapescript 2.3.

'I come from a long line of failures, but I am the first one in the family to become a total failure.'

Language focus: *used to*

a We can use *used to* to talk about the past. Look at tapescript 2.3 and find examples.

b When do we use *used to*? How is it different from the past simple?
➤ Check your ideas in **Grammar Reference 2.4**.

c Complete these sentences with *used to* to make true statements about Kathy and Bill.
1 _____ be married.
2 _____ work with Harry Clarkson.
3 _____ be slimmer.
4 _____ teach English.
5 _____ talk about becoming a teacher.
6 _____ live in Birmingham.

d Write down four things that you used to do or have. Tell your partner.

5 Imagine that you meet an old friend after five years.

a Work with a partner. Decide together what your lives used to be like.

b On your own, decide what has happened in the last five years. Think about:
- work or study
- family
- house
- mutual friends

c Make the conversation with your partner. Greet each other and talk about your lives since you last met.

6 Write a letter to a friend. Bring them up to date with your news and ask about theirs.

100 Roman Way
Repton
Derbyshire
DE65 6GD

Dear _____ ,
How are you? I'm so sorry that I haven't written for such a long time, but I've just been so busy ...

Pronunciation
Vowels; /ə/ in words

1 The IPA: Vowels

a Look at the list of IPA symbols on the inside back cover. Match the words to the correct vowel sounds.

three	/ɒ/
look	/ɔɪ/
flat	/ɜ:/
done	/ɪe/
want	/iː/
roll	/æ/
save	/ʌ/
boy	/ʊ/
earn	/ɑ:/
part	/əʊ/
year	/eɪ/

b What are these words?

/keɪm/   _____
/niːd/   _____
/wɜːk/   _____
/ʃəʊ/   _____
/dʌz/   _____
/sɒŋ/   _____
/dɪˈsaɪd/   _____
/bɔːt/   _____

c 📼 *2.4* Listen, check your ideas, and repeat.

2 /ə/ in words

a 📼 *2.5* Listen to these words and answer the questions.

1 Where is the stress in each word?
2 How are the endings *-al, -tion, -our, -ant, -er, -re, -ure* pronounced? Why?

natural	colour	station
important	furniture	centre
expedition	final	over
weather	wider	theatre	future

b 📼 *2.5* Listen again and repeat.

Extension: Reading and listening
Second Chance

1 Look at the title of the article and the photographs.

a What do you think the story is about?

b Discuss your ideas with the class.

2 Read the article and number these events in the correct order.

☐ make a lot of money   ☐ start a new venture
☐ go scuba-diving for treasure   ☐ work in Oklahoma
☐ give up his job   ☐ talk things over with his wife
☐ make a discovery   ☐ move to Florida
☐ sell the company

3 Read the story again.

a What do you think the 'crazy idea' was? Work in groups and discuss your ideas.

b 📼 *2.6* Listen and check your ideas.

4 What was the significance of each of these items in the story?

- ten cents
- washing machine
- neighbours
- 2,500
- 80,000–100,000
- Hawaii
- half price
- yacht

Vocabulary file: Phrasal verbs and idioms

Find expressions in the text which can replace the words in this list.

1 didn't reach
2 began his working life
3 tried
4 trying to find
5 discussed
6 leave
7 a risk
8 my job was
9 succeeded

---

5 What happens in the factory?

a Put these verbs in the correct order.

pack	whiten	sell	count	unload	dry
spray with an acrylic		clean	take out	send	

b What happens to the ones that aren't used?

c 📼 *2.6* Listen again and check your ideas.

6 Look at the story again.

a Answer these questions.
1 Is the golfer Jim Reid?
2 Why does Jim smile?
3 What do you think of Jim?

b Were your first ideas about the story right?

c Do you know any more people who have made money from unusual ideas? Tell the class.

Second Chance

The golfer put his ball on the tee. He looked at the flag, swung the club, and the ball flew into the air. But it fell short of the green and landed 'plop' in a lake. Jim Reid smiled. 'It's a nice sound, isn't it?' he said. Jim likes going to golf courses. And why not? He has recently sold his company for $5 million and now he has plenty of time and money to do exactly what he wants.

But it hasn't always been so. Jim started out in Oklahoma, and then in 1971 he moved to Florida where he worked as a surveyor for Walt Disney World for ten years. In his free time he used to go scuba-diving, looking for treasure among the shipwrecks that had lain for centuries around the Florida coast. Then one day he had a go at diving in a different place and made a discovery that was to change his life. When he went home that day, he talked the matter over with his wife, Beverley. It seemed like a crazy idea and Jim would have to give up his job, but they decided to go for it.

'It was a bit embarrassing at first when people asked me what I did for a living,' says Jim, 'and it wasn't easy.

Some of the places are over 15 metres deep. You're down there in the dark for hours with the snakes and the eels – and your imagination.' Stepping on broken glass and sharp pieces of metal was a constant hazard and Jim was once struck by lightning while underwater. But the gamble paid off. In fact, the new venture was successful beyond their wildest dreams and ten years later Jim and Beverley were multi-millionaires.

W

If, like
then o
who, so
and the
questio
Sunday
blue da
people
once sh

I was
dinner
with fo
calls. T
simple.
sat on
surprise
she can
your v
said. '
it's an
was on
worrie
their
We st
sitting
the po
my off
rather
meeti
most
are,
Anyw
interr

3 Your future

Grammar
Talking about the future

Grammar in use

1 🔊 3.1 **Read and listen to the dialogues. Discuss these questions.**
   1 Who are the people talking?
   2 What are they talking about?

2 **Complete these sentences with the correct subjects.**
   1 _____ are arriving at 2 o'clock.
   2 _____ will call back later.
   3 _____ is going to win the race.
   4 _____ is going to have a party.
   5 _____ will put more money into education.
   6 _____ can't come to the phone.
   7 _____ is meeting some visitors tomorrow.

And here comes Karlsson. The others are at least ten metres behind her. This brilliant young athlete is going to win and we're going to see a new world record.

What are you doing tomorrow, Claire?

I'm meeting those visitors from France.

That's OK. They aren't arriving till 2.00. Can we get together at 11.00?

Hello, it's David. Is Jane there?

Yes, but she's in the bath.

Oh, well, I'll call back in about half an hour.

What are you going to do for your birthday, Sandy?

I'm going to have a party.

Great!

And what will your government do about unemployment?

We will put more money into education and training and ...

Yes, but that won't produce new jobs.

Rules

1 There are three main ways of talking about the future. Look at the table.

a Next to each use, write the number of the dialogue which illustrates that use.

b Match each use to the correct form.

Dialogue number	Use	Form
	a general prediction	*going to*
	a plan or intention	
	a prediction with present evidence	the future with *will*
	an arrangement for a specific time in the future	the present continuous with a future time expression
	a spontaneous decision	

2 Look at each dialogue again.

a Explain why each form is used.

b Sometimes more than one future form is possible. It depends on the emphasis we want to give. Could any of the other forms be used in the dialogues?

➤ Check the rules for future forms in **Grammar References 3.1** to **3.4**.

Practice

1 Some of the future forms in these sentences are incorrect. Find and correct them.

1 **A** Are you doing anything this afternoon?
   B Yes, I'll play tennis.
2 **A** I can't find my pen.
   B Oh, I'm going to help you look for it.
3 In the future I believe that people are living on Mars.
4 **A** Shall we go to the beach?
   B No, it's raining this afternoon.
5 If I see David, I'll invite him to dinner.
6 **A** Will you go to Sarah's party on Saturday?
   B Yes. Is Alma going?
7 **A** Are you really going to leave your job?
   B Yes, I'm going to tell my boss today.
8 **A** I see they've knocked down that old factory. What will they build there?
   B They'll make it into a shopping centre.
9 **A** Will you be in tomorrow morning?
   B No, I'll go to the airport at 10.00. My parents are going to arrive at 12.30.
10 **A** Where are you going?
   B I'll visit my grandmother.

2 Complete the conversations.

a Put the verbs in brackets into an appropriate future form. Sometimes more than one form is possible.

Sally's car

Monday
Meg Hi, Sally. _____ (do) anything tomorrow?
Sally I _____ (go) to the dentist's in the morning, but I _____ (not do) anything in the afternoon.
Meg Do you fancy a game of tennis about 2.00?
Sally OK. I _____ (see) you about 2.00 at the park.

Tuesday morning
Sally Oh! The car won't start! I _____ (have to) get the bus, but I _____ (be) late for my appointment.
Mother If you hurry, you _____ (get) the 10 o'clock bus. I _____ (phone) the dentist's and say that you _____ (be) late.

Tuesday afternoon
Meg Hi, Sally. Where's your car?
Sally It's broken down again, and it _____ (cost) a lot to repair. I _____ (sell) it.
Meg _____ (get) a new one?
Sally No, I can't afford it. I _____ (get) a bike instead.
Meg Well, that _____ (keep) you fit.
Sally It certainly will, and I _____ (save) a lot of money, too.
Meg OK. So _____ (play) tennis?
Sally Yes. I'm ready when you are.

b 📼 *3.2* Listen and compare your answers.

3 Work with a partner. Ask and answer about the future, using appropriate future forms.
- after the lesson?
- on Saturday night?
- for your holiday next year?
- when you retire?
- on your next birthday?
- at the weekend?
- when you have finished learning English?

EXAMPLE
A *What are you **going to do / doing** after the lesson?*
B *I'm not sure. I think I'll go to the café.*
   OR
B *I'm going to the cinema.*

Reading
2050

1 **What do you think the future holds for the world in 2050?**

a Work with a partner. Make some predictions.

b Discuss your predictions with the class.

2 **Look at the twelve texts. There are six predictions for the twenty-first century and six likely results. Read the texts and match the predictions to their results.**

Language focus: Expressing probability

Most of the predictions in the texts are definite.
*The earth's climate **will** become warmer.*

However, the results are less definite.
*We **might** see wars over the control of rivers and lakes.*

a Find five different ways (3 modal verbs and 2 adverbs) of showing that the results are not definite.

b Put the verbs and adverbs in the chart.

most likely		least likely
p_____	c_____	m_____
	m_____	p_____

c Look at texts A and J. Where do the adverbs go in relation to the verb?

➤ Check your ideas in **Grammar Reference 3.5**.

---

3 **According to the texts, what could happen to**
- the United Nations?
- the industrialized countries?
- Africa?
- banks and offices?
- the tiger?
- the environment?
- water?
- cars?

Vocabulary file: Word association

Match a word in column A with an associated word in column B.

A	B
control	decline
climate	genetic engineering
agriculture	extinct
succeed	drought
animal	famine
increase	petroleum
old people	power
scientist	fail
oil	pension

---

4 **Discuss these questions.**

a Compare your ideas from **1** with the predictions in the text. Are any of them similar?

b Which predictions in the text do you agree with? Give your reasons.

c Which of the ideas do you find
- the most encouraging?
- the most worrying?
- the saddest?
- the most important?

5 **Write your own predictions for the future.**

a Work in groups. Discuss one of these topics:
- society
- communication
- medicine
- the environment
- international relationships
- space travel

b Write about what will happen and what the likely results will be.

'When you replace the hip is there any chance of replacing the rest of him at the same time?'

'The salesman said that this was the ideal car for life in the fast lane.'

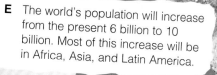

E The world's population will increase from the present 6 billion to 10 billion. Most of this increase will be in Africa, Asia, and Latin America.

I At the same time, however, the expensive social problems of a young society – crime, drugs, divorce – could decline.

A Many of the larger mammals may become extinct in the wild. And some, such as tigers and black rhinos, will possibly survive only in zoos.

F This could produce a change in the international balance of power, as the countries in these regions demand more control in international organizations like the United Nations and the World Bank.

J But this probably won't matter, because scientists will use genetic engineering to produce oil from plants like sunflowers.

B The earth's climate will become warmer. This will create major problems for agriculture and we will see droughts and famine in Africa. We might even see these problems in southern Europe.

G In the industrialized countries there will be more and more old people. The costs of providing pensions and medical care for them will rise steeply.

K The future looks bad for the world's animals. We will continue to destroy huge areas of the rain forest and other important natural habitats.

C Attempts to produce an electric vehicle will fail and we'll continue to use our normal cars. Around the middle of the century, however, the world's supplies of petroleum will run out.

H With new technology people won't need to be in the same place to communicate easily. They'll be able to stay at home and do everything by computer and videophone.

L Patterns of work may change. People might decide that they don't actually need to go to banks, offices, schools, universities or shops, any more.

D There will be serious racial conflicts as large numbers of people move to try and find food. Water will become a valuable resource and we might see wars over the control of rivers and lakes.

3 Your future

Vocabulary
The weather

1 Match the words and symbols.

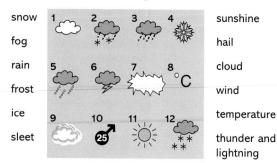

snow   sunshine
fog   hail
rain   cloud
frost   wind
ice   temperature
sleet   thunder and lightning

2 Now match these adjectives with types of weather. Each adjective can be used more than once.

> heavy   light   thick   strong   high   low

3 Here are more adjectives for describing the weather.

> fine   wet   dry   sunny   hot   cold
> warm   cool   windy   rainy   stormy
> cloudy   dull   humid   clear   bright

a Which adjectives do you normally associate with
- holidays?
- Britain?
- Australia?
- Russia?
- Christmas?
- March?
- November?

b 3.3 Listen to the weather forecast. Which types of weather are mentioned?

4 What's the weather like?

a Match the words with a suitable verb to describe a change in the weather.

rain	warm up a bit
a bit dull	calm down
rather chilly	stop
windy	brighten up
sunny	cool down
foggy	clear
very hot	cloud over

b Work with a partner. Make conversations about the weather, using the information above and these expressions.

> now   at the moment   soon
> You never know.   I think   later

EXAMPLE
A *What's the weather like?*
B *It's raining at the moment, but I think it might stop soon.*

Listening and speaking
Making plans

1 Look at the photographs. What are the people doing?

a 3.4 Listen. You will hear seven conversations. In the first column of the table, write the letters of the photographs in the correct order.

	Activity	Weather	Action
1			
2			
3			
4			
5			
6			
7			

b Compare your answers with a partner. Answer these questions.
1 What is said about the weather in each case?
2 What do the people decide to do?

c 3.4 Listen again and complete columns 2 and 3 of the chart.

Conversation pieces

1 Asking about the weather

a Complete these expressions from the conversations.

What's the _____ like?

What's the _____ (for the weekend)?

What's it like _____ ?

b Write two more ways of saying *Let's see what the weather's like...*

_____

_____

c 📼 *3.4* Listen and check your answers.

2 Making suggestions

a Work with a partner. How many ways of making suggestions can you remember from the conversations?

b Complete the table. Write the expressions in the correct column.

+ infinitive	+ infinitive without *to*	+ *-ing* form

c Check your answers, using tapescript 3.4.

d Roleplay the conversations with a partner, using tapescript 3.4.

2 Make conversations about these situations.

a Work with a partner, following the diagram.
- go for a picnic/ warm but dull/ brighten up later/ get things ready
- game of golf/ possibly foggy in the morning/ play in the afternoon
- swimming/ sunny/ cloud over later/ go now
- go for a walk/ possible snow/ put warm clothes on

A   B

Make a suggestion

        Ask about the weather

Give the information

        Suggest action

Agree

b Make more conversations for these situations.
- You want to have a barbecue at the weekend, but the weather's changeable.
- You want to take the dog for a walk, but rain is forecast.
- You want to go to the theatre and you need to drive there, but it's foggy.
- You want to play tennis, but it's too hot.

Pronunciation
Consonants; /ə/ in sentences

1 The IPA: Consonants

a Look at the list of IPA symbols on the inside back cover. Match the correct sound to the letters.

know	/dʒ/	/j/	**ph**one
house	/s/	/t/	**fi**t
ni**ce**	/ʃ/	/f/	**c**ar
jam	/h/	/tʃ/	**y**es
she	/n/	/k/	wa**tch**

b Complete the sentences with *voiced* and *voiceless*.

/p/ /t/ /k/ /f/ /s/ /h/ /θ/
These sounds are _____ .
/b/ /d/ /g/ /v/ /z/ /l/ /r/ /m/ /n/ /w/ /ð/
These sounds are _____ .

c 3.5 Listen and tick (✓) the words you hear.

path	bath	sat	sad
to	do	pig	big
cave	gave	rice	rise
loose	lose	leaf	leave
fan	van	back	bag

2 /ə/ in sentences

a In sentences, words that are not essential to the meaning often have a reduced /ə/ sound, especially prepositions with -o- or -a-, auxiliary verbs, and words like *and, or, that,* and *than*.

> **EXAMPLE**
> /ə/   /ə/
> *I was taking it to the kitchen.*

b Each of these sentences contains words with a reduced vowel sound. Circle them.
  1 It will be dull and cloudy at first.
  2 You can see the rain coming in from the west.
  3 It's going to be warmer than yesterday.
  4 Let's go to the beach at the weekend.
  5 How about a game of tennis or something?
  6 She said her friend was from Texas.

c 3.6 Listen, check, and repeat.

Extension:
Reading and listening
A year out

1 Read the information. Compare it to your own country.

Education in England and Wales

Children start primary school when they are 5 years old. From 11 to 16 they go to secondary school. When they are 16 they take the General Certificate of Secondary Education (GCSE) exams. At the age of 16 they can leave school or study for two more years in the sixth form. Here, they study three subjects for the qualification called A-levels. At the age of 18 they can go on to study at a university. Most university courses last three years. Students can apply to any university in the country and many young people choose to study away from home.

2 Look quickly at the article *A year out*. Answer these questions.
  1 What is it about?
  2 Do young people do this in your country?

3 Read the article. Answer these questions.
  1 What examples are given of things to do in a year out?
  2 What are the benefits?
  3 What must you check before you decide to take a year out?
  4 How do universities feel about it?
  5 What do you think the expression *the university of life* means?

4 A radio DJ is talking to a group of young people about their plans for their year out.

a 3.7 Listen. Which of these do the young people mention?
  • work in a children's camp
  • do community work
  • travel round Europe
  • work in a department store
  • join an expedition
  • be a tour guide
  • be a ski instructor

b Write what the people are going to do in the second column of the table.

Name	Plan	Reasons
Rosie		be a challenge
		earn some money
Christopher		be a change
		find out what it's like
Helen		do something useful
		meet interesting people
Martin		become more independent

c 3.7 Listen again. Match each person's plans to the reasons given.

d Describe each person's plan.
> **EXAMPLE**
> *… is going to … , because he/she thinks it will …*

EDUCATION NOTEBOOK

A year out

Y ou've just finished your A-levels and you've got a place at university, but you'd really like a break from the academic world. Why not think about taking a year out? While most students go straight from school to university, more and more young people today are choosing to spend a year at 'the university of life' first. There are lots of things to choose from. You could work in a bank or do community work. You might even do something adventurous, such as joining an expedition to the Amazon rain forest. The experience will broaden your horizons and teach you new skills. It may also

by TONY HALPIN
EDUCATION CORRESPONDENT

give you the chance to earn some money, which will be very helpful when you eventually start your studies. If you're interested in taking a year out, you must make sure that the university will hold your place for you till next year. Most are quite happy to do this, as they find that year-out students are more mature, confident, and independent. But don't forget: it's a year out not a year off. Your university will want to know what you're going to do. They won't be very pleased if you just want to do nothing for a year. So what would you do with a year out?

'The university of life'

5 What is the significance of these things in the people's plans?
- management
- hotel
- conservation
- £20
- Alaska
- January
- £3,000

Language focus: *would*

a Look at these sentences. What is the difference in meaning?

What will you do with a year out?
What would you do with a year out?

b Why is *would* used in the last sentence of the article?

c How do we make positive and negative statements with *would*?

➤ Check your ideas in **Grammar Reference 3.6**.

d What would you do with a year out? Discuss your ideas with a partner. Think about
- things that you could do.
- reasons for doing them.

6 Imagine you are going to take a year out.

a Choose one of your ideas from **Language focus d**.

b Work in a group. One student is the DJ, the others are young people. Roleplay a radio interview about your plans.

4 Relationships

Grammar
Relative clauses

Grammar in use

1 Read the text and answer these questions.
 1 What does Eduard Spranger suggest motivates people?
 2 Which of the types does Conrad represent?
 3 What aspects of his life demonstrate his type?
 4 How do you feel about him?

2 Discuss these questions.
a What motivates you to do things? For example, are you motivated by money or power, or do you like to be helpful to other people?
b Do you think that the same things motivate other people?

Rules

1 Look at these sentences from the text.
Are you the kind of person <u>that likes to help other people</u>?
Does the salary <u>that you earn</u> motivate you?

a Each of the sentences has
  • a main clause   • a relative clause
  Which clause is underlined?
b A relative clause gives us information about the noun in the main clause. What do the relative clauses in the example sentences describe?
c Where does the relative clause go in the sentence?
d Underline more examples of relative clauses in the text. What does each one describe?

2 A relative clause normally starts with a relative pronoun.
a What is the relative pronoun in the sentences in **1** above?
b Underline the relative clauses in these sentences. What are the relative pronouns?
Conrad is the kind of person who thinks everything should be useful.
He thinks he deserves the high salary which he earns.
c Look at the relative clauses in the text. Complete the rule with *that, which, who.*

> We use _____ for people. We use _____ for things.
> We can use _____ for people and things.

d Look at the relative clauses that you underlined in the article. Replace *that* with *who* or *which.*
➤ Check the rules for relative clauses in **Grammar Reference 4.1**.

Values

Are you the kind of person that likes to help other people? Does the salary that you earn motivate you? The German psychologist, Eduard Spranger, suggested that there are six main types of people: aesthetic, social, religious, economic, political, and theoretical. These types are based on the values that motivate people.

Conrad, for example, is the kind of person who thinks everything should be useful. His high-powered job as the sales director of a large international company is very important to him, and he thinks he deserves the high salary which he earns. He collects works of art, but he only buys things that have a commercial value. Conrad sees himself as someone who knows what he wants. The clothes that he wears are stylish and the car that he drives is fast and expensive.

Practice

1 Here are the other five types that Spranger identifies.
a Complete the texts. Put these relative clauses in the correct places, using *that* as the relative pronoun.

 1 govern the universe
 2 take place next year
 3 concern him
 4 she has sold
 5 he got for his birthday
 6 she wants
 7 needs support or a shoulder to cry on
 8 are sick
 9 she thinks are wrong with society
 10 he leads
 11 genuinely likes people
 12 she gets from her involvement in politics

Selina is an artist. Some of the paintings _____ have fetched high prices, but Selina is not very interested in money. As long as she has enough for the things _____ , she's content.

Bjorn is fascinated by the laws _____ . When he was a child he loved to study the stars with a telescope _____ . Today he works in the science department of a university.

Clara is the kind of person _____ . She's always ready to help anyone _____ . Her job as a nurse gives her the opportunity to help people _____ .

Katrin loves the feeling _____ . She wants to change the things _____ . She has decided to stand in the local elections _____ .

Tamas is interested in the deeper meaning of life. The questions _____ are: Why are we here? What is the purpose of life? The life _____ is very simple and he meditates for at least two hours a day.

b Change the relative pronouns to *who* or *which*.

c 🔊 *4.1* Listen and check your answers.

2 Which type does each person represent?

a Match the people to the other types identified by Spranger.

b Most people are a combination of types. Which ones do you associate yourself with and why?

3 Write a description of one of the characters.

a Think about the details of that person's life:
- the kind of house that he/she lives in
- the things that he/she owns
- the car that he/she drives (if any)
- the kind of people that he/she associates with
- the things that he/she does in his/her free time
- the kind of partner that he/she has (if any)
- the holidays that he/she would take

b Write a description without saying who the character is.

> **EXAMPLE**
> *… lives in a house that … The things that he/she owns are …*

c Give your description to another student. Can he/she guess who it is?

4 We often use relative clauses to describe something when we don't know its name.

a Match the definitions with the objects.

It's a tool that you use in the garden.	a whale
It's a large animal that lives in the sea.	honey
It's a kind of make-up which is usually red.	a spade
It's a camera that you make videos with.	a skyscraper
It's someone who makes things with wood.	a ruler
It's a kind of food which bees make.	a saucepan
It's something which you draw straight lines with.	a camcorder
It's a piece of land that's almost an island.	a carpenter
It's something that you cook things in.	a peninsula
It's a building that's very tall.	lipstick

b Work with a partner. Describe an example of each of these things. Your partner must guess what it is.
- a kind of job
- an animal
- a game
- a piece of furniture
- a place
- a tool
- an everyday object
- a kind of food
- a famous person
- an item of clothing

Vocabulary
Communicating

1 Match the verbs and nouns.

express	eye contact
pay	a message
hold	your head
impress	a question
make	an opinion
fold	a rule
achieve	your arms
send	a compliment
nod	an answer
ask	a conversation
follow	other people
give	a result

2 Complete the sentences with these verbs. Which verb can you replace with *talked*?

> thought introduced said asked
> heard told agreed spoke listened

1 I _____ John about his new job.
2 I _____ Mary a joke.
3 I _____ to Mr Saul about the report.
4 I _____ hello to the neighbours.
5 I _____ with Carla on the matter.
6 I _____ Sasha to Walter.
7 I _____ to Pierre's story.
8 I _____ of something to say.
9 I _____ a funny story on the radio.

3 How many different forms of communication can you name? Complete the spidergram.

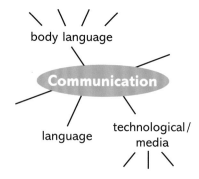

Reading
Successful small talk

1 Read the first paragraph of the article.

a Which action would you choose?
b Do you know people who are good conversationalists?
c What is *small talk*?

2 Look at the seven headings from the article.

a What advice do you think will be under each heading?
b Look quickly at the article and write the paragraph headings in the correct place.
  ● Pay compliments
  ● Turn the spotlight on others
  ● Keep it light
  ● Silence your inner critic
  ● Use friendly body language
  ● Start with the obvious
  ● Pay attention

3 Read the article again. Why should or shouldn't you
  ● try to impress people?
  ● only talk about important things?
  ● pay compliments?
  ● stand with your arms folded?
  ● ask questions?
  ● think about what you're going to say next?
  ● ask people about their personal problems?
  ● express your opinions forcefully?

4 Imagine you are strangers at a party.

a Find a partner. Talk to him/her for five minutes. Try ideas from the article.
b Move on and talk to another partner.
c Were you able to apply some of the rules?

5 The article is written for a British or American audience.

a How appropriate is the advice to your culture?
b Discuss these questions with regard to your culture.
  1 Who should start conversations?
  2 Is it acceptable to talk to strangers?
  3 What things should or shouldn't you talk about?
  4 Is it acceptable to maintain eye contact with someone you are talking to?
  5 Is it polite to disagree with someone publicly?

6 Write some advice for conducting polite conversations in your culture.

a Include details about
  ● topics that strangers usually talk about.
  ● topics to avoid.
  ● any conventions for who normally speaks first.
  ● any rules about body language, e.g. touching, shaking hands, eye contact.
b Give your advice to other students to read.

The secret of successful small talk

You're at a cocktail party. There are lots of people there, but there's nobody that you know. What do you do?

a   Turn around and leave.

b   Walk up to someone and introduce yourself.

c   Wait patiently until somebody comes to talk to you.

d   Try to think of something interesting to say to someone.

The good conversationalist would choose b. We all know people like that – people who can talk to anyone about anything. How do they do it? Well, the good news is that there is no great secret to small talk. There are just some simple techniques that anyone can use to start a conversation and keep it going.

1 _____

In the film *Annie Hall*, Diane Keaton and Woody Allen have just met and they want to impress each other. While they are talking their inner thoughts appear in sub-titles on the screen. 'Listen to me – what a jerk.' 'He probably thinks I'm stupid.' Thoughts like these kill a conversation. So don't try to impress other people. Just relax and be yourself.

2 _____

When you talk to someone you show that you are interested in them. So you don't have to talk about deeply important things. Just talk about simple things like the weather or a television programme that you saw last night. If the other person wants to talk, these obvious things will soon lead into other more interesting topics.

3 _____

TV journalist Barbara Walters recalls that when she was younger she met the author, Truman Capote. She wanted to tell him that she liked his book. However, she thought that he must be tired of hearing that, so she just mumbled 'How do you do?' and turned away. She forgot that everybody likes to receive a compliment and it's an easy way into a conversation, especially if you follow it up with a question: 'I really liked your book. How long did it take you to write it?' 'That's a nice jacket. Where did you buy it?'

Language focus: Reduced relative clauses

a   Look at these sentences.

He was the first person that I saw.
He was the first person that spoke to me at the party.

b   In which sentence is *that*
   • the subject of the relative clause?
   • the object of the relative clause?

c   In which sentence can you omit *that*?

d   Make a rule for when you can omit the relative pronoun in a relative clause.

e   Find sentences in the article where the relative pronoun can be omitted.

➤   Check your ideas in **Grammar Reference 4.2**.

4 _____

Your face and your body can communicate much more than your words. If you stand with your arms folded or if you keep looking around the room, the conversation will quickly end, because you will look uninterested. Instead, you should make eye contact, keep an open posture and smile. If you send out friendly messages, you will get friendly messages back.

5 _____

A Victorian lady once compared the two British prime ministers, Gladstone and Disraeli. 'When you speak to Mr Gladstone,' she said, 'you think he is the most interesting man in the world. But when you speak to Mr Disraeli, you feel that you are the most interesting woman in the world.' People like to talk about themselves and they will think you are fascinating if you ask questions that allow them to do so.

6 _____

But people often don't listen properly. They are too busy thinking about the next thing that they themselves want to say. Good conversationalists listen carefully and they show that they are listening, too. They ask questions, nod their head in agreement or say things like 'Oh, that sounds exciting'.

7 _____

There are some topics that you should avoid. Don't ask people about personal problems, money or religion. It's also a good idea to avoid the kind of statements that say 'I'm right. You're wrong.' It's all right to express your opinions, but soften your comments with expressions such as 'I'm afraid I have to disagree with you there.'

So, there is no secret to successful small talk. Just follow these simple rules and you'll soon find that you can hold a pleasant conversation with anybody about anything.

Listening and speaking
Conversations

1 **Look at the photographs and discuss these questions.**
   1   Where are the people?
   2   What do you think they are talking about?

2 📼 **4.2 Listen to these four conversations and match them to the correct pictures.**

3 **What can you remember?**

a Answer the questions.
   1   What is the score?
   2   Who scored the goal?
   3   Whose party is it?
   4   What are the names of the two speakers at the party?
   5   Who is the man in the pink jacket?
   6   Who has been to the club?
   7   What's its name?
   8   Why can't they go?
   9   Who is the man from Australia?
   10 What does he do?

b 📼 **4.2** Listen again and check your ideas.

Language focus: Question tags

a Complete these sentences from the conversations with the correct question tag.

isn't it?	can it?	doesn't she?	is it?
shall we?	have they?	didn't he?	

They haven't scored, _____

But that isn't her husband with her, _____

It's a lovely day, _____

Paula always picks the right day for a party, _____

Well, it can't be Brad Conran, _____

Let's go to that new club, _____

John said it was good, _____

b 🔊 *4.2* Listen again and check your ideas. What do you notice about the intonation?

➤ See **Pronunciation** for question tag intonation.

c How do we form question tags? Answer these questions.
1 When is the tag negative or positive?
2 How do we make the tag when the verb is *to be* or an auxiliary verb?
3 How do we form the tag when the verb does not have an auxiliary verb?
4 When the subject is a pronoun we use the pronoun in the tag. What do we do when the subject is a noun?
5 What is the tag for a sentence with *Let's ...*?

➤ Check your answers in **Grammar Reference 4.3**.

d Complete these tags. Which conversation is each one from?
1 Well, they aren't going to win now, _____?
2 The bride looks lovely, _____?
3 He works in television, _____?
4 I told you I was out of touch, _____?
5 I think it's my round, _____?
6 Well, it won't be open tonight, _____?

e Check your answers in tapescript 4.2.

4 Imagine you are having a conversation at a party.

a Write down some comments to make about the party, using question tags.

b Write down some things that you think you know about your partner. Here are some possible ideas:

born in/ works/ lives/ likes/ used to/ can/ married/ children/ has got

c Work with your partner. Have a conversation at the party and find out if your ideas about your partner are correct, using question tags.

EXAMPLES
A It's a nice party, isn't it?
B Yes, it is.
A You work in a bank, don't you?
B Yes, that's right. And you are a student, aren't you?

d Find another partner and have another conversation.

Pronunciation
Vowels; question tags

1 Vowel sound pairs

a 🔊 *4.3* Listen and repeat these words. What do you notice about the vowel sounds?

hat /æ/	heart /ɑ:/
fit /ɪ/	feet /i:/
shot /ɒ/	short /ɔ:/
full /ʊ/	fool /u:/

b 🔊 *4.4* Listen and tick (✓) the words you hear.

will	wheel
cat	cart
pot	port
cot	caught
pull	pool
sit	seat
not	nought
back	bark

c 🔊 *4.4* Listen again and repeat.

2 Question tag intonation

Question tags can have falling or rising intonation, but the meaning is different.

a 🔊 *4.5* Listen to the difference.

It was Brazil, wasn't it?

It was Brazil, wasn't it?

b Complete the rules with *falling* and *rising*.

> A _____ intonation means that you think the statement is true. You expect the other person to agree.
>
> A _____ intonation means that you are not sure whether the statement is true. It is more like a real question.

c 🔊 *4.6* Listen to these question tags. Mark the intonation.
1 You're away next week, aren't you?
2 He's pretty good at tennis, isn't he?
3 You can't play golf, can you?
4 The restaurant isn't closed, is it?
5 They're in room 234, aren't they?
6 She went swimming, didn't she?
7 The meeting's at four, isn't it?
8 You haven't got a map, have you?

d 🔊 *4.6* Listen again and repeat.

Extension: Reading and listening
Season's greetings

1 **Look at the text and pictures. Discuss these questions.**
    1 Do you celebrate this festival in your country?
    2 Is it the biggest festival of the year?
    3 If not, what do you celebrate?

2 **Read the text quickly.**

a Put these days in the correct order and give the dates.
    ☐ New Year's Day   _____
    ☐ New Year's Eve   _____
    ☐ Christmas Eve   _____
    ☐ Boxing Day   _____
    ☐ Christmas Day   _____

b Match these items to the correct day.
    • turkey   • *Auld Lang Syne*
    • winter sales   • crackers
    • Father Christmas • sport
    • sacks   • Christmas pudding

3 **Read the text again.**

a How many of the things mentioned can you see in the pictures?

b Find all the information in the text about
    • Christmas trees. • entertainment.
    • fruit.   • shops.
    • presents.   • families.
    • parties.   • modern developments.

4 **What does the British Christmas sound like to you? Is there anything that you find strange or unusual about it?**

5 🔊 **4.7 Listen to some people talking about Christmas. Answer the questions for each person.**
    1 How do they normally celebrate it?
    2 How do they feel about it?

6 **Think about the biggest festival of the year in your country.**

a Discuss these questions.
    1 What is it?
    2 How do you celebrate it?
    3 What traditions are there?
    4 How are these traditions changing?
    5 How do you feel about the festival?

b Write a description of the festival, using the questions above.

7 **What do you think?**

a Why do we have traditions and customs? Do you think they are important?

b What other events have a lot of traditions associated with them?

Christmas is the biggest festival of the year in most of Britain. Celebrations start properly on 24 December, Christmas Eve, although there have been several weeks of preparation beforehand. The Christmas tree and all the presents, food, drinks, and decorations have been bought. Christmas cards have already been sent to friends and relations. About a week before Christmas, people usually put up their decorations and decorate the Christmas tree with lights, various coloured decorations and an angel on the top. Family presents are usually put under the tree.

Christmas is a family celebration and many of the customs centre on children. When they go to bed on Christmas Eve, children hang up a pillow case or a sack for their presents. (Traditionally, it should be a stocking, but a stocking wouldn't hold enough to satisfy today's kids.) While the children are asleep, so the custom goes, Father Christmas, or Santa Claus, comes (but only to children who have been good). He travels from the North Pole in a sleigh which is pulled by reindeer. After landing on the roof, Father Christmas climbs down the chimney and puts presents in the sacks that the children have left out.

Christmas Day is the biggest day of the holiday. On Christmas morning (often very early!), children open the presents that were in their sacks. Some families go to church. The traditional Christmas dinner consists of roast turkey with potatoes and various other vegetables. This is followed by Christmas pudding – a dark, rich mixture of flour, fruit, sugar, nuts, and brandy. Before the dinner people usually pull crackers – small rolls of paper that have gifts, jokes, and party hats inside. Needless to say, large quantities of beer, wine, and spirits are also drunk.

How the rest of the day is spent varies a lot from family to family and may include opening the rest of the presents that are under the tree, playing games, going for a walk or just going to sleep in an armchair! And there is always a special schedule of films and other programmes on television.

December 26, which is called Boxing Day, is also a holiday. On Boxing Day most people go out to see friends, watch sports events, go to the theatre to see a pantomime, or increasingly nowadays, go shopping. Most of the large stores start their winter sales on Boxing Day now. But the Christmas holiday is still not over. In fact, many offices and factories close for the whole Christmas period from 24 December to 2 January. On New Year's Eve there are a lot of parties and at midnight everyone joins hands to sing *Auld Lang Syne*. Then after New Year's Day to sleep it off, that's Christmas over for another year.

5 The law

Grammar
The passive

Grammar in use

1 **Look at the text and answer the questions.**
1   What has happened?
2   Who probably won't solve the crime?
3   Who are the 'experts'?
4   What will happen to the evidence?

2 **What kind of evidence do you think is collected?**

Rules

1   Underline all the verbs in the passive.

a   How do we form the passive? Label both parts of the verbs in these examples.

	_____	_____	
The evidence The things	is are	collected. taken	to the police laboratories.

b   Find two examples of the negative form of the passive in the text. Which part of the passive shows the negative?

2   **How do we make different tenses in the passive?**

a   Look at the text again. Find examples of the passive in these tenses.
* the past perfect   _____
* the past simple   _____
* the present perfect _____
* _will_   _____
* _would_   _____

b   Which part of the passive changes to show the tense?

3   **When do we use the passive?**

a   Find passive sentences in the text where we don't know who does the action.

b   If we want to show who does the action, we use an agent. Find examples in the text.

c   Complete the rule with _action_ and _agent_.

> We use the passive when the _____ is more important than the _____ .

d   Translate the text into your own language. Do you use the passive in the same way?

➤   Check the rules for the passive in **Grammar Reference 5.1**.

Evidence

A woman has been murdered. Her body was discovered at seven o'clock this morning. She had been stabbed. What happens next? In fiction, the crime would probably be solved by a brilliant detective. But in real life crimes aren't usually solved like that. Most criminals are caught by scientists.

The police have been called, but the room isn't touched until the experts arrive – the pathologist, the photographer, and the detective. Then the evidence is collected and the things are taken to the police laboratories. Here they will be examined by forensic scientists. The evidence will be used to find and try a suspect.

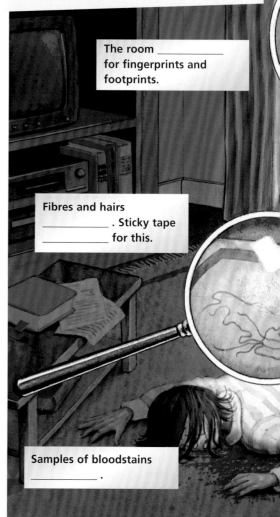

The room _____ for fingerprints and footprints.

Fibres and hairs _____ . Sticky tape _____ for this.

Samples of bloodstains _____ .

Practice

1 Complete the sentences around the picture. Put these verbs in the passive. Use some more than once.

search	take	check	photograph	match
collect	find	pick up	make	use	examine

2 Many things are used to solve crimes.

a How do you think these things are used?
- tyreprints
- teeth
- insects
- DNA
- guns
- paint

b What other things are used to solve a crime? How?

What evidence is collected?

The garden _____ for footprints and weapons.

Windows and doors _____ for marks.
Plaster casts _____ of any marks. Sometimes tools _____ . They _____ against the plaster casts.

Pieces of broken glass _____ .

The body _____ .
Then it _____ to the mortuary. There it _____ by the pathologist.

3 Read what happened next in the murder case.

a Change the sentences into the passive, keeping the same tense. Omit the agent where it is not important.

EXAMPLE
A suspect was arrested yesterday.

1 The police arrested a suspect yesterday.
2 Someone murdered the victim at 6 o'clock.
3 A neighbour had seen the suspect near the house at 5.30.
4 The police searched the suspect's house.
5 They found some bloodstains.
6 The forensic scientists have examined the bloodstains.
7 Two detectives are questioning the suspect.
8 They will probably charge him with murder.
9 They will take him to court tomorrow.

b 🔊 *5.1* Listen and check your answers.

4 Tell the story of a robbery, using this information. Make sentences in the active or passive.
- Two days ago/ record shop in the High Street/ rob
- Some money and several CDs/ steal
- A man and a woman/ see/ near the shop at 10.30.
- The burglars/ break/ a window at the back of the shop
- However, not much/ steal/ because the burglars/ set off/ the alarm
- The police/ call/ a neighbour
- The shop/ examine/ forensic scientists
- Some hair/ find/ on the broken window
- The next day/ the shop assistants/ question/ the police
- One of the assistant's hair/ match/ the hair on the window
- She and her boyfriend/ arrest
- They/ identify/ the witness

5 Think of a crime.

a Work in groups. You can choose a real-life crime or one from television, a book, or a film. What happened? How was it solved? Write the story.

b Tell your story to another group.

Vocabulary
Crime and the law

1 Work in pairs. Make a list of all the crimes you can think of. Compare your list with the class.

2 Match the verbs and nouns. Some verbs may go with more than one noun.

call	a victim
commit	a suspect
arrest	a witness
murder	sentence
examine	the police
solve	the police
try	a crime
catch	prison
pass	the law
break	a criminal
question	a criminal
send to	evidence
give	

3 Look at the actions in 2. Who does each one?

EXAMPLE
A lawyer or a detective questions a witness.

4 Look at this list of crimes. Work in groups and put them in order of seriousness.

- [ ] assault
- [ ] vandalism
- [ ] blackmail
- [ ] murder
- [ ] fraud
- [ ] shoplifting
- [ ] speeding
- [ ] burglary
- [ ] kidnapping
- [ ] drug trafficking

Reading
Sentenced to two years of fun

1 Read the newspaper article.

a Answer these questions.
   1 What happened to Mr Singh?
   2 What will happen to the boy?

b Discuss these questions.
   1 How do you feel about the sentence?
   2 What do you think should happen to the boy?
   3 Why do you think the judge made the decision?

Sentenced to two years of fun

By Arthur Campbell

It was a brutal assault in which an elderly man was almost killed. Yesterday the 17-year-old thug who did it was sentenced to two years at Winfell Grange, a luxury country home where all kinds of sports and games will be provided. If the boy, who can't be named, behaves himself, he'll be taken on a trip to Paris. The cost to the taxpayer of his detention will be £1,000 a week.

When they heard the judge's sentence, the victim's family were very angry. Mr Singh, 61, had been hit several times with a piece of wood and was in hospital for weeks after the attack. He has only just started walking again, still suffers headaches and is afraid to leave his house.

Winfell Grange, where the boy will be sent, aims to give young people a purpose in life. The boy will have his own room with a television and will have access to computers, table tennis, motorcycles, golf, and a swimming pool. Education will be provided at the local school.

Winfell Grange: detention centre or holiday camp?

2 **Look at the parts of two letters to the newspaper about the case.**

a Sort the parts to make the two letters.

b Number the parts in the correct order.

3 **Look at the letters again and discuss these questions.**
1 What arguments are given for and against the boy's sentence?
2 Which arguments do you agree with?
3 Would you change your ideas about the sentence now?
4 Whose fault was the crime?

A 1 If you didn't know it was true, you'd think it was a joke. A young thug almost murders an old man and he is sentenced to two years in a place where most people would be happy to spend their holidays.

B 1 Most people have read the newspaper articles about the young man who was sent to Winfell Grange for assaulting an old man, and it's easy to understand the anger that people feel about the apparent injustice of it. But very few people really understand the truth behind the headlines.

☐☐ Providing televisions, computers, and holidays for young criminals is an insult to all the law-abiding young people who can't afford these things. For beating up an old man, this young thug should be punished, not sent to a holiday camp. In some countries he would be beaten with a cane until he was unconscious. He'd certainly think twice about committing another crime after that.

☐☐ Young people who have been abused like this are angry with society and punishing them will only make them angrier. At Winfell Grange the young men are treated well for the first time in their lives. We have to show them that society does care about them, so that they can become responsible and law-abiding adults.

☐☐ First of all, it must be understood that Winfell Grange is not a holiday camp. The boys there follow a strict daily routine and they have to work hard to earn the rewards of motorcycle racing and a trip to Paris. We aren't dealing with young thugs, as the press like to call them, but angry and frightened young men, whose lives have been badly damaged by their childhood.

☐☐ And why has he been sent there? Well, we are told that the boy isn't really a criminal. He's just an angry young man. He shouldn't be punished. He should be taught how to control his anger. What rubbish! I feel angry when I read about what this young man has done, but I'm not going to go out and assault someone because of it.

4 **Here are two more cases.**

a Work in groups. What do you think should happen? What sentences should be given? Why?
1 A bomb exploded in a busy shopping centre. Three people were seriously injured. A terrorist organization fighting for independence said that they planted the bomb.
2 A woman was found guilty today of murdering her husband. The court was told that the man had been violent towards his wife and had often beaten her up. Last February she stabbed him while he was asleep.

b Now compare your ideas with the information from your teacher.

Language focus: Modal verbs and the passive

a Look at these sentences.
The boy should be punished.
The boy can't be named.

b Complete the rule with *past participle*, *modal verb*, and *be*.

When we use a modal verb with the passive, we use
_____ + _____ + _____ .

➤ Check the rules for modal verbs and the passive in **Grammar Reference 5.1**.

c Complete the sentences with the items in brackets.
1 Young criminals _____ (mustn't / name) in the press.
2 You are less likely to commit a crime if you think you _____ (might / catch).
3 People who commit crimes of violence _____ (should / punish).
4 Young people _____ (can't / send) to prison.
5 The victims of crimes _____ (should / help).
6 Some people think that capital punishment _____ (should / bring back)

☐☐ No, feeling angry isn't an excuse for committing a crime. Perhaps the boy in this case has had a hard life. But he can still tell the difference between right and wrong. Thousands of other people have difficult childhoods, thousands of people are poor, but they don't become criminals.

☐☐ In this particular case, his father left home when the boy was only two. He was neglected by his mother and often left alone in the house for days. When he was seven years old he was so badly beaten up by his stepfather that he was in hospital for ten weeks. Three years later he came home one day and found that his mother had tried to commit suicide. He was taken away and put in a children's home. This boy's case is not uncommon, and many are much worse.

Listening and speaking
Reporting an incident

1 **What do you think has happened to the man's car?**

a Look at the photograph. Choose from these ideas.
  - It's been damaged.
  - It's been stolen.
  - It's been broken into and the radio has been stolen.
  - Another car has run into it.
  - It's been towed away.
  - A bag has been taken from the back seat.
  - It's been blocked in by a lorry.

b 📼 **5.2** Listen and check your ideas.

2 **How much can you remember?**

a Mark these sentences *True* (✓) or *False* (✗).
  1 The car was parked in Samwell Road.
  2 The car is a BMW 540e.
  3 The car is red.
  4 The registration number is P67 HKL.
  5 The car had been parked there for three hours.
  6 A lorry ran into the car.
  7 The car is now at the police station.
  8 The man and the police officer are standing in Hilton Road.
  9 The number 24 bus goes to Hilton Road.

b 📼 **5.2** Listen again and check your ideas.

Language focus: Questions in the passive

a Look at these questions from the conversation.

Where was the car parked?
Has it already been found?

b How do we make questions in the passive?

c Find more questions in the passive in tapescript 5.2.

d Write the questions in the passive in the correct tense.

1 There was a crash on the motorway yesterday.

_____ ?
(anyone/ kill)
No, but two people were hurt.

_____ ?
(take/ to hospital)
Yes, they were.

2 My car was stolen.

_____ ?
(find/ yet)
Yes, I've just got it back.

_____ ?
(it/ damage)
No, it hasn't.

3 That man's been found guilty.

_____ ?
(When/ he/ sentence)
Tomorrow.

_____ ?
(he/ send/ to prison)
Yes, I think he will.

4 A woman has been arrested for that murder.

_____ ?
(charge/ yet)
No, she hasn't.

_____ ?
(being/ question)
Yes, she is.

3 **Make conversations for these situations. Work with a partner, following the diagram. Take it in turns to be the police officer and the person reporting a problem.**
- Your motorcycle has been stolen.
- Your dog has disappeared.
- Someone has broken into your car and stolen something.
- You've found a bag.

A

Ask what the problem is

Ask for more details

Say what you will do

B

Explain the problem

Provide the information

Pronunciation
/ɜ:/; word linking (1)

1 The /ɜ:/ sound

Many words in English have the /ɜ:/ sound, but it can be spelt in different ways.

a Tick (✓) the words with the /ɜ:/ sound.

bird	word	warm	worth
curl	heard	first	pure
occur	storm	girl	beard
stir	world	calm	fire
worm	birthday	third	

b 📼 **5.3** Listen, check, and repeat.

c In the spelling of words with the /ɜ:/ sound, which consonant is always present?

2 Word linking (1)

a 📼 **5.4** Listen to these expressions. What happens to the words that start with vowels?
forensic evidence   shop assistant

b Mark the links in these sentences.
1 He was an old man.
2 I feel angry when I read about it.
3 He died soon afterwards.
4 He's run into the back of my car.
5 It's been towed away.
6 She's a police officer.

c 📼 **5.5** Listen, check, and repeat.

d 📼 **5.6** Now read and listen to these sentences. What happens to the words beginning with vowels here?

/j/
There are too many of them.

/w/
How often do you come here?

/r/
I've been here for an hour.

e Mark the links in these sentences.
1 There's a cow in that field.
2 What's the colour of the car?
3 It's my own book.
4 I parked my car in this street.
5 We decided to stay all day.
6 Now it's time to go.

f 📼 **5.7** Listen, check, and repeat.

Extension: Reading and listening
Who killed Harry Squires?

1 Read the story and name the people in the picture.

Who killed Harry Squires?

At around 10.30 on the evening of 9 June millionaire businessman, Harry Squires, was murdered in his sitting room. His business partner, Julian Clayton, was wounded in the attack. There were three other people at the house at the time: Harry's wife, Martina, his sister, Belinda Ewers, and her husband, Craig.

According to their stories, at the time of the murder, Martina Squires was reading in the library. Belinda Ewers was upstairs in her bedroom. She wasn't feeling well and she had gone to bed early. Craig Ewers was in the garden. He was having a cigarette. Harry Squires wouldn't allow smoking inside the house. Harry Squires himself and Julian Clayton were discussing business in the sitting room. It was a warm evening and the French windows were open.

Suddenly a shot was fired. It was quickly followed by a second shot and a scream. Belinda Ewers arrived at the sitting room first. Harry Squires was already dead and Julian Clayton was lying on the floor. His hand was bleeding and he was holding a handkerchief around it. Soon afterwards Martina Squires arrived. While she and Belinda were helping Julian, Craig Ewers entered the sitting room through the French windows. He was holding a gun in his hand. The police were called.

Preliminary investigations showed that Harry Squires and Julian Clayton had almost certainly been shot with the gun that Mr Ewers had brought in. The bullets had been fired from the direction of the garden. The only fingerprints on the gun were Mr Ewers'.

2 What do you think?
a Make a note of any facts you think are significant.
b Who do you think is the prime suspect? Why?

3 Here are some notes from the detective's notebook.
a Why is each of these facts significant?
b Who do you think committed the murder?

It seemed an open and shut case, but later investigations revealed some interesting facts.

1 When Belinda Ewers went to the sitting room, she was fully dressed. Her bed had not been disturbed.

2 The gun belonged to Harry Squires. It had disappeared three days before the murder on the day that the Ewers had arrived.

3 Belinda arrived at the sitting room before Martina.

4 The light in the library was switched off.

5 The back door was open.

6 Mrs Squires had soil on her shoes.

7 Nobody seemed unhappy about the murder. Harry Squires had been hated by everybody in the house and many other people, too.

8 Harry Squires and Julian Clayton were arguing in the sitting room. Their voices could be heard in the garden.

4 🔲 *5.8* Listen to these interviews with the people involved.
a Note down any important facts.
b What motive did each person have for killing Harry Squires?
c Do any of the facts change your ideas about who committed the murder?

5 🔲 *5.9* Listen. The detective will reveal the murderer.

6 Write a short newspaper article about the murder with the title below, using all the information that you have.

Squires' murder solved!

6 Travel

Grammar
Conditionals; time clauses

Grammar in use

1 📼 *6.1* **Listen to Bill and Marie discussing their holiday and answer these questions.**
1   What aspect of the holiday are they discussing?
2   What are the two possibilities?
3   Which do Bill and Marie want?

2 **What are the arguments for and against each form of travel?**
a   Complete the table.

Form of travel	for	against
1 _____		
2 _____		

b   Which would you choose? Why?
c   How do you think they will resolve the argument?

Rules

1   **The conversation contains two types of conditional sentence.**

a   Complete these sentences from the conversation.
If we _____ by coach, it _____ a lot cheaper.
If we _____ two weeks for the holiday, the coach _____ all right.

b   What form of the verb is used
   • in the *if* clause?
   • in the main clause?

c   What is each type of conditional called?

2   **When is each type of conditional used?**

a   Look at the example sentences and answer these questions.
   1   Is it possible to go by coach?
   2   Do they have two weeks?

b   Which sentence is talking about
   • a possible situation?
   • an imaginary situation?

c   The same verb forms can also be used with time clauses, using the conjunctions *when, as soon as, until, before,* and *after.*

   EXAMPLE
   You'll be able to sleep when we're on the plane.

d   Find more examples of each type of conditional and underline any other time clauses in tapescript 6.1. Say why each example is either a first or a second conditional.

➤   Check the rules for conditionals and time clauses in **Grammar References 6.1, 6.2,** and **6.3**.

Practice

1 What are the advantages and disadvantages of different forms of travel?

Make sentences using items from each column.

EXAMPLE

If we go by coach, it will be cheaper.
If we fly, we'll get there quicker.

A	B
fly	be cheaper
	get there quicker
	be more comfortable
go by coach	be able to see things on the journey
	cost more
	not be bothered by traffic jams
take the train	be more relaxing
	take longer
	not be able to take a lot of luggage
drive	be able to leave when we like

2 Things can sometimes go wrong on holiday.

a What would you do in these situations?

EXAMPLE

If I lost my credit cards, I'd phone the credit card company immediately.

1 You lose your credit cards.
2 A stranger asks you for a lift.
3 Your hotel is overbooked.
4 You get toothache in the middle of the night.
5 You lock yourself out of your hotel room.
6 Your plane is hijacked.
7 Your passport is stolen.
8 Your hotel room is too noisy.
9 An armed mugger demands your wallet.
10 Your car breaks down on a lonely road at night.
11 A dog bites you.

b Work with a partner. Ask and answer about the situations. Then ask questions to find out more information.

EXAMPLE

A What would you do if you lost your credit cards?
B I'd phone the credit card company immediately.
A What would they do? / What would you do if you didn't know their number?

3 Rewrite these sentences with time clauses, using the conjunctions in brackets.

EXAMPLE

We'll have dinner before we go out.

1 We'll have dinner, and then we'll go out. (before)
2 They'll send us the report, but they'll need to finish the survey first. (after)
3 We'll go to the travel agency, but we'll look at the brochures first. (before)

4 She hasn't arrived yet, so I'll wait. (until)
5 I'll get back, and then I'll drop you a line. (when)
6 She'll get to her hotel and then she'll phone us immediately. (as soon as)

4 Look at the conversations.

a Decide whether each incomplete sentence should be a first or second conditional. Some have time clauses.

b Complete the sentences with the correct form of the verbs in brackets.

1 A Do you think you've had an interesting life?
  B Oh yes. If I _____ (have) my time again, I _____ (do) exactly the same.
2 A Can you tell Sally I won't be here tomorrow?
  B OK. I _____ (tell) her if I _____ (see) her.
  A No, on second thoughts I _____ (wait) until she _____ (come) back.
3 A I think I'll go out this evening.
  B Well, if you _____ (take) the car, you _____ (need) to put some petrol in it. Will you be late?
  A Yes. You _____ probably _____ (be) in bed when I _____ (get) back.
4 A Can you lend me £10?
  B No, I'm sorry.
  A But I need it urgently, and I _____ (pay) you back as soon as I _____ (get) paid.
  B Look, I _____ (lend) it to you if I _____ (have) it, but I'm broke.
5 A This letter's important. It must get there by tomorrow.
  B OK. If you _____ (leave) it there, I _____ (post) it for you.
  A You won't forget?
  B Don't worry. I _____ (see) to it before I _____ (go) to lunch.

c Explain your choice of conditionals.

d 🔲 *6.2* Listen and compare your answers.

e Work with a partner. Practise the conversations.

5 Try some creative thinking.

a Write down some ideas for these imaginary situations.

b Discuss your ideas with a partner.

1 What would life be like if people had three legs instead of two?
2 What would happen if everyone in the world got flu at the same time?
3 What would people do if there was no television or radio?
4 What would or wouldn't you do if you were nine years old again?
5 What would life be like if we could read other people's minds?

Vocabulary
Phrasal verbs (1)

1 **Look at these phrasal verbs and answer the questions.**

a Can you work out what these phrasal verbs mean from the meanings of each part?

*He **ran away** from home.*
*They **took** their coats **off**.*
*They **set off** early in the morning.*
*She **looks after** her granddaughter.*

b Some phrasal verbs have an object (transitive) and some do not (intransitive). Look at these sentences. Which verbs are transitive?

*Your son has really **grown up**.*
*Could you **pick up** that pen?*
*I think I'll **turn** the TV **off**.*
*It's time to **get up**.*

c With some transitive verbs the two parts can be separated. Which of these sentences are correct?

*I'm **looking for** my glasses.*
*I'm **looking** my glasses **for**.*
*I'm **looking** them **for**.*
*I'm **looking for** them.*

*They **put** the meeting **off**.*
*They **put off** the meeting.*
*They **put** it **off**.*
*They **put off** it.*

➤ Check the rules for phrasal verbs in **Grammar Reference 6.4**.

2 **Work with a partner.**

a Can you work out the meanings of these phrasal verbs from the two parts? Which of them are transitive? Check your ideas in a dictionary.

1 She really stands out from the rest.
2 Just kick off your shoes and dance.
3 I fell over in the street.
4 We decided to set up a business together.
5 'Lindsay isn't here. She's just gone out.'

b Complete these sentences with the phrasal verbs in brackets. Give both the separated and the unseparated forms where possible.

1 The baby _____ his chair. (has fallen off)
2 Could you please _____ the form? (fill in)
3 The witness _____ the robber easily. (picked out)
4 I'd like to stay for a few days. Can you _____ me? (put up)
5 The soldiers _____ the train. (blew up)
6 Could you _____ the radio? (turn down)
7 She's just _____ the plane. (got on)

Reading
Culture clash

1 **Discuss these questions.**
1 Have you ever been to another country or had contact with people from another culture?
2 Have you ever had any experiences that were caused by cultural differences?

2 **Read the first paragraph and answer the questions.**
1 What do your responses show about your culture?
2 Do you think people from other cultures would give the same response?

3 **Read the rest of the article quickly and answer these questions.**
1 What differences is it about?
2 In what context do these differences emerge?
3 Who does this cause problems for?

4 **The text describes two ways in which cultures differ.**

a Complete the scale.

_____ | less mobile
universalist | _____

b Read the text again. For each of the four types of society or culture find
- the distinguishing feature.
- the effects on behaviour.
- countries or regions that have the culture.
- how the opposite kind of culture sees it.

5 **Discuss these questions.**
1 What do you think are the plus and minus points of the different types of culture?
2 What do you think of the Indian traveller's problem?
3 Where would you put your country on the scale in **a**?

6 **Look at these situations. What would you think or do? Make notes, then discuss in groups.**
1 You are working in a foreign country. A colleague from your own country comes to see you. He/She is only in town for a day and would like to see some of the interesting places. You are very busy and would have to take the rest of the day off to show him/her around.
2 You are in a queue in a bank. A local politician comes in. The bank clerk invites him/her to come to the front of the queue.
3 You have a meeting. When you arrive, you find that the person that you are meeting has taken the day off to go to a cousin's wedding.
4 You are in the 'no smoking' section of a restaurant. Some people at the next table start smoking.

Culture clash

You've just got on a plane for your long-haul flight to Australia. The flight is full and there's someone sitting in the seat next to you. You know that you're going to spend the next twenty hours or so next to your fellow passenger. What would you like to happen:

- You start a conversation with the other person and really get to know him/her?
- You sit quietly next to each other and perhaps just before you land you'll say how nice it was to meet?
- You wait for the other person to start a conversation?

Would it make a difference if the other passenger was
- older than you?
- younger than you?
- of the opposite sex?
- from a different culture?

Vocabulary file: Synonyms

Find words or expressions in the article which mean the same as:
- a flight between continents
- someone who is travelling with you
- male, if you are female
- are different
- moving
- often
- lasting a long time
- It isn't enjoyable.
- in different places

These are questions from a cross-cultural workshop which helps business people to avoid misunderstandings when they deal with people who come from different cultures. Ideas about polite behaviour vary from one culture to another and it's easy to cause offence, or feel offended, if you don't know what other cultures expect.

Some societies, such as America and Australia, for example, are mobile and very open. People here change jobs and move house quite frequently. As a result they have a lot of relationships that often last only a short time, and they need to get to know people quickly. So it's normal to have friendly conversations with people that they have just met, and you can talk about things that other cultures would regard as private.

At the other extreme are more crowded and less mobile societies where long-term relationships are more important. A Malaysian or Mexican businessperson, for example, will want to get to know you very well before he or she feels happy to start business. But when

you do get to know each other, the relationship becomes much deeper than it would in a mobile society.

To Americans, both Europeans and Asians seem cool and formal at first. On the other hand, as a passenger from a less mobile society put it, it's no fun spending several hours next to a stranger who wants to tell you all about his or her life and asks you all sorts of embarrassing questions that you don't want to answer.

Cross-cultural differences aren't just a problem for travellers, but also for the airlines that carry them. All airlines want to provide the best service, but ideas about good service vary from place to place. This can be seen most clearly in the way that problems are dealt with.

Some societies have 'universalist' cultures. These societies have a strong respect for rules, and they treat every person and situation in basically the same way.

'Particularist' societies, on the other hand, also have rules, but they are less important than the society's unwritten ideas about what is right or wrong for a particular situation or a particular person. So the formal rules are bent to fit the needs of the situation or the importance of the person.

This difference can cause problems. A traveller from a particularist society, India, is checking in for a flight in Germany, a country which has a universalist culture. The Indian traveller has too much luggage, but he explains that he has been away from home for a long time and the suitcases are full of presents for his family. He expects that the check-in clerk will understand his problem and will bend the rules for him. The check-in clerk, however, expects that if she explains the rules, the customer will understand. If he was allowed to have too much luggage, it wouldn't be fair to the other passengers. But the traveller thinks this is unfair, because the other passengers don't have his problem.

Listening and speaking
Checking in

1 Read this information about Mr Brown's flight.

> Mr Brown is flying to New York. He has an important meeting tomorrow morning. He doesn't smoke and when he's travelling he likes to look out of the window. He's taking one suitcase and a briefcase. His wife packed the suitcase. Last time he went, she forgot his electric razor, but this time she remembered it. She put his personal stereo in his suitcase, too. Mr Brown drove to the airport, parked his car and checked in straight away.

2 Mr Brown is checking in at the airport.

a Look at the dialogue in 3.

b Write what you think Mr Brown says.

c 🔊 *6.3* Listen and check your ideas.

3 🔊 *6.3* Listen again and complete the conversation.

Mr Brown	Do I check in here for New York?
Clerk	Yes. Could I see your ticket and passport, please?
Mr Brown	_____
Clerk	Thank you. How many pieces of luggage are you checking in?
Mr Brown	_____
Clerk	Did you pack the case yourself?
Mr Brown	_____
Clerk	Does the bag contain any electrical items?
Mr Brown	_____
Clerk	I'm afraid you can't take electronic items in hold baggage. You'll have to take the personal stereo in your hand baggage, I'm afraid.
Mr Brown	_____
Clerk	Thank you. Has the case been unattended at any time since your wife packed it?
Mr Brown	_____
Clerk	Fine. Would you like smoking or non-smoking?
Mr Brown	_____
Clerk	And would you prefer a window or an aisle seat?
Mr Brown	_____
Clerk	Here you are. Here's your boarding card, ticket, and passport. Boarding is at 18.40 from gate 23. Have a pleasant flight.
Mr Brown	_____

4 🔊 *6.4* **Listen to three more conversations and complete the table.**

	1	2	3
Destination Baggage Smoking Seat Boarding time Gate			

5 Roleplay conversations at the check-in desk.

a Work with a partner. Practise the conversations, using tapescript 6.4. Take it in turns to be the customer and the check-in clerk.

b Make more conversations, using this information.
- Singapore/ smoking/ aisle/ packed own case/ nothing electrical/ 16.40/ gate B11
- Sydney/ non-smoking/ window/ mother packed case/ hairdryer/ 10.00/ Gate 26

Conversation pieces: Check-in problems

a Complete the sentences with these expressions.

I'm afraid	while I had a meeting
is overweight	only smoking seats
over there, please	is closed
as hand baggage	isn't valid
I'm sorry, sir	while you're waiting

I'm sorry, sir. There are _____ left.

_____ there's a three-hour delay on this flight. Here's a voucher for a drink _____ .

Yes, I left it at the hotel reception, _____ this morning.

None. I'd like to take both of these _____ .

I'm afraid you're too late. The flight _____ .

_____ . Your ticket _____ for this flight. You'll have to go to the airline ticket office.

I'm afraid your luggage _____ . Could you go to the excess baggage counter _____ ?

b Look at the completed sentences and answer the questions.
1. Who would say each one?
2. Where would it occur in the check-in conversation?
3. How would the other person respond?
4. What won't they be able to do?
5. What will they have to do?

6 Imagine the most frustrating check-in possible. Work with a partner. Make a new conversation, using some of the ideas from Conversation pieces.

Pronunciation Diphthongs; questions with choices

1 Diphthongs

Some English vowel sounds consist of two sounds together called diphthongs. The first sound moves smoothly into the second, so that it sounds like one sound.

a Match the diphthongs to the words.

/eɪ/	boy
/əʊ/	there
/ɔɪ/	day
/aʊ/	go
/aɪ/	how
/eə/	here
/ɪə/	fly

➤ Check your answers in the IPA chart on the inside back cover.

b Try saying the individual sounds first and then put them together.
EXAMPLE
/e/ + /ə/ = /eə/

c Choose the word with the diphthong.

say	said	done	down
wine	win	car	care
toy	story	bean	fear
blow	blue	noise	knees

d 🔊 *6.5* Listen, check, and repeat.

2 Questions with choices

a 🔊 *6.6* Listen to these questions and mark the intonation.

Do you want to go to Paris?

Do you want to go to Paris or Rome?

b Mark these questions with a rising or a falling intonation.
1. Would you like a window or an aisle seat?
2. Do you like flying?
3. Do you have one suitcase or two?
4. Would you like to go by plane, train, or car?
5. Have you been to Athens?
6. Do you usually travel business or economy class?

c 🔊 *6.7* Listen, check, and repeat.

Extension: Reading and listening
A day out

1 What is your idea of a good day out? Discuss these questions.
1 Where would you go?
2 Who would you go with?
3 What would you do?

2 Look at the leaflet and answer these questions.
1 What is it for?
2 What kind of people is it aimed at?
3 Which place is it about?
4 What are the names of the four attractions described?

3 Write the names of the correct place(s).
1 Where can you learn about life in the past?
2 Where can you go underground?
3 Where can you see how honey is made?
4 Where is there a Fun Centre?
5 Where can you have a ride on a toboggan?
6 Where are dogs not allowed?
7 Where can you see a ghost?
8 Where are there some animals?
9 Where are there guided tours?
10 Where can you learn to windsurf?

Vocabulary file: Working out meanings

a You may not have understood all the language in the leaflets. Do you think all the words are necessary for understanding the texts? Why/Why not?

b What do you think these things are? Try to guess from the context.
  • an infoline
  • the A379
  • all-inclusive admission
  • wheelchair access
  • toddlers
  • playzones
  • hands-on technology
  • takeaway meals

c Find some unknown words that you think are important for the meaning. Look them up in a dictionary. Do they help you to understand the leaflet better?

---

4 Which of these features do the different places use as selling points?
  • technology
  • cleanliness
  • variety
  • uniqueness
  • facilities for the disabled
  • awards it has won
  • suitable for all weathers
  • special admission charges
  • beautiful scenery
  • safety
  • educational value

5 Which things do these words describe? Why do you think they are used?
  • electrifying
  • fascinating
  • superb
  • extraordinary
  • unspoilt
  • extensive

6 The Wilson family are discussing which place to go to.

a 🔊 *6.8* Listen. Where does each person want to go?
  • Mr Wilson
  • Mrs Wilson
  • Sasha
  • Robert

b What do they finally decide?

c 🔊 *6.8* Listen again. What arguments does each person put forward?

7 Discuss these questions.
1 What do you think are the most attractive features of each place?
2 What do you think are the least attractive features?
3 Which of the places would you choose to spend a day? Why?

8 Work in groups. Think of an attraction for a good day out and write an advertisement for it.

Morwellham Quay

Nr. Tavistock off the A390

AA award winner "Leading Day Out" Most facilities under cover

This riverside village is the **ONLY PLACE IN THE WORLD** where your family can • Travel by train a mile underground in a **COPPER MINE**

- **RIDE A WAGONETTE** drawn by Shire Horses
- Play Games of the Past and **HANDS-ON** 19th C. technology
- See baby farm animals/shire horses at our **FARM**
- Take **GUIDED TOURS** of the Port, Ships, Cottages, Workshops, School and Ghosts! • Enjoy daily events, **MAZEY DAY** (miner's holiday fun) • Experience **LIFE ABOARD SHIP/AT THE MINE** (for children, limited spaces, first come) • **MUSEUMS** • **VIDEO SHOWS**,

restaurants, shops and much more. All inclusive admission, Family ticket Great value (2 adults, with up to 2 children 5–16 years). Info line: (01822) 833808.

Open 10am–5.30pm. Winter (1st Nov–Easter) 10am–4.30pm copper mine & grounds only (closed Christmas week). Last admission 2 hours before closing time. Average visit 5–6 hours. Dogs on leads.

PLYMOUTH DOME

The Hoe, Plymouth, PL1 2NZ
Telephone: Plymouth (01752) 600608

The Award-Winning Centre on Plymouth Hoe – exploring Plymouth's great Maritime Heritage

Atmospheric reconstructions and high-tech equipment take you on an extraordinary journey through time; through the sights and smells of Elizabethan Plymouth; on the voyages of Drake, Cook and the Pilgrim Fathers; and through the tragic devastation wrought by the Blitz on Plymouth. "Hands-on" computers, TV, Radar and satellite technology give you a fascinating view of the bustling modern harbour. This stunning £3.5 million centre, overlooking Plymouth Sound, has already won ten awards including the England for Excellence "Tourism for All" Award.

Open daily from 9am seven days a week throughout the year. Closed Christmas Day. Full Wheelchair access. Facilities for hearing and visually impaired people. Quality Gift Shop and Coffee Shop.

Children under 7 are free. Discounts for families, children and senior citizens. Call Plymouth (01752) 603300 for School and Group rates. Discounts for groups, schools, coaches and families. Allow at least 2 hours for your visit.

FAMILY DAYS OUT

Woodlands LEISURE PARK

DARTMOUTH
A FULL DAY OF VARIETY SET IN 60 GLORIOUS ACRES
1995 – 500m TORNADO TOBOGGAN RUN

12 Electrifying Playzones
- Mighty Commando Course
- Slippy Dipper • Action Track
- Amazin' Matrix • Astroglide

NOW 34,000 sq.ft. Undercover Play
- Bigger Circus Playdome
- Triple Dropslide • Smugglers Ballpool • New Fun Centre
- Big Farm Complex

- Fascinating Honey Farm **Toddlers Paradise**
- 4 Extensive Play Areas plus Indoor Wonderlands
100's of Animals & Birds • Woolly Llamas • Silky Rabbits
- Bristly Pigs • Pretty Ponies • Multitudes of Birds
- Café • Picnic Area • Great Gift Shop

Open Daily 9.30 to Dusk.
Five Miles West of Dartmouth on A3122

Info line (01803) 712598
Woodlands Leisure Park, Blackawton, Totnes TQ9 7DQ

IN GLORIOUS DEVON

BLACKPOOL SANDS

Set in an unspoilt, sheltered bay with its superb golden beach, turquoise blue sea and magnificent pines, Blackpool Sands is the ideal place to relax and enjoy the views or to swim and sail. But don't just take our word for it, come and see for yourself!

Relax or play, it's South Devon's most beautiful beach any day!

RURAL BEACH AWARD

GOOD BEACH GUIDE Marine Conservation Society

- ✔ Safe swimming and wonderful watersports
- ✔ Beach cleaned daily in main season (no dogs)
- ✔ Delicious takeaway meals (mid March to October)
- ✔ Paddling/boating pond and putting green
- ✔ Beach goods shop, with deck chair hire
- ✔ Sailing/windsurfing tuition and boat hire

TEL: INFOLINE 01803 770606 (APRIL – OCTOBER)

Signposted from Dartmouth on the A379 between Stoke Fleming and Strete

1995 BEST KEPT BEACH AWARD

7 Entertainment

Grammar

The present perfect simple and continuous

Grammar in use

1 Discuss these questions.
  1 In the last seven days how much time have you spent watching TV?
  2 What are your favourite programmes?
  3 Would you miss the TV if you didn't have one? What would you do instead?

2 Read the text. What did the family do? What effects has it had?

Are you a telly addict? We aren't!

Have you ever spent a year without a television? A year ago the Benson family decided that they were spending too much time in front of the box. So they got rid of it. And they have been living without a television for almost a year now. So how have they been spending their free time?

'We found it very hard for the first few weeks,' says Mrs Louise Benson. 'We didn't know what to do with our free time. But since then it's been fine. We've done so many things that we hadn't done for such a long time. Last year, for example, we didn't go out to the cinema or the theatre once, but this year we've seen at least a dozen films and plays. And I've even joined the local drama society.'

Daughter Emily has been learning to play the piano, husband Rob has taken up tennis and son Mark has been going to judo classes. And they've all read several books. Mark: 'Before we got rid of the telly I only read comics, but this year I've read about ten novels and five or six other books, too. This week I've been reading a book on UFOs. It's very good and I've nearly finished it.'

So, haven't they missed the box at all? Emily says she has had a few problems: 'I don't like it when I go to school and all the kids are talking about a programme that they've seen. Actually, I've just been watching a programme round at my friend's house.'

As Rob Benson put it, 'We've all started doing so many interesting things that we wouldn't have time to watch TV now.'

Rules

1 What do you know about the past simple and the present perfect tenses?

a Look at the list of uses. Complete them with the correct names of the tenses.

> We use the _____ tense to talk about
> 1 an event in a time frame that comes up to the present, e.g. *this year, this month, today.*
> 2 a past event with a present result.
> 3 experiences in your life.
>
> We use the _____ tense to talk about
> 4 events in a time frame that ended in the past, e.g. *last year, last month, yesterday.*
> 5 completed past events.

b Match the example sentences to the uses.
☐ *Last year we didn't go out to the cinema or the theatre once.*
☐ *This year we've seen at least a dozen films and plays.*
☐ *So they got rid of it.*
☐ *Have you ever spent a year without a television?*
☐ *I've joined the local drama society.*

2 Every tense in English has a continuous form.

a You already know the two most common continuous tenses:
• the present continuous
• the past continuous
Find an example of each tense in the text. When do we use them?

b Now find examples of another common continuous tense – the present perfect continuous.

c How do we form the present perfect continuous?

3 Compare the present perfect simple and continuous.

Look at the examples and questions below and identify the uses.
I've read a book on UFOs this week.
I've been reading a book on UFOs this week.
1 Which sentence shows
• an activity that is still happening?
• an activity that has finished?

I've just been watching a programme at my friend's house.
I've just watched a programme at my friend's house.
2 Which sentence emphasizes
• the actual process of the activity?
• the result of the activity?

➤ Check the rules for the present perfect continuous in **Grammar Reference 7.1**.

Practice

1 Here are some of the Bensons' activities.

a What is the difference between last year and this year?
EXAMPLE
Last year they didn't go out, but this year they've been out a lot.
Last year Mark only read comics and magazines, but this year he's read lots of books.
• go out   • play tennis
• read   • watch TV
• see plays   • start new hobbies
• learn to play a musical instrument

b 🔲 *7.1* Listen and compare your answers.

c Compare last year and this year for yourself.

2 In some of these sentences both forms are correct, in others only one form is correct. Delete the forms that are incorrect.
1 We*'ve lived* / *'ve been living* here for five years.
2 I*'ve always liked* / *'ve always been liking* Mozart.
3 They **have worked** / **have been working** at the factory for a year.
4 I*'ve forgotten* / *'ve been forgetting* their names.
5 He's a famous author. He*'s written* / *'s been writing* two best sellers.
6 I*'ve played* / *'ve been playing* tennis all day.
7 I*'ve written* / *'ve been writing* a letter and I've almost finished now.
8 Have you ever **won** / **been winning** the lottery?
9 Good. They've finally *arrived* / *been arriving*. We*'ve waited* / *'ve been waiting* for an hour.
10 Have you **seen** / **been seeing** my glasses? I*'ve looked* / *'ve been looking* for them all morning.

3 Think about your life.

a Look at the times below. Which tense would you use for talking about each one?
• this year   • on your birthday
• recently   • since your birthday
• last month   • last summer
• on Saturday   • for the last five years
• today   • yesterday

b Think about something that you did/have done/have been doing at these times.

c Tell your partner about your activities.

4 Write a letter to a friend.

a You can write about your real life or imagine that you have had a big change in your life, e.g. you've gone to work or study abroad, you've got a job or changed your job, you've got married.

b Your letter should answer these questions.
• What have you done so far this year?
• How has this year been different from last year?
• What have you been doing recently?
• What have you been doing today?

c Give your letter to your partner to read.

Vocabulary
Entertainment

1 Complete the spidergram.

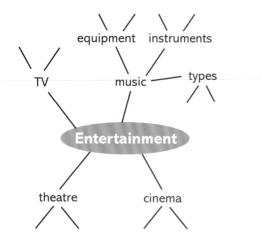

2 Where would these words go in your spidergram?

a CD   a hi-fi   an album   a stereo
rock (and roll)   a play   horror   jazz
the top twenty   a ballad   a concert
crime   heavy metal   classical
box office   a musical   a romance
a camera   a hit   folk   a thriller
a programme   country (and western)
a comedy   a stage   a tour
a whodunnit   a show

3 Talk to other members of the class and find out about their tastes in entertainment. Here are some possible questions. Add some more.

1 What kind of music do you like best?
2 Who are your favourite artists? .
3 Have you got any of their albums?
4 Have you ever seen them live?
5 What kind of films do you like best?
6 Do you prefer to watch films at the cinema or on video?
7 Do you ever go to concerts/ the theatre?
8 Do you play a musical instrument yourself? What?

Reading
I'm so lucky!

1 Look at the article and photographs.

a Who is the text about?

b What do you know about her?

2 What is each paragraph of the article about?

a Look at these paragraph topics.
  • a typical day in her life
  • her early life
  • why she has been successful
  • her feelings about life
  • Emilio's early life
  • her family life
  • the accident
  • how she became a pop star
  • her recovery from the accident

b Look quickly at the text. Choose the six correct topics and match them to the paragraphs. Justify your choice.

3 Read the text in more detail. What part does each of these play in the story?
  • two metal rods
  • *Miami Sound Machine*
  • *Cuts Both Ways*
  • Emilio
  • a lorry
  • fans
  • Nayib
  • Havana
  • the clinic
  • Castro
  • Miami University
  • Star Island

4 Discuss these questions.
1 In what ways has Gloria struggled in her life?
2 In what ways has she been lucky?
3 What does Gloria mean when she says *We live right on the edge*? How does her life illustrate this? Can you give examples from your own life to support it?
4 Gloria is described as not 'the typical rock star'. Why? What do you think of her image?
5 Nayib's experience of life has been very different from his parents. In what ways? What problems could this cause?

5 A reporter interviewed Gloria to write the article.

a Work with a partner. Look at the article and write down what questions you think the reporter asked to get the information.

b One person is the reporter, the other is Gloria. Roleplay the interview.

6 Write an article about a superstar.

a Choose or invent another international star.

b Write a magazine article about his/her life. Your article should have four or five paragraphs. Choose from the paragraph topics in **2**.

I'm so lucky!

The concert had been a great success and now Gloria Estefan was asleep in the bus that was taking her to the next town on the tour. Her husband and manager, Emilio, was making calls on his mobile phone and her son, Nayib, was talking to his personal tutor at the back of the bus. Suddenly the peace was shattered when a huge lorry crashed head-on into the bus. Gloria was thrown to the floor, her back broken.

☆ ☆ ☆ ☆ ☆

When she left hospital several weeks later Gloria was in a wheelchair. Her spine was held together by two long metal rods. She can still feel them when she lies down. At the time, it was feared that the high-kicking Conga Queen of Miami might never walk again, but for Gloria giving up was never an option. She started a long and tough exercise programme, and just over a year later she had recorded a new album and was back on stage in her biggest ever tour. 'My only thought was that I owed it, not only to my family, but also to my fans,' she says. 'I've been doing it for them, to show that it is possible to do the impossible, in my own small way.'

☆ ☆ ☆ ☆ ☆

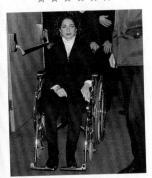

Gloria leaving hospital

To those fans, Gloria's return to health was close to a miracle, but Gloria has always been a fighter. She was born in 1957 in Havana, Cuba, where her father worked as a policeman at the president's palace. After Castro's revolution two years later, the family had to leave Cuba quickly and they settled in Miami. Life in the United States was not easy for the young Gloria, because her father became very ill and she had to look after him while her mother went out to work to support the family.

☆ ☆ ☆ ☆ ☆

Gloria wanted to be a psychologist, but while studying at Miami University, she met Emilio Estefan and joined his band, the *Miami Sound Machine*, as a singer. Three years later when Gloria was still only 21, they got married. A brilliant businessman who had also emigrated from Cuba after his family had lost everything, Emilio turned the shy, overweight Gloria into an international superstar. Her record, *Cuts Both Ways*, sold an amazing 10 million copies worldwide. She has been making successful records ever since, both in English and Spanish.

☆ ☆ ☆ ☆ ☆

Although she is now one of the richest and most successful artists in America, Gloria Estefan is not the typical rock star. She's never had anything to do with drugs or alcohol, and her marriage to Emilio, who was her first and only love, is blissfully happy. Her biggest worry is her son, Nayib. She doesn't want him to become spoilt by having too much money. A few years ago, when Nayib was behaving very badly, she took away all his toys. 'I left only his books. He lived like that for a year. I told him he was going to have to realize what it was like to have nothing.'

☆ ☆ ☆ ☆ ☆

Gloria has a lot to smile about – a $6 million mansion on Star Island, Miami, her own yacht, and enough money to buy anything she wants. But she has also had to struggle hard in her life. Gloria herself, however, doesn't see it that way. 'Everybody's life is tough sometimes, and other people have had far worse problems than me. I've always felt very lucky to have what I have. I certainly felt this when I had to go to the clinic after my accident and saw all the terrible things that had happened to other people in the course of their normal lives. It showed me that we live right on the edge.'

The Estefans' house on Star Island

Listening and speaking
Stating your views

1 🔊 **7.2 You are going to hear part of a radio phone-in programme. Read and listen to the presenter's introduction and answer these questions.**

1 What topic is the phone-in about?
2 What evidence is presented about the scale of the problem?
3 Is this an issue in your country?
4 What do you think about the problem?

‘A recent survey revealed that in one week on British TV 401 people were killed and 119 were wounded. There were also 29 cases of bad language. The survey included both terrestrial and satellite channels. Similar research in the United States showed that the average American child watches 8,000 murders and 100,000 other acts of violence while still at junior school. What effect has this been having on our children? American psychologists, Huesmann and Eron, maintain that watching violence on TV 'is one of the major causes of aggressive behaviour, crime and violence in society'. In several recent trials it has been shown that the defendants had got their ideas from watching violent videos. So do you agree that what children see on TV affects their behaviour? Should we have stricter controls on what can or can't be shown? Or should people be able to watch anything that they want? We'd like to hear your views, so please call us. ’

2 🔊 **7.3 Listen to the phone-in.**

a Number these opinions in the order that you hear them.

b Which two opinions are not expressed?

☐ It is difficult to control what children watch.
☐ Only sick people watch violent films.
☐ Television should show real life.
☐ People should be allowed to watch anything that they want.
☐ Children can tell the difference between fantasy and reality.
☐ Children naturally act out scenes from films and TV programmes.
☐ There is too much unnecessary violence on TV.
☐ Children need to learn that life isn't always pleasant.
☐ People blame TV for violence so that they can censor it.
☐ There's too much bad language on TV.

3 What examples or evidence does each speaker give to support his/her views?

a Note down your ideas and compare them with a partner.

b 🔊 **7.3 Listen again and check your ideas.**

Conversation pieces: Expressing opinions

Complete the expressions with these words:

simply	see	believe	wouldn't	support
have	would	can't	in	mind

think

I _____ (that) …

maintain

_____ say

To my _____ , …

_____ my opinion, …

As I _____ it, …

I agree with …

I'd like to _____ …

I'm sorry, but I _____ agree (with …)

I'm afraid I _____ to disagree (with …)

I _____ don't agree (with …)

I _____ agree (with …)

Note: You can agree/disagree with a person or an idea.

EXAMPLES

I don't agree with you/ the last caller (on that).
I don't agree with censorship/ that view/ what you said.

➤ Look at tapescript 7.3 and check your answers.

4 Discuss these questions.

1 Which of the views do you agree/disagree with? Why?
2 Should the content of TV be controlled?
3 What sorts of things would you not want to see on TV?
4 What sorts of things would you not want children to see?
5 How can programmes, especially satellite programmes and videos, be controlled?

5 Make a radio phone-in programme.

a Work in a group. You can continue with the topic above, or choose another one. Here are some ideas.
1 The number of foreign programmes on TV should be limited.
2 Young people watch too much television.
3 The standards of TV have deteriorated.

b Prepare your opinions individually. Decide the order that people will speak in. One student is the presenter who asks each caller to speak in turn. Each caller must first agree or disagree with the last caller, before stating their views.

c Roleplay the phone-in programme. If possible, use a cassette player to record your programme, and play it to the class.

Pronunciation
Syllables; word linking (2)

1 Syllables

a Often, not every part of a word is pronounced. How many syllables are there in these words?
wanted   /ˈwɒntɪd/
seemed   /siːmd/
secretary   /ˈsekrətrɪ/
interesting /ˈɪntrəstɪŋ/

b Normally two vowels together form one syllable, but sometimes they are pronounced as separate syllables. How many syllables are there in these words?
cream   /kriːm/
create   /krɪˈeɪt/

c How many syllables do these words have?

camera	☐	realize	☐	married	☐
poem	☐	rhythm	☐	reaction	☐
business	☐	scientist	☐	idea	☐
economy	☐	figures	☐	various	☐
languages	☐	beautifully	☐	information	☐
appeared	☐	experience	☐	coloured	☐
opened	☐	someone	☐	finished	☐

d 🔲 **7.4** Listen, check, and repeat.

2 Word linking (2)

We saw on page 45 that when a word starts with a vowel sound we normally run on the consonant sound from the previous word, even if the consonant is not normally pronounced. What happens when two vowel sounds come together at the end and the beginning of two words?

a 🔲 **7.5** Listen to these sentences.

/j/
He isn't here.

/w/
Are you upstairs?

/r/
I've been to China and India.

b Mark the extra consonants in these sentences.

1 He was too old.
2 I was there for two hours.
3 We ate three eggs.
4 We went to America in June.
5 He's got blue eyes.
6 So do I.
7 So is he.
8 Oh, I am.

c 🔲 **7.6** Listen, check, and repeat.

Extension: Reading and listening
Rock and roll will never die

1 Discuss these questions.
1 Do you like rock music?
2 What artists do you know?
3 What do you think are the characteristics of rock music?
4 What do you know about its origins?
5 Do you recognize the person in the photograph?

2 Look quickly through the article and find
- three examples which show that pop music has become an international language.
- three things that combined to create rock and roll.
- three reasons why the electric guitar was so important.

Rock and roll . . .

Switch on a radio or walk into a hotel lobby anywhere in the world and you'll probably hear the same songs. Many of these songs, by artists such as Elvis Presley, the Beatles, or Abba, are far from new, but date from the fifties, sixties, and seventies. Yet back in the 1950s people thought that this kind of music would be just a brief fashion. 'It will never last,' people said. In fact, pop music has become a worldwide language and its stars are international icons with sell-out concerts wherever they go.

Modern popular music started when two very old musical traditions were brought together in the southern United States. White music came from the old folk songs which were taken to America by the early European settlers, especially those from Scotland and Ireland. The music has a clear melody and the songs normally tell a story. Black music was brought to America from Africa by the black slaves. Their music had a strong, driving rhythm.

The two traditions were first brought together in the early part of the twentieth century in jazz and blues music. However, like most other things in America at the time, music was segregated. Black people listened to black musicians and white people listened to white bands. By the 1950s attitudes were starting to change and people were looking for a new sound that would really combine black and white music. That new sound was provided by a simple but revolutionary invention – the electric guitar.

The electric guitar had three big advantages. Firstly, it was easy to play. Secondly, you could sing and play at the same time, but most importantly of all, it was LOUD.

In late 1954 a young man called Elvis Aaron Presley burst upon the airwaves of the world. Combining the rhythms of Africa and the melodies of Europe with the volume and raw energy of the electric guitar, the new sound had arrived.

They called it rock and roll.

. . . will never die

3 **Read the article and answer these questions.**
1 When did rock and roll start?
2 What did people say about it at the time?
3 Why did rock and roll start in the USA?
4 What were the different characteristics of traditional African and European music?
5 Who was the first rock star?

4 **You will hear an interview with someone who works in the music industry.**

7.7 Listen and mark these statements *True* (✓) or *False* (✗).
1 The man's name is Alan.
2 He's a singer.
3 By 1961 rock and roll had almost died.
4 Pop music hasn't changed much since the Beatles.
5 The man likes Abba.
6 He thinks that modern songs are better than the earlier ones.
7 The man's children are teenagers.
8 A lot of the latest hits are new recordings of old songs.
9 His favourite song is by the Rolling Stones.

5 **What can you remember?**

a Try and answer these questions.
1 What does Alan say about these people? Match the names and information.

Elvis Presley	was in jail
Buddy Holly	were great
Chuck Berry	became a preacher
Little Richard	rescued rock and roll
Jerry Lee Lewis	joined the army
The Beatles	added something new to pop music
Abba	married his cousin
Madonna	died in a plane crash
Michael Jackson	
The Rolling Stones	

2 What reasons does he give for his choice of record?
☐ the lyrics ☐ the guitar
☐ the rhythm ☐ the singer's voice
☐ It's fun. ☐ the melody
3 Which of these types of music does he mention?
☐ rave music ☐ Brit pop
☐ soul ☐ reggae
☐ mainstream pop ☐ heavy metal
☐ heavy rock ☐ disco music

b **7.7** Listen and check your answers.

6 **What do you think?**

a Work in groups and discuss these questions.
1 Who are the ten greatest pop stars ever?
2 What is the best song?

b Compare your ideas with the class.

7 **7.8 Complete the song with these words, then listen and check.**

leader down trees tonight rhythm come
sitting woods guitar music made play
stop name boy man read used

Johnny B Goode

Way _____ in Louisiana close to New Orleans

Way back up in the _____ among the evergreens

There stood a log cabin _____ of earth and wood

Where lived a country _____ named Johnny B Goode

Who never ever learnt to _____ and write so well

But he could play a _____ just like ringing a bell.

Chorus
Go, go Johnny, go, go (x4)
Johnny B Goode.

He _____ to carry his guitar in a gunny sack

Go sit beneath the _____ by the railroad track.

Engineers would see him _____ in the shade

Strumming to the _____ that the drivers made.

People passing by they would _____ and say

'Oh my, but that little country boy can _____.'

His mama told him, 'One day you will be a _____

And you will be the _____ of a big old band.

People will _____ from miles around

Just to hear you play your _____ when the sun goes down.

Maybe some day your _____ will be in lights

Saying Johnny B Goode _____.'

8 Time out

Grammar
Question forms; indirect questions

Grammar in use 1

1 **Read this information and discuss these questions.**

1 Do you have similar events in your own country?

2 Why do you think quiz nights are held?

> In Britain many pubs and clubs hold quiz nights. People normally play in teams of 3–5. You pay a small fee to enter the quiz and there is usually a prize for the winning team. Questions are divided up into topics – sport, music, history, general knowledge and so on. The questions may be read out or printed on a sheet of paper which is given to each team. Quiz nights are very popular.

2 **Here are some quiz questions. What is the topic?**

a In groups, answer the questions.

b 🔊 *8.1* Listen and check.

1 **Where is Mount Fujiyama?**

2 **Who wrote *Sense and Sensibility*?**

3 **Which country won the football World Cup in 1994?**

4 **What language did Jesus speak?**

5 **How many strings has a mandolin got?**

6 **Where does Arnold Schwarzenegger come from?**

7 **How fast can a cheetah run?**

Rules

1 **Here is a basic rule for making questions in English.**

> In English we can make a statement into a question by inverting the subject and
> * the verb *to be*.   * an auxiliary verb.   * a modal verb.

a Find examples for the rule in the quiz questions.

b How do we form questions when the positive form of the verb doesn't have any of the above? Find examples in the quiz questions. Which two tenses do this?

2 **Look at quiz question 2.**

a Does this question follow your rules in **1**? What is the subject of the question?

b Complete the rule.

> When the question word (or expression) is the _____ , we use the positive form of the verb to make a question.

c Find another example to illustrate this rule in the quiz questions.

3 **Look at quiz question 6.**

a Where is the preposition in the question?

b Complete this question with the preposition *to*.
Where was Columbus trying to get?

➤ Check the rules for question forms in **Grammar Reference 8.1**.

64

Practice

1 **Some of these questions are incorrect. Find and correct them.**

1 Who did build the Eiffel Tower?
2 How died Martin Luther King?
3 Which war ended in 1945?
4 Which animal does live the longest?
5 What for do you use an abacus?
6 Which country comes from *paella*?
7 Who invented the camera?
8 Where the 1996 Olympics were?
9 Where to did Marco Polo travel?

2 **Here are some quiz answers.**

1	radio	**5**	Antarctica	**9**	1914
2	65 million years ago	**6**	5	**10**	8
3	John Wilkes Booth	**7**	1992	**11**	India
4	Paul McCartney	**8**	tennis	**12**	2062

a Match these items to the answers.

> Abraham Lincoln   the Taj Mahal   basketball
> Marconi   penguins   Andre Agassi   dinosaurs
> a spider   the First World War   Halley's comet
> *Yesterday*   the Barcelona Olympics

b Write the questions, using the information.

EXAMPLE
1   What did Marconi invent?

3 **In groups, make your own quiz. Write five general knowledge questions. Give your questions to another group to answer.**

Grammar in use 2

1 **A team is discussing the quiz questions.**

a Look at these parts of their discussion. Choose the correct form.

b ▣ *8.2* Listen to the discussion and check your choices.

2 **Has the team got the right answers?**

Rules

1 **Look at the indirect questions in Grammar in use 2. Indirect questions are statements or questions which contain another question.**

a What word order is used in the indirect question?
   • statement word order   • question word order

b Look at the indirect question about Italy. What word has been added? Why? What form of question is this?

c Look at the last three questions in the quiz in **Grammar in use 1**. Make statements about the questions with these expressions.

> I (don't) know   I can/can't remember   I've no idea

➤ Check the rules for indirect questions in **Grammar Reference 8.2**.

Practice

1 **Look at your corrected questions for Practice 1 above. Say whether you know the answers.**

EXAMPLES
I know who built the Eiffel Tower.
I've no idea how Martin Luther King died.

2 **Look at the people's questions. Make indirect questions, using these expressions.**

> doesn't know   wants to know   can't remember

EXAMPLE
Simon wants to know what day it is.

Simon	What day is it?
Claire	Is it raining?
John	Can Sally play tennis?
Mrs Pines	Where does Mr Jackson work?
Ann	What's the time?
Peter	How long have the Clarks lived here?
Mr Walters	What time will we arrive?
Betty	Has the hotel got a gym?

3 **How well do you know your partner?**

a Write down whether you know or don't know these things about him/her. Add some more.

EXAMPLE
I know how old he/she is.
I've no idea whether he/she likes classical music.

1 How old is he/she?
2 Does he/she like classical music?
3 When is his/her birthday?
4 What job does he/she do (or want to do)?
5 Has he/she ever been abroad?
6 What is his/her favourite food?
7 Does he/she play any sports?
8 Has he/she got any brothers or sisters?
9 Does he/she believe in ghosts?
10 Has he/she got a pet?

b Work with your partner and check your ideas.

Vocabulary
Compound nouns; sport

1 Compound nouns are very common in English.

a Look at these examples.

football boots   a car seat   a sports shop

b Choose the correct compound noun.

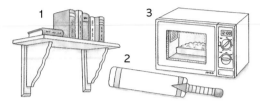

1 a shelfbook/ a bookshelf
2 a cricket bat/ a bat cricket
3 an oven microwave/ a microwave oven

c What are these called? Write the compound nouns.
- a shop that sells souvenirs
- a shop that sells software for computers
- someone who owns a restaurant
- a machine that sends and receives faxes
- an animal that you find on farms
- someone who teaches science

d Answer the questions.
1 Would you eat a *packet of crisps* or a *crisp packet*?
2 What's the difference between a *bottle of milk* and a *milk bottle*?
3 Would you drink a *teacup* or a *cup of tea*?

➤ Check the rules for forming compound nouns in **Grammar Reference 8.3**.

2 Look at these nouns to do with sports.

a Make as many compound nouns as possible. The nouns can be used more than once.

tennis	golf	football	race	racing	ski

boots	ball	club	circuit	racquet	poles	kit
horse	slope	car	course	court	track	pitch

b Complete the table.

place	equipment

Reading
Fit for life or fit to drop?

1 Look at the title of the article and the pictures.

a What is this section about?

b What are the people doing in the pictures?

2 Each paragraph is about a different place.

a Match these places to the correct paragraph.

Russia	Australia	Hong Kong
Spain	the United States	

b What clues are there in the texts that indicate the places?

c Which one seems closest to attitudes to fitness in your country?

3 Read the article again.

a What reasons are given for taking exercise? What other reasons can you think of?

b Which place do you think has the healthiest attitude to exercise and which has the least healthy attitude?

> ### Vocabulary file: Fitness
>
> **a** What do you think these expressions mean? Most of them are illustrated in the pictures.
> - to pump iron
> - a couch potato
> - a beer belly
> - an exercise bike
> - an aerobics video
> - the lycra and leotard brigade
> - a gym(nasium)
> - to work out
> - a jogger
> - to get off your backside
>
> **b** Find other terms in the text associated with fitness. Can you think of any more?

4 What part does exercise play in your life?

a Discuss these questions.
1 Do you take regular exercise?
2 If you exercise, what do you do and how often?
3 Do you think exercise is important or unimportant?
4 Do you think you are typical of people in your country?

b Write a short text summarizing your attitude to exercise and the part it plays in your life.

Fit for life or fit to drop?

A recent report showed that 60% of adults here are overweight, at least 40% are completely sedentary, and only 20% do enough exercise. 'Everyone knows why we have the problem,' says a former basketball star. 'We're a nation of couch potatoes. We sit around and watch television too much.' And yet while the people get fatter, they are surrounded by images of the perfect body. The guilt is enormous, and as a result there is a billion dollar market in diet books, aerobics videos, and all kinds of exercise machines. Alas, buying the exercise bike doesn't keep you fit. You actually have to use it. The simple fact is that Mr and Mrs Average need to eat less and get off their backsides more often.

It's 3 a.m. in the City Gym, and men and women are bending, stretching, running, and lifting weights. The City Gym has 5,000 members and it never closes. You might think from this that this is a nation of slim and super-fit people. Certainly the country has a reputation for sport and healthy outdoor living. But the truth is rather different, according to one health expert. 'Gymnasiums are full of the lycra and leotard brigade – mostly single young people,' he says. 'In fact, about one in three men is a sedentary slob with a beer belly.' But people certainly know what they should do for a healthy lifestyle. The government spends about $240 million a year on education in health and fitness. That's $14 for every man, woman, and child.

The slim, blonde TV presenter looks terrifyingly fit. Her new lifestyle programme about exercise and diet is popular all over the country and her classes at a gym in the capital city are always full. But if you're wondering whether this is part of a new attitude to health, it isn't. 'People here don't exercise to improve their health,' says our blonde TV presenter. 'It's all about looking good.' So while the women sweat in the aerobics class to keep their figures trim, the men pump iron to build up their muscles and look more macho. Nobody would dream of jogging through the streets. Few people can afford the new healthy lifestyle at the moment. The traditional fatty diet doesn't help and membership at a gym can cost up to $2,000 a year.

They come here in huge numbers. Every weekend they put on their tracksuits, leave the stress of the capital city behind and drive out into the hills. Here they can find fresh air, beautiful scenery, forests, rivers, and, most important of all, thousands of restaurants. Don't be fooled by the tracksuit. It's frequently worn with high-heeled shoes and jewellery. 'I can tell you what the favourite sport of our people is,' says a local restaurant owner. 'It's sitting at a table to eat.' This does not mean that they take no exercise. This country has produced some famous international athletes and you can regularly see joggers in the streets of the cities. But people have a very relaxed attitude to exercise. Even the really fit don't take it so seriously. It's just part of enjoying life.

When an international survey decided that this was the most stressful place in the world, people here weren't worried – they were proud of it. In most places when people meet they ask how you are. Here they ask whether you are busy or if you are travelling much. Life here is fast. People work hard and they have the same attitude towards exercise. And with modern technology you don't have to choose between keeping fit and sitting at your desk. You can keep in touch with your clients by mobile phone while you're jogging in the park or working out in one of the many gyms.

Enjoy Fitness

Listening and speaking
Making polite requests

1 Look at these responses.

a Where do you think they take place?

☐ At seven in the dining room, but you can get it earlier in your room, if you wish.

☐ Certainly, which room is it, please?

☐ If you give me the keys, I'll get one of the porters to see to it for you.

☐ You need to dial 9 for an outside line, then 00 and the code for the country you want.

☐ Let me see. Ah yes, there's a fax and a phone message.

☐ Yes, it's on the second floor. Turn left when you come out of the lift.

☐ Certainly. What would you like?

☐ Oh, I'm very sorry about that. I'll get some sent up straight away.

☐ No, they're provided at the poolside.

b Look at the photographs. What do you think the requests could be?

2 📼 **8.3 Listen to the requests and choose the appropriate response for each one. Put the numbers of the requests in the boxes.**

3 📼 **8.4 Now listen to the complete dialogues.**

a Check your answers.

b Match the dialogues to the correct photographs.

ROOM
SERVICE
MENU

Conversation pieces:
Polite requests for information

a Look at tapescript 8.4.

b Which expressions are used to introduce the requests?

c There are two types of request.
• a request for information
• asking someone to do something
Which type of request do we use indirect questions for?

d Change these questions into polite requests for information.
1 What time is it?
2 Where do you live?
3 When does the train arrive?
4 Am I on the right road for Longton?
5 How do we get to the park from here?
6 Will the flight from Paris be on time?
7 Do you have a gymnasium here?

e How would you make these requests in your own language? Would you use an indirect form? Why/Why not?

f Work with a partner. Practise the dialogues, using tapescript 8.4.

➤ See **Pronunciation** for polite intonation practice.

4 🔲 *8.5* **Listen to the conversations. What do the people want to know?**

5 **Work with a partner. Make conversations for these situations. Use expressions from Conversation pieces.**
1 You're in the street. Where can you buy a newspaper?
2 You're in a hotel. You want to book a wake-up call for 6.15.
3 You phone the station. When is the first train to London?
4 You're in a hotel. Has the hotel got a sauna?
5 You're in the street. How do you get to the station?
6 You're in a hotel room. The TV isn't working.
7 You're in a restaurant. Where are the toilets?
8 You're reading a menu. What is the soup of the day?

Pronunciation
/ʃ/, /tʃ/, /dʒ/; polite intonation

1 The sounds /ʃ/, /tʃ/, /dʒ/

a Write the words in the correct column.

/ʃ/	/tʃ/	/dʒ/
cushion	cheaper	journey

package passenger insurance admission
efficient attraction Japan coach feature
condition jewellery much lecture station
culture check-in stranger national luggage
hijack section special beach speech

b 🔲 *8.6* Listen, check, and repeat.

c Look at your completed table. Can you identify any spelling patterns for each sound?

2 Polite intonation

Requests can sound polite or impolite depending on how you say them.

a 🔲 *8.7* Listen to this request said in two different ways, and answer the questions.

Could you tell me where the restaurant is?

1 Which one sounds more polite?
2 Which one has the rising intonation?

b 🔲 *8.8* Listen and tick (✓) the requests that sound polite.
1 ☐ Could you tell me how much these socks are, please?
2 ☐ Could you tell me whether they're ready yet?
3 ☐ Do you think you could turn the light off, please?
4 ☐ Would you mind closing the door, please?
5 ☐ Could you tell me where the newspaper is?
6 ☐ Do you think I could have a drink, please?
7 ☐ Could I have the bill, please?
8 ☐ Would you mind waiting a minute, please?

c Practise saying the requests politely.

Extension: Reading and listening
Ironman

1 Look at the title and photographs.

a Discuss these questions.
  1 What are the people doing?
  2 Who or what is *Ironman*?

b Look at the article and check your ideas.

2 Read the article and answer these questions.
  1 What is the full name of the event?
  2 What kind of event is it?
  3 What does it consist of?
  4 Where does it take place? Why?
  5 When did it first start?

3 Look at these ways of describing the event and competitors.
  - psychologically demanding
  - growing in popularity
  - gruelling
  - dedicated

a What evidence is given in the text to support these descriptions?

b Think of some other sports. How would you describe them and the people who do them?

Vocabulary file: Synonyms

Find words or expressions in the text that mean the same as:
- big waves
- one after the other
- very hard
- people who compete in a race
- becoming more popular
- was the idea of
- was discussing
- incredible
- started slowly
- races to decide who goes into the final
- anyone can take part

---

4 Work with a partner.

a Write down six things that you would like to know about the race.

EXAMPLES
I would like to know why people do it.
I wonder what sort of diet they eat.

b 📼 *8.9* Listen to an *Ironman* competitor on a TV phone-in programme. Are your questions answered?

5 Discuss these questions.

a What do you think of the *Ironman* race and the people who compete in it?

b Would you like to do it? Why/Why not?

Language focus:
Adjectival expressions with numbers

a Arrange these words into expressions from the article.
  - 180/ road/ race/ a/ kilometre
  - Honolulu/ 42/ the/ marathon/ kilometre
  - training/ programme/ hour/ a/ twelve

b Check your ideas in the article.

c What do you notice about *kilometre* and *hour*?

d What would you call these?
  1 a race of a hundred metres
  2 a bicycle that costs two thousand dollars
  3 an event that lasts two weeks
  4 a competitor who is fifty years old
  5 a flight that lasts four and a half hours
  6 a journey of two thousand miles
  7 a river that is three miles wide
  8 training shoes that cost two hundred pounds
  9 a marathon that lasts three days
  10 a prize of a million dollars

'The trouble is I can never get fit enough to use the equipment.'

'I'm not saying you are out of condition, but the machine appears to be laughing!'

Ironman

Find out what you need to push your body to the limits of endurance. It's all in the name of a new sport that's taking the world by storm.

Imagine what it is like to swim four kilometres through the pounding surf and surging currents of the Pacific Ocean. Do you think you'd feel tired? How about a 180-kilometre road race on a bicycle in the tropical heat of Hawaii? Tired again? Then what about running a marathon in the same conditions? What? Still tired? Now try to imagine what it feels like to do the swim, the bike race, and the marathon 'back to back', with no breaks in between, against the toughest, fittest, and most dedicated athletes in the world.

Well, if you're wondering whether such a gruelling race exists, let me tell you, it does. In an event that lasts at least nine hours, each of 1,500 competitors strives to achieve one of the most physically, emotionally, and psychologically demanding titles in the whole of sport: *Ironman*. *Ironman* is a version of the new sport of triathlon – a combination of swimming, cycling, and running – that is rapidly growing in popularity.

The first *Ironman* competition was thought up by an American, John Collins, back in 1977. Under the umbrellas of a Hawaiian beach bar, a group of friends was debating which of the local sporting events was the toughest – the four-kilometre Waikiki rough-water swim, the 180-kilometre round-Oahu bike race, or the 42-kilometre Honolulu marathon. As often happens, they couldn't agree, and so to settle the argument Collins suggested the unbelievable: why not try to do them all, one after the other, on the same day?

And so the Hawaiian *Ironman* triathlon, as the new event was known, was born. It got off to a slow start with only 12 entrants in the first year. Now, however, the contest is so popular that selection heats are held at events around the world in order to limit the number of participants in the final to 1,500.

The event is open to anyone – male or female, old or young, but you have to be superbly fit and, more importantly, you have to

be dedicated. Apart from the race itself, imagine what the training does to your lifestyle. Competing at this level requires a special diet and a 12-hour training programme every day. And yet every year thousands of people dream of becoming *Ironman*.

9 All in the mind?

Grammar
-ing forms

Grammar in use

1 Look at the story and answer these questions.

1 When and where did the incident take place?
2 Who are the people in the picture?
3 What is the girl wearing?
4 What is its significance in the story?

2 Do you believe the story or do you think there is a rational explanation?

Rules

1 What uses of -ing forms do you know already?

a Underline all the -ing forms in the text. Find examples of
- a continuous tense.
- a gerund (verb used as a noun).
- *there is/are* + noun + *-ing*.
- *see* + noun + *-ing*.
- an adjective.
- *start* + *-ing*.
- *after* + *-ing*.

b Do you know other verbs which use the same construction as *see*?

c Do these sentences mean the same?
The doctor stopped writing out the prescription.
The doctor stopped to write out the prescription.

d What other verbs can take -ing and/or the infinitive?

The shawl

This story happened in Philadelphia towards the end of the nineteenth century. One winter evening Dr. S. Weir Mitchell sat down in an armchair and started reading a book, but after an exhausting day at the surgery, he soon fell asleep. A short while later he woke up suddenly when he heard the door bell ringing. There was a girl standing on the doorstep. It was cold and snow was falling, but she was wearing only a thin shawl around her shoulders and she was shivering. 'My mother is very ill,' she said. 'Please come'.

Walking through the dark and snowy streets was not easy, but eventually they came to an old apartment building and the girl led the doctor up to a room on the third floor. There was a woman lying on the bed and the doctor recognized her as a former servant of his. After examining her, he took out his notepad and looked around for the girl. 'Where's your daughter?' he asked the woman. 'I need her to go for some medicine.'

'My daughter?' she said in surprise. 'My daughter died a month ago.' 'But that's impossible,' said the doctor. 'She came to fetch me. I saw her. She was wearing a shawl.'

'My daughter's shoes and her shawl are in there,' said the woman, pointing to a small cupboard. The doctor stopped writing out the prescription and went to the cupboard. He saw the girl's shawl lying on the shelf. It was folded and dry. It clearly had not been worn that night.

2 **Translate these sentences into your own language. What forms do you use?**

There was a girl standing on the doorstep.
He could hear the doorbell ringing.
The doctor stopped writing out the prescription.

3 **Do these sentences mean the same?**

After he had examined her, he took out his notepad.
After examining her, he took out his notepad.

a Do you know any other conjunctions like *after* which can be used with an *-ing* form?

b We can't use the same construction with this sentence. Why not?
After the doctor had told her his story, the woman started crying.

➤ Check the rules for *-ing* forms in **Grammar References 9.1**, **9.2**.

Practice

1 **Complete the text.**

a Put a noun and a verb from each column in each gap.

the ghost	watching
an old woman	moving
something	screaming
someone	living
nobody	walking
eyes	covering
lights	whispering
our young son	standing
voices	shining

The haunted house

We loved the house when we first moved in. Then two years after moving in, I woke up suddenly one night. There was *an old woman* *standing* at the foot of our bed. She was crying. I tried to shout, but I couldn't. I could feel _____ _____ my face.
Terrified, I watched _____ _____ towards the wall. After it had disappeared, I turned to wake my husband, but suddenly I heard _____ _____ in the next bedroom. I ran to see what was wrong. He had seen _____ _____ through the wall from our room. It was an old woman. After that we didn't like living in the house any more. It felt as if there were _____ _____ us all the time. Strange things started happening. We saw _____ _____ , and we heard _____ _____ in the middle of the night. We sold the house, but the new people didn't stay there very long. There is _____ _____ there now.

b 🎧 *9.1* Listen and check your answers.

2 **Change these sentences where possible, using *after/ before/ while + -ing*.**

1 While he was reading a book, the doctor fell asleep.
2 After he had been asleep for a short while, the doorbell rang.
3 Before he followed the girl, the doctor fetched his bag.
4 After she had led the doctor upstairs, the girl pointed to a room.
5 While the doctor was with her mother, the girl did not appear.
6 Before he wrote out the prescription, the doctor looked around for the girl.
7 After he had opened the cupboard, the doctor saw the shawl on the shelf.

3 **Work with a partner. Your partner will give you one of the words below. Close your eyes and describe the picture that the word creates in your mind. Use these constructions.**

There is/are + noun + -ing
I can see/ hear/ smell + noun + -ing

- holiday
- accident
- Christmas
- Africa
- spring
- birthday

4 **Work with a partner. Use the *-ing* form or the infinitive. Tell your partner about something that you**

- forgot to do.
- have stopped doing.
- can't stand doing.
- must remember to do.
- often imagine doing.
- sometimes feel like doing.
- remember doing as a child.
- tried but gave up doing.
- would like to start doing.
- are considering doing.
- wouldn't like to do.

5 **Most people know at least one ghost story.**

a Tell a story that you know.

b Write the story, or invent one, using as many *-ing* forms as possible.

Vocabulary
Strong adjectives

1 **Look at these two types of adjective.**

a Match the adjectives to their strong equivalents.

Base	Strong
big	amazing
tiring	hideous
frightening	terrifying
cold	fascinating
ugly	brilliant/wonderful
surprising	impossible
strange	terrible/awful
difficult	exhausting
interesting	uncanny
good	huge
bad	freezing

b Which type of adjective can be used with *very*, and which type can be used with *absolutely*?

2 **Work with a partner. Talk about these things, using *very/absolutely* and the adjectives above.**

> ghost stories   UFOs   the Pyramids
> the North Pole   horror films
> witches   telepathy   exams
> summer holidays   the sea

EXAMPLE
A *I think ghost stories are absolutely terrifying.*
B *Oh, I think they're very interesting.*

'For heaven's sake Maureen, not everybody wants to see photographs of the grandchildren.'

Reading
Coincidence

1 **Discuss the questions.**

a What coincidences have happened to you or people that you know?

b How do you explain these coincidences?

2 **Read the article and answer the questions.**

1 What strange coincidences happened to these people or things?
 • Jason Pegler   • the *Titanic*   • an architect
2 What two scientific explanations are given for coincidences?
3 What other explanation is suggested?

3 **Match these topics to the correct paragraphs.**

☐ Coincidences and memory
☐ The strange coincidences concerning the *Titanic*
☐ Why do coincidences happen?
☐ An incident that is difficult to explain
☐ An explanation of probability
☐ An example of an amazing coincidence

Vocabulary file: Phrasal verbs; synonyms

a Match the phrasal verbs from the text and the definitions.

broke down	stuck
set off	phoned
pinned up	happened
called up	discover
turned out	stopped
bumping into	stopped working
find out	gone
looking at	considering
pulled up	meeting

b Find words or expressions in the text which mean the same as:
• to repair
• someone that you work with
• a friend that you share
• only
• very large
• a large passenger ship
• impossible to sink
• the first time that a ship sails
• a large piece of ice
• very strange
• to kill yourself

4 **Discuss these questions.**

1 Do you agree with the explanations in the article?
2 Think of coincidences that have happened to you or that you have heard about. Can the ideas in the article explain them?
3 How would you explain the story of the architect?

COINCIDENCE:
Is it more than just chance?

Sue Hamilton was working alone in her office in July 1992 when the fax machine broke down. After trying unsuccessfully to fix it, she decided to call her colleague Jason Pegler, who had set off home a little earlier. Finding his home number pinned up on a noticeboard, she called him up and began to explain the problem. But Jason quickly stopped her. 'I'm not at home,' he explained. 'I just happened to be walking past this phone box when I heard the phone ringing, so I answered it.' The number Sue had found on the noticeboard wasn't Jason's phone number. It was his employee number. Amazingly, it turned out to be the same as the number of the phone box that Jason was walking past when she called.

Strange coincidences like this fascinate us. We've all had similar, though perhaps less dramatic, experiences such as bumping into someone that you know when you're on holiday. There is also the 'small world' phenomenon, where you meet a stranger and find out that you have a friend in common. Are such experiences merely coincidences or is there some kind of unknown force making these things happen?

Most scientists maintain that coincidences are just the results of the laws of probability. For example, one famous coincidence concerns the sinking of the *Titanic*. In 1898 a book was published in America called *The Wreck of the Titan*. It told the story of the *Titan*, a huge 46,000 ton liner, which its builders claimed was unsinkable. On its maiden voyage from England to New York in April, it struck an iceberg in the North Atlantic and sank. There were not enough lifeboats on the ship and many of the passengers drowned. Fourteen years later on 15 April 1912, the unsinkable 45,000 ton *Titanic* sank on its maiden voyage from England to New York after hitting an iceberg. Half the passengers drowned because there were not enough lifeboats.

It seems like an uncanny prediction, but was it? First of all, if you're going to write a book about a ship, isn't it likely that you would choose the biggest ship in the world? And which would be more dramatic, its first voyage or its 23rd, an ordinary ship or an unsinkable ship, everyone survives or there aren't enough lifeboats? Secondly, some facts are the natural results of other choices. A huge liner would probably have a name that meant 'huge', wouldn't it? And what was a common danger in the North Atlantic? Icebergs, of course. Looking at things in terms of probability, the strange coincidences don't seem so strange after all.

Another way of explaining coincidences is that we notice them simply because they are unusual. So you remember meeting your neighbour when you're on holiday, and you think that's amazing, but you don't remember all the times that you go on holiday without meeting one of your neighbours.

It must be said, however, that some coincidences are hard to explain in terms of probability or selective memory. Take the case of the young architect who in 1971 tried to commit suicide by jumping in front of a London Underground train. The train pulled up just in time and the architect survived. But the train driver hadn't stopped the train. A passenger who had no idea what was happening had pulled the emergency cord. Talking about the incident later he said that he had suddenly felt 'driven' to stop the train. Pure chance or a mysterious force? Can we really be certain?

Listening and speaking
Agreeing and disagreeing

1 🔊 *9.2* **Listen to three conversations and answer the questions.**
   1 How many people are there in each conversation?
   2 What topics are they discussing?

2 🔊 *9.2* **Listen again. How many people**
- saw the TV programme?
- believe in ghosts?
- have seen a UFO?
- saw the light?
- think it was an aeroplane?
- can remember their dreams?
- think that dreams have a meaning?
- can return to the same dream?

Conversation pieces: Agreeing and disagreeing

a Complete the table with the correct responses.

Oh, I didn't.   *Oh, I can.*
Oh, I don't.   *Nor/Neither have I.*
Nor/Neither can I.   *So did I.*
So do I.   *Oh, I have.*

	Agree	Disagree
I believe in ghosts.		*Oh, I don't.*
I can't remember my dreams.		
I've never seen a UFO.		
I saw an interesting TV programme.		

b 🔊 *9.2* Listen again and check your ideas.

c Complete the rules with these words:

negative   so   nor   positive   subject   disagree

> To agree with a positive statement we use:
> _____ + auxiliary verb + _____ .
> To agree with a _____ statement we use:
> _____ + auxiliary verb + subject.
> To _____ with a positive statement we use:
> (Oh) subject + negative auxiliary verb.
> To disagree with a negative statement we use:
> (Oh) subject + _____ auxiliary verb.

d Where can you put *Me, too/neither.* in the table in **a**?

➤ Check the rules in **Grammar Reference 9.3**.

e How would you agree or disagree with these statements?
1 I'm not from this town.
2 I can speak Russian.
3 I haven't got a pet.
4 I finished my homework yesterday.
5 I get up at 7 o'clock.
6 I'll be at the party.
7 I wouldn't like to be a politician.
8 I'm going to have lunch.

f 🔊 *9.3* Listen to some statements. Agree or disagree with each one. Then listen and check each answer.

3 Discuss these questions.

a Work with a partner and give reasons, details, or examples to explain your opinions.
1 Have you ever seen a ghost?
2 Would you sleep in a haunted house?
3 Were you frightened of anything when you were a child?
4 Do you ever watch horror films?
5 Will you read your horoscope today?
6 Are you superstitious?
7 Can you remember a dream that you had last night?
8 Do you know anyone who has seen a UFO?
9 Do you think there is life on other planets?

b Work in a group. Discuss your opinions. Are there any students in the group that hold similar views on any of the topics?

Pronunciation
-o-; reduced words

1 The vowel -o-

The vowel *-o-* can be pronounced in several different ways.

a Write the words in the correct column.

/ɒ/	/ɔː/	/ʌ/	/əʊ/
got	boring	done	go

> offer   golf   woman   won   do
> opponent   topic   wonder   boy
> knowledge   short   popular   so
> born   hockey   does   polo   cost
> towel   ago   once   sport   lord
> score   both   porter   hotel
> only   front   gone   phone
> some   spoke   motor   other   worry
> among   normal   slow   women

b Five of the words do not go in any of the columns. Which are they?

c 🔊 *9.4* Listen, check, and repeat.

2 Reduced words

We have already noted that in natural speech
• vowel sounds may be reduced.
• words are run together.
In some common expressions this means that some syllables disappear completely.

a 🔊 *9.5* Listen to this sentence. What do you hear?
Do you like jazz?

b 🔊 *9.6* Listen and repeat these sentences.
/wʊdʒə/
1 Would you like a drink?
/vju:/
2 Have you got the time?
/gənə/
3 I'm going to have a shower.
/wɒnə/
4 I don't want to go out.
/dʃi:/
5 What time did she get here?
/dʒə wɒnə/
6 Do you want to dance?
/kəz/
7 I can't go out because I'm broke.

c Practise saying them.

Extension: Reading and listening
Memory

1 How good is your memory? Do these tasks, but don't write anything down.

a ▣ **9.7** (1) Listen to the people in the photographs introducing themselves.

b ▣ **9.7** (2 and 3) Now listen and try to remember the information that you hear.

c Look at the list of words at the bottom of the page for a minute.

2 Look quickly at the article and choose the best title.
- ☐ People who have lost their memory
- ☐ Why we need a memory
- ☐ Why our memories get worse as we get older
- ☐ How to improve your memory
- ☐ Factors that affect memory

3 Look at the first two paragraphs. Give more examples of things that would be impossible without a memory and things that we use our memory for.

4 Read the article and answer the questions.
1 What are the five factors that affect how well you remember something?
2 What example is given to illustrate each one?

5 Discuss these questions.
1 Can you think of any more factors that affect your memory?
2 Can you give examples from your own life to illustrate the points in the text?
3 What is your earliest memory?
4 What implications do the ideas in the text have for learning a language?

6 How well do you remember the tasks you did in 1?

a Answer the questions.
1 In the quiz show photographs, what are the people's names and jobs? Where is each one from?
2 What was the telephone number?
3 Write down as many of the words as you can.
4 Draw a small map to show how to get to the station.

b Compare your ideas with a partner.

c ▣ **9.7** Listen to the cassette again and check your ideas. Look at the list of words. How well did you do?

7 ▣ 9.8 Listen to someone giving some techniques for improving your memory. Try the techniques with the tasks in 1.

| rocket | book | sugar | yellow | bicycle | long | bag |
| television | bananas | kick | trousers | horse | | sun |

78

Try to imagine life without a memory. It would be impossible. You couldn't use a language, because you wouldn't remember the words. You couldn't understand a film, because you need to hold the first part of the story in your mind in order to understand the later parts. You wouldn't be able to recognize anyone – even members of your own family. You would live in a permanent present. You would have no past and you wouldn't be able to imagine a future.

Human beings have amazing memories. Apart from all our personal memories about our own lives, we can recall between 20,000 and 100,000 words in our own language as well as possibly thousands more in a foreign language. We have all sorts of information about different subjects such as history, science, and geography, and we have complex skills such as driving a car or playing a musical instrument. All these things and countless others depend on our memory.

How well you remember things depends on many different factors. Firstly, some people naturally have better memories than others, in just the same way as some people are taller than others, or have different colour eyes. Some top chess players, for example, can remember every move of every game that they have ever seen or played.

Secondly, research shows that different things are stored in different parts of the brain. Ideas, words, and numbers are stored in the left-hand side, while the right-hand side remembers images, sounds, and smells. In most people one side of the brain is more developed than the other, and this may explain why some people can remember people's faces easily, but can't remember their names.

Thirdly, we all remember exciting, frightening, or dramatic events more easily. This is because these experiences produce chemicals such as adrenaline, which boost your memory. They say that anyone who is old enough to remember knows exactly where they were on Friday 22 November 1963, when radio and TV programmes around the world were interrupted with the shocking news that John F. Kennedy, the President of the United States, had been assassinated.

Fourthly, the context in which you learn something can affect how well you remember it. Tests on divers, for example, showed that when they learnt things underwater, they could also remember those things best when they were underwater.

Lastly, the more often you recall a memory the more likely you are to remember it. If you don't use it, you'll lose it. A telephone number that you dial frequently will stay in your memory easily, but you will probably have to write down one that you use only now and again.

10 Your health

Grammar
Modal verbs

Grammar in use

1 Look at the title and photograph. What is the article about?

2 Read the article. What does it say about smoking in these places?
- public transport
- public places
- offices
- the street
- bars and restaurants
- homes
- the United States

3 What do you think of the situation in the text? Compare it to your own country.

Rules

1 The text contains several modal verbs and their past and future forms.

a Find examples of them in the text.

b Complete these sentences with modal verbs from the text.
1 New York smokers _____ go out into the street.
2 You _____ only find a few bars where smoking is allowed.
3 You _____ smoke in most restaurants.
4 'Smokers _____ be able to smoke at work,' say non-smokers.
5 Soon restaurants _____ all be non-smoking.
6 Some people think that smoking _____ be banned in people's homes.
7 One day smoking _____ be illegal in the USA.

Last gasp for smokers

It was a normal day and in their New York office, Ken Schwarz and his colleagues stopped for their coffee break. But while Ken's colleagues were able to sit at their desks and drink their coffee, Ken had to go outside. He couldn't stay inside, because he wanted to smoke. If the smokers of the Big Apple want to enjoy a cigarette, the authorities have decided they must go out into the street or up onto the rooftops.

Throughout the United States, the number of places where people are allowed to smoke has gradually become smaller and smaller. First it was banned on trains, buses, and planes, then in public places such as theatres and airports. Now you

From GEORGE GORDON in New York

Driven outside to smoke in NY

can't smoke in any workplace. Non-smokers are definitely winning the battle. 'Why should we breathe their smoke?' they say.

If they're lucky, smokers can still find some bars and restaurants where they can light up a cigarette, but it may soon be banned there, too. Anti-smoking groups even think that smoking ought to be banned in people's homes. Under new plans you won't be able to smoke in any house where there are more than ten visitors in a week, or where there are children.

In 1996, nicotine was classed as a drug, like cannabis, cocaine, or heroin. In the country that gave tobacco to the world, smoking might one day be illegal. And then Ken will have to give up.

2 When do we use modal verbs? Complete the table. (Some modal verbs may have more than one meaning.)

ability	
obligation	
advice	
probability	
permission	

3 Are these statements true of modal verbs?
- The 3rd person singular ends in -s.
- They never have -ed or -ing forms.
- They have no infinitive form.
- They are followed by an infinitive with to.
- To make questions subject and modal verb are inverted.
- To make negatives we add not.

4 If we want to use *can* and *must* in the past or the future we need to use different verbs.

a Which verbs are used to replace *can* and *must* in the past and future?

b Find examples in the text.

➤ Check the rules for modal verbs in **Grammar Reference 10.1**.

Practice

1 Look at these comments about smoking.

a Complete them with *can/can't, must, should/shouldn't,* or *ought to*. Sometimes more than one is possible.

1 I _____ understand why people smoke. It tastes horrible.
2 If people get ill from smoking, they _____ pay for the treatment. Why _____ I pay more taxes for it?
3 Smokers _____ have to go outside to smoke. Employers _____ provide places for them to smoke.
4 I'm sorry, sir, but you _____ put the cigarette out. You _____ smoke here. It's a non-smoking area. If you want to smoke you _____ go outside.
5 The government _____ ban smoking completely so that we _____ all breathe clean air.
6 Why _____ anyone else decide whether I _____ smoke in my own home? It's ridiculous.

b 🔲 *10.1* Listen and compare your answers.

2 Complete the sentences, using this information and *will/won't be able to* or *will/won't have to*.

> export more to other countries   have children
> put extra taxes on cigarettes   look for new jobs
> go outside   smoke while they're waiting
> get life insurance   pay out huge sums of money

1 People with illnesses like lung cancer are claiming compensation from the tobacco companies. If the people win, the tobacco companies _____ .
2 Thousands of people are employed in the tobacco industry. If fewer people smoke, they _____ .
3 The cost of treating illnesses caused by smoking is rising. The government _____ .
4 Insurance companies don't want to take on the extra risks of people who smoke. Smokers _____ .
5 Some tobacco companies are paying to build smoking lounges at airports, so smokers _____ .
6 If smoking in the USA declines, the tobacco companies _____ .
7 Some offices are going to provide places for smokers, so they _____ .
8 If smoking is banned in homes, smokers _____ !

3 Think about times in your life when you had to do something that you didn't like.

a Write down five things.

EXAMPLE
When I was younger I had to go to bed early, so I couldn't watch the TV programmes that I liked.

b Compare your answers with a partner.

4 Here are some possible future developments.

a Discuss each one. Do you think we will be able to do these things? Do you think we should do them? What will we have to do to achieve/ control/ stop them?
- use animal parts for medical transplants
- choose the gender and other characteristics of a baby
- stop the ageing process
- control the growth of the world's population
- start colonies on other planets
- stop global warming

b Choose one of the topics and write a paragraph about it. Include as many modal verbs as you can.

Vocabulary
Medical terms

1 Complete the table with the medical terms. Use a dictionary to help you.

> flu bandage infection germ
> sore throat thermometer cold
> temperature hay fever rash
> prescription tablets injection
> stomach ache plaster X-ray
> earache sprain pills virus
> cough mixture disease pain
> cut headache bruise ointment
> fracture painkillers medicine
> eye drops allergy low-fat diet
> high cholesterol antibiotics
> high blood pressure

illness/problem	treatment

2 Some words for describing illness or treatment are uncountable.

a Complete the sentences with *a/an*, *some*, or nothing. Use your dictionary.

1 We've got _____ flu.
2 She's got _____ cold.
3 You need _____ medicine. I'll give you _____ injection.
4 I've got _____ headache and _____ sore throat.
5 My sister's got _____ earache.
6 My father's suffering from _____ high blood pressure.
7 I've got _____ cough. I need _____ cough mixture.
8 You've got _____ temperature. Stay in bed!

b Read the *Dirty body* text in the **Reading** section. What expressions do we use to count uncountable names of illnesses?

Reading
What's good for you?

1 What are all of these articles about?

2 Read the articles.

a Match the items in column A and column B.

b Which text does each pair of items go with?

A	B
being cheerful	heart attacks
low-fat diets	a shorter life
keeping a pet	minor illnesses
eating citrus fruit	suicide
washing frequently	turning orange
getting up early	lower blood pressure

3 One of the articles is a hoax, but the others are all genuine.

a Read the articles again. Which one do you think isn't genuine? Why?

b Discuss your ideas with other members of the class.

c 🔊 *10.2* Listen. You will hear which one isn't genuine. Compare your ideas.

4 Choose three of the genuine articles. For each one complete as much as possible of the table.

	1	2	3
cause			
effect			
explanation			
evidence			

Vocabulary file: Synonyms

Match the words and their synonyms.

a link	a research team
results	a study
researchers	findings
research	a connection
assert	reinforce
confirm	show
reveal	claim

5 Discuss these questions.
1 Which article do you think is the most interesting?
2 Would you change your lifestyle on the basis of this kind of evidence?
3 What is your advice for a healthy life? Write a list of do's and don'ts.

1 Dirty body – healthy body

Do you like to be clean? Italian doctors think it could be making you sick. 'Bathing removes our natural protection from germs,' asserts Dr Giancarlo Pagnozzi. 'Nature gave us protection, but we keep washing it away.'

For seven years researchers studied 300 people. One half took a bath or shower every day using soap and deodorant. The other half washed once a week in plain water. The super-clean team had several minor illnesses including 873 colds, 167 cases of flu, 49 sore throats, 27 attacks of bronchitis, and various skin diseases. The dirty group had only 29 colds, 3 cases of mild flu, and one sore throat – but no friends.

2 A miserable life won't kill you

Laughter is not the best medicine for a long life, according to researchers. Dull, cautious, conscientious people are 30 per cent less likely to die early than the cheerful and easy-going.

The discovery comes in a 60-year study of more than 1,000 American men and women. One reason might be that cautious people are less likely to smoke, drink, take drugs, or drive fast. They take fewer risks and are more careful about their health.

3 EARLY RISERS BITE THE DUST

A 30-year study in New Zealand has revealed that the person who gets up early is less likely to survive the day than the one who lies in bed till after 8 or 9 o'clock. A research team studying a group of 500 people found a significant link between early rising and heart disease.

'We don't fully understand the link,' said Dr Prudence White, 'but we know that the risk of a heart attack is highest in the early morning. Perhaps if you're lying in bed you stand more chance of surviving an attack.'

Another possibility is that people who get up early in the morning are more likely to eat a traditional cholesterol-rich breakfast of sausages, eggs, and bacon. So it seems we no longer need an excuse for lying in bed longer. Good news at last!

4 Pets on prescription

In the future if you go to your doctor with high blood pressure, he or she might prescribe not medicine but a cat or a dog. Australian scientists have found that owning a pet brings lower blood pressure and lower cholesterol. The results are confirmed by research at Cambridge University, which showed that people who were given cats and dogs to look after were ill less often than people who did not have a pet. Researchers believe that keeping a pet helps because it reduces stress.

Language focus:
Expressing possibility and probability

a There are several expressions in the texts with similar meanings. Complete the expressions with these words.

possibility	risk	believe	thought
may	seems	likely	according

This | could / _____ / might | be making you ill.

This | _____ / appears | to …

Researchers | think / _____ | that …

It is | believed / _____ | that …

It's also possible
Another _____ is | that …

_____ to researchers …
Researchers claim that …

These people | run a greater _____ / stand more chance / are more _____ to die. | of dying.

b Use the expressions above and the information in your chart from **4**. Briefly summarize each of the articles you chose.

5 What's good for the heart might not be good for the mind

Low-fat diets prescribed to reduce heart disease may be bad for mental health, a report claims. A low level of cholesterol appears to affect a person's mood and increases the risk of suicide, according to researchers. The new findings reinforce an earlier US study which showed a connection between low cholesterol and depression.

6 Oranges and lemons

Fruit is generally thought to be good for you, but a recent medical report claimed that people who eat large amounts of citrus fruit (oranges, lemons, grapefruits) run the risk of turning orange.

Listening and speaking
At the doctor's

1 Look at the picture. What is wrong with the people?

2 🔲 *10.3* Listen to four of the patients' conversations with the doctor. Answer these questions.
1 Which of the people in the picture do you hear?
2 What is wrong with them?
3 What is the doctor's diagnosis? Choose from this list.

☐ flu   ☐ an infection
☐ a sprain   ☐ depression
☐ a virus   ☐ a fracture
☐ an allergy   ☐ high blood pressure

3 What can you remember?
a Complete the chart.

	patient	symptoms	started	treatment
1				
2				
3				
4				

b Compare your ideas with a partner.
c 🔲 *10.3* Listen and check your ideas.

Conversation pieces: Polite enquiries and recommendations

a What expressions does the doctor use to:
 1 ask
   ● what the patient wants.
   ● when the problem started.
 2 suggest
   ● having an X-ray.
   ● going to the hospital straight away.
   ● staying off work.
 3 say
   ● how long the illness will last.
   ● that the ear is infected.
   ● how often to take the medicine.
 4 ask the patient to
   ● show him his wrist.
   ● take his shirt off.
   ● put the thermometer under his arm.

b 🔲 *10.3* Listen again and check your ideas.
c Work with a partner. Practise the conversations, using tapescript 10.3.

Language focus:
must, mustn't, have to, needn't.

a Complete these sentences from the doctor's conversation with Mr Scales.

You _____ take more exercise.

You _____ do too much exercise at first.

You _____ exercise every day.

b Match the sentences to these meanings.
- It doesn't matter whether you do this or not.
- It's important that you do this.
- It's important that you don't do this.

c Translate the sentences into your own language.

d Look at this dialogue and answer the questions.

Mr Scales: *What do I have to do?*

Doctor: *You must take more exercise.*

1 Why does the doctor use *must*?

2 Why does Mr Scales use *have to*?

➤ Check the rules for *must* and *have to* in **Grammar Reference 10.1**.

e What does the doctor tell Mr Scales? Use *must, mustn't,* or *needn't* and this information.

EXAMPLE

You must lose weight.
- lose weight
- give up work
- spend more time at work
- eat a lot of fat
- cut out all fat
- make an appointment with the lifestyle consultant
- relax more
- have more tests
- smoke
- go jogging every day
- go to the hospital

f Say whether the other patients *have to, mustn't,* or *don't have to*
- go back to see the doctor again.
- take some medicine.
- make another appointment.
- stop taking the tablets.
- go to work.
- go to the hospital.
- stay in bed.
- have an X-ray.
- keep warm.

4 Choose other patients from the waiting room picture. Work with a partner and take it in turns to roleplay their conversations with the doctor.

Pronunciation
-i-; strong and weak forms

1 The vowel -i-

a The vowel -i- is normally pronounced in one of three ways, as shown in the table.

/ɪ/	/aɪ/	/ɜː/
lift	write	first

b Write these words in the correct column.

prize stir girl little bird birthday thin video will hi-fi miss active lip price fine alive drive light olive give fill title direct like high item nice third office

c 📼 *10.4* Listen, check, and repeat.

d Look at the table. How is -i- normally pronounced when it is followed by
- a double consonant?
- a single consonant at the end of the word?
- a consonant + -e?
- -r followed by a consonant or at the end of a word?

2 Strong and weak forms

a Some prepositions and auxiliary verbs have a strong form and a weak form. In most situations we use the weak form. However, when the preposition or auxiliary comes at the end of the sentence we use the strong form.

EXAMPLES

/frɒm/ *Where are you from?*   /frəm/ *I'm from Scotland.*

/wə/ *Were you on holiday last week?*   /wɜː/ *Yes, we were.*

b Circle the weak forms and underline the strong forms of the auxiliaries and prepositions in these dialogues.

1 **A** Which hotel are you staying at?

  B We're at the *Black Bull.*

2 **A** Who are you waiting for?

  B For John.

3 **A** Can you speak Japanese?

  B Yes, I can.

4 **A** Do you know who this card is from?

  B Yes, I do. It's from Sharon.

5 **A** Was that your new CD you were listening to?

  B Yes, it was.

c 📼 *10.5* Listen, check, and repeat.

d Practise the dialogues with a partner.

Extension: Reading and listening
Sentenced to death

1 **Read the information and compare it to your own country.**

In Britain, if you are ill you can receive free treatment on the National Health Service (NHS) or you can pay for private treatment. With the NHS, the country is divided into a number of local health authorities. As more and more treatments become available, these health authorities often have to decide which cases should have priority.

2 **Look quickly at the article and answer the questions.**
1 Who is it about?
2 What is wrong with her?
3 Explain the headline.

3 **Read the story and complete the sentences with the correct names.**
1 _____ needs treatment for cancer.
2 _____ thinks that the local health authority should pay for the treatment.
3 _____ thinks further treatment would not be good for Child B.
4 _____ thinks further chemotherapy should be tried.
5 _____ has agreed to carry out the treatment.
6 _____ has refused to pay for the treatment.
7 _____ explained the health authority's decision.
8 _____ says he won't give up.

4 **Answer these questions.**
1 Why can't Child B be named?
2 What form of cancer has she got?
3 How many times has she had the disease?
4 What treatments has she had so far?
5 Why has the health authority refused to pay?
6 What are the girl's chances of survival?

5 **Discuss these questions.**
a How do you feel towards
   • Child B?   • her father?   • the health authority?
b Would you feel differently if
   • it was not a child but an adult?
   • you were waiting for treatment from the same health authority?
   • she was a member of your family?

Vocabulary file: Collocations

Match the verbs and nouns. Some verbs can go with more than one noun.

diagnose	a row
consult	a disease
cure	a transplant
receive	a specialist
carry out	a doctor
cause	treatment

---

6 **What do you think happened to Child B?**

a ▣ *10.6* Listen to a radio news item about her and answer the questions.
1 When was the news item?
2 Child B's name is
   ☐ Jackie Boone.   ☐ Janet Bourne.
   ☐ Jane Brown.   ☐ Jaymee Bowen.

b **Tick (✓) the correct answers. More than one may be correct.**
☐ The treatment was not carried out and Child B died.
☐ An anonymous donor provided the money for the treatment.
☐ The health authority changed its mind.
☐ Friends and neighbours collected the £75,000.
☐ A revolutionary new treatment saved her.
☐ She was completely cured.
☐ She survived for a few months but then died.
☐ Her treatment is continuing.

7 **Discuss these questions.**
1 If there is a limit to how much money should be spent, which of these should get priority? Work in groups and agree on an order of priority.
   • people who injure themselves doing dangerous things
   • people with conditions that are not life-threatening such as hip replacements
   • people with illnesses caused by smoking, alcohol, or drugs
   • premature babies
   • children
   • old people
   • criminals
   • adults with dependants
   • people with valuable skills
2 Should there be cash limits on health spending, or should treatment always be provided however small the chance of survival?
3 Should people have to pay for their own medical treatment?

Sentenced to death

BY SARAH BARCLAY

'If we spend money on one patient, it's money that won't be available for other patients.'

Yesterday the girl at the centre of a row over health spending lost her fight to receive the treatment for cancer that she needs. Child B, who can't be named to protect her from publicity, needs expensive treatment, and her local health authority has refused to pay for it. The case has caused considerable debate over priorities in the health service.

Child B has been suffering from leukaemia since she was only six years old. When the disease was first diagnosed, she was given chemotherapy and the treatment, seemed to be successful. For three years she was free of symptoms, but then the cancer returned in a much more serious form. This time, Child B received a bone marrow transplant from her younger sister. Again it worked. When doctors said that she was free of the disease, her father took her and her sister on holiday to Disneyland.

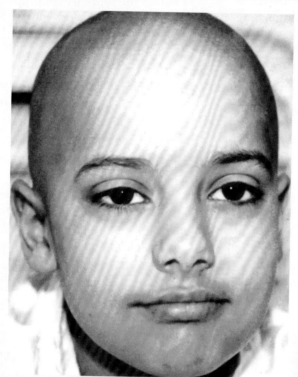

Child B during one of the chemotherapy sessions to treat her cancer

That's when the really bad news came. Child B's local health authority said it would not pay for the treatment. The Chief Executive, Stephen Thornton, said: 'If we spend money on one patient, it's money that won't be available for other patients. In this particular case we felt that the chances of survival were so low that it would be a waste of money.'

Yesterday afternoon, Child B's father said that they would not give up. 'The doctors tell me that there's only a 10 per cent chance of survival,' he said. 'But I think those odds are better than nothing. I'm not prepared to just go home and watch my daughter die.'

Then in January this year the leukaemia returned, and since one transplant had already failed, there was little chance of a cure. The specialist who had been treating Child B, Dr Valerie Broadbent, believed that putting her through the pain of more chemotherapy and keeping her in hospital would not be in her best interests.

Her father, however, didn't agree and he desperately consulted other specialists. Finally, he found Professor John Goldman, head of leukaemia research at Hammersmith hospital, who believed that further chemotherapy could work, and a private clinic in Harley Street, London, agreed to carry out the treatment. But it would cost £75,000.

Child B before the cancer returned, leading a normal life

Child B being hugged by her desperate father

11 Priorities

Grammar

Causative *have*; *make/let/get*

Grammar in use

1 📻 *11.1* **Read and listen to the story and answer the questions.**
  1 Where does the story take place?
  2 What does the man do every week?
  3 Why does the customs officer stop him?
  4 What does he find?
  5 Why does the customs officer stop working on the customs desk?
  6 How does he finally get the man to tell him the truth?
  7 What has the man been smuggling?

2 **This is a very old story that exists in many different versions. Do you know another version?**

Crossing the border

The customs officer was suspicious when the man appeared at the border crossing. He made him open his suitcase, but there was nothing valuable in it. So the officer let him cross the border. Every week after that the same thing happened. The man arrived and the customs officer stopped him and searched his suitcase. Sometimes he made the man wait for several hours, hoping he would confess, but he always had to let the man go. He was sure that the man was smuggling something, but he never found anything.

The years passed and the customs officer became a senior customs officer. He no longer worked on the customs desk, but every week from his office window he saw the man arrive, and every week he had the man stopped and searched by the customs officer, but nothing was ever found.

Then the day came when the senior customs officer was to retire, and he decided that before he left he would get the man to tell the truth. So he got the customs officer on the desk to stop the man and had him brought to the office. 'I am retiring tomorrow,' he said. 'I know that you have been smuggling all these years. Please tell me what it is. You have my word that I won't tell anyone.' The man looked at him, smiled, and said, 'Suitcases.'

Rules

1 **Match the sentences and pictures.**

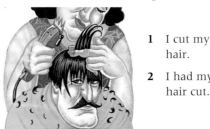

  1 I cut my hair.
  2 I had my hair cut.

a Now look at these two sentences and answer the questions.
  The customs officer stopped the man.
  The senior customs officer had the man stopped.
  1 Who stopped the man in each case?
  2 Replace *the man* with a pronoun. What kind of pronoun is used?

b We call the second sentence a causative *have*. When do we use the causative *have*?

Complete the rule with *object, past participle,* and *have.*

We form causative *have* with _____ + _____ + ._____ .

Find another example in the story.

2 Complete these sentences from the text.

He _____ the man _____ for several hours.
So the officer _____ him _____ the border.
He would _____ the man _____ the truth.

a Translate the sentences into your own language. Do you use different verbs for each sentence?

b What is the difference in meaning? Complete the sentences below so that they mean the same as the sentences above.
  1 The officer asked (or persuaded) the man to _____ .
  2 The officer allowed the man to _____ .
  3 The officer compelled the man to _____ .

c In what way is the construction of sentences with *get* different from *make* or *let*?

➤ Check the rules for causative *have* and *make/let/get* in **Grammar References 11.1** and **11.2**.

Practice

1 What did the senior customs officer have done?
He got the officer on the desk to
  1 stop the man. *He had the man stopped.*
  2 empty his suitcase. *He had his suitcase emptied.*
  3 check his passport.
  4 search his clothes.
  5 question him.
  6 send his details to the police.
  7 follow him.

2 Look at these signs.

a What can you have done in each place?

EXAMPLE
You can have your hair cut here.

b What have you had done in the last few months? Make a list, then compare it with your partner.

3 Say what happened in each conversation, using *make, let,* or *get*.

EXAMPLE
Sandra got the secretary to type a letter.

  1 **Sandra** Could you type this letter, please?
    Secretary Yes, of course.
  2 **Daughter** Can I go to the party tonight, Mum?
    Mother Yes, but don't be back late.
  3 **Police officer** OK, Maloney. Drop the gun and put your hands against the wall.
  4 **Father** Have you finished your homework?
    Son Er, no. I was going to go out. I …
    Father Well, go and finish it now!
    Son Oh, all right.
  5 **Kate** Do you think you could lend me £10? I'll pay you back.
    Colin OK. Here you are.
  6 **Jack** Could I use your computer for a while, please?
    Peter Sure. Help yourself.
  7 **Solicitor** Could you just sign the document at the bottom there, please?
    Client There you are.
  8 **Robber** Hand over the money. Now!
    Bank clerk OK, OK. Don't shoot. Here it is.
  9 **Mr Winston** Would you mind working late tonight, Charles?
    Charles No, that's OK.
    Mr Winston Thank you. We're very busy.

4 What would you *get/make/let* someone (to) do if
  • you were in a cinema and someone behind you kept talking?
  • someone was dropping litter in the street?
  • your neighbours' dog bit you?
  • a waiter in a restaurant spilt coffee on your best jacket?
  • you saw two young boys vandalizing a phone box?
  • your friend asked if he/she could borrow your car?
  • a stranger asked if he/she could use your mobile phone?

Vocabulary
Noun formation

1 Many abstract nouns are formed from verbs. Look at these examples.

explain   explanation
agree   agreement

2 Use a dictionary. Complete the table.

verb	noun
destroy	_____
_____	introduction
_____	creation
survive	_____
_____	production
establish	_____
protect	_____
examine	_____
_____	imagination
decide	_____
suggest	_____
_____	concentration
compensate	_____
support	_____
injure	_____
_____	appearance

3 Complete the sentences, using words from above.

1 We need to make a _____ about next year's _____ targets, so I would like to _____ a meeting on Friday.

2 If we can't reach an _____ with the local people about the _____ of these animals, they won't _____ .

3 We must put an end to the _____ of the forests and _____ new national parks.

4 The woman got £1,000,000 _____ for the _____ that she suffered in the crash.

Reading
Di-Di's story

1 Look at the first photograph and answer the questions.
1 What is the animal?
2 What is the woman doing with it?
3 Where do you think the picture was taken?
4 How do you feel when you see the picture?

2 Read the article.

a Who or what are these? What role do they have in the story?
- Taiwan
- Mrs Chang
- Shylie
- Dr Willie Smits
- Di-Di
- Wanariset
- Marcus Phipps
- Indonesia

b Who do you think the writer is?

3 Explain what has happened to the orang-utans. Put these events in the correct order.
☐ Baby orang-utans are captured in Indonesia.
☐ Baby orang-utans are sold as pets.
☐ The orang-utans are released into the forests.
☐ Adolescent orang-utans are abandoned.
☐ The Wanariset Centre is established.
☐ The orang-utans grow up.
☐ Baby orang-utans are smuggled into Taiwan.
☐ People want baby orang-utans as pets.
☐ The orang-utans learn to live together.
1 *The Naughty Family* is on TV.
☐ Orang-utans are flown back to Indonesia.

Vocabulary file: Synonyms
Find words in the text which mean the same as:
- very unusual
- something that a baby wears
- the toilet
- very surprised
- death of a species
- the ones that are still there
- very fast
- to import illegally
- teenage
- from the Netherlands
- to watch
- up till now
- to set free

4 Discuss these questions.
1 Find examples in the text which illustrate these comments from the author.
- It was my introduction to an extraordinary story of love and sadness.
- Di-Di, like all orang-utans, is very intelligent.
- It hides a story of death and destruction.
2 What have you learnt about orang-utans from the story?
3 How do you feel about Di-Di's story? Who is most to blame for the problem?
4 What do you think about these animal issues?
- keeping animals as pets
- blood sports
- trapping animals for fur
- factory farming

WILDLIFE MAGAZINE

Di-Di's story

'Mrs Chang has looked after Di-Di like her own daughter for more than six years,' explained Marcus Phipps, of the Taiwan Orang-utan Foundation. When we rang the doorbell of the apartment, the door was opened, not by Mrs Chang, but by the orang-utan, Di-Di. It was my introduction to an extraordinary story of love and sadness.

Di-Di, like all orang-utans, is very intelligent. 'Go to the toilet,' said Mrs Chang. 'Take off your nappy first.' Di-Di responded immediately by taking off her nappy, running into the bathroom and going to the loo. I watched, amazed. 'Now flush the toilet and wash your hands.' Di-Di responded to everything that Mrs Chang said. 'She understands about 75 per cent of our daily conversation,' explains Mrs Chang. 'That's about 500 words. I think she's very special and I love her very much.'

'I think she's very special and I love her very much.'

It's a touching sight, but it hides a story of death and destruction which has brought one of our nearest relatives close to extinction. Most of the world's remaining 30,000 orang-utans live in Indonesia. In the 1980s their numbers began to fall rapidly, as the forests where they live were destroyed. At the same time in Taiwan a children's soap opera, called *The Naughty Family*, was becoming very popular. The star of the programme was a young orang-utan called Shylie. It created a demand for baby orang-utans as pets. When the adult orang-utans were hunted and killed in Indonesia, the young apes were captured and smuggled into Taiwan where they were sold for $2,000–$5,000 each.

Di-Di is one of about 1,000 baby orang-utans that found their way into Taiwanese homes. Only about 280 have survived. But survival has brought its own problems, for while a baby orang-utan may be cute and cuddly, an adolescent ape is not. Many of them were taken to Taipei zoo, or simply abandoned onto the streets of the city. Eventually a Dutch scientist, Dr Willie Smits, established a centre at Wanariset in Indonesia to return the orang-utans to the wild. It was this that we had come to observe, for now it was Di-Di's turn to go home.

Three months later Di-Di and eleven other orang-utans were flown to Indonesia and taken to the Wanariset Centre. Mrs Chang went with us. Di-Di was not very happy. Mrs Chang and Dr Smits got her to go into the large new cage where she would learn to live with other orang-utans. But then Mrs Chang had to say goodbye. 'This is a much better place for you. You'll be much happier here, Di-Di. I love you. You be a good girl now. Mummy is going now.'

It was a sad moment, but three days later Di-Di was getting used to her new home. She couldn't climb very well at first, but she learnt quickly. The biggest problem for the Wanariset Centre is preserving the forests to provide homes for the apes. The timber industry is very powerful in Indonesia, and the government provides very little money to protect the forests. To date more than 50 apes have been released, but there are still 200 more at the Wanariset Centre. Dr Smits and his team are looking for new areas of forest where they can be released and protected.

Di-Di pushes her finger through a hole in the door and Mrs Chang touches it.

Now the big day has arrived when Di-Di and the other orang-utans are going to be released. It seems strange when we look at her to think that a year ago she was wearing children's clothes and playing the piano. The cage has been taken deep into the forest and as we watch from a treehouse, the cage door is opened. Di-Di comes over to the treehouse. She knows that Mrs Chang is with us. But we can't let her come in. She has to forget Mrs Chang and go to her friends. Di-Di pushes her finger through a hole in the door and Mrs Chang touches it. It is their last goodbye. Then Di-Di is gone. When we leave, the thirteen orang-utans are playing in the forest – playing as if they had never been away.

Listening and speaking
Dealing with problems

1 **Look at this list of situations.**

a Have any of these ever happened to you?
1   Your watch has stopped.
2   You've left something at a hotel.
3   You've bought some theatre tickets but you want to return them.
4   You've damaged your car.
5   You're in a restaurant. There's something wrong with the food.
6   You're in a hotel. The people in the next room are very noisy.
7   You've bought something and it's faulty.
8   You've just got on a plane. Someone has been allocated the same seat as you.

b Imagine you had these problems. What would you do in each situation? Who would you speak to about each problem?

2 📼 *11.2* **Listen to five conversations and tick (✓) the five situations that you hear from the list in 1.**

3 📼 *11.2* **Listen again and complete the table.**

problem	action offered	choice made

Conversation pieces: Polite expressions

a Complete the expressions, using tapescript 11.2.

Introducing the problem:

I wonder _____

Excuse me, I'm _____

I'm sorry to _____

Expressions which mean the same as *Do you want* … :

Would you _____?

Do you _____?

Would you _____?

Asking someone to do something:

Would you _____?

Could I _____?

Could you _____?

b Work with a partner. Practise the conversations, using the table in **3**.

Language focus: *need + -ing*

a Choose the correct forms to complete the sentences.

The battery needs	replace. to replace. replacing.

Do you need a new one	put in? to put in? putting in?

➤ Check your ideas in **Grammar Reference 11.3**.

b Look at the problems below and say what needs doing, using the correct verbs.

EXAMPLE
The door handle needs tightening.

change	tighten	repaint	refill	clean
replace	repair	wash	cut	

1 The door handle is loose.
2 The side of the car has been scratched.
3 The light bulb has gone.
4 Your trousers are dirty.
5 You can't see through the windows very well.
6 The brakes aren't working properly.
7 The gas bottle is empty.
8 My hair's getting long.
9 The tyre's got a puncture.

4 Look at the other situations in the list in **1**. Work with a partner. Decide what you would do and roleplay the conversation for each situation.

5 Here are some further complications.

a Match each problem to a situation in **1**.
- The plane is fully booked.
- The gloves haven't been found.
- The smoked salmon is too salty, too.
- The shop doesn't have the correct size of battery.
- You've lost the receipt.
- The theatre has a *no refund* policy.
- The noise continues.
- The garage can't do the repair today.

b Make new conversations for some of the situations, including the new complications.

Pronunciation
-ea-; corrective stress

1 The vowels *-ea-*

a The vowels *-ea-* can be pronounced in several different ways. The commonest ways are shown in the table.

/ɜ:/	/ɪə/	/e/	/iː/
heard	fear	dead	bean

b Complete the table with these words.

head appear bead early bread clean ear
dearest weak earth read easy please
gear learn hear weather year rear
leather heavy speak seat lead search

c 🔊 *11.3* Listen, check, and repeat.

d Two of the words can go in two of the columns. Which words are they? What is the difference in meaning between the two pronunciations?

e Look at the table. How is *-ea-* normally pronounced when it is followed by:
- *-r*
- *-r* + another consonant
- *-th*
- *-l*

f Now look at these exceptions. How are these words pronounced?

pear beard wear beneath yearly

2 Corrective stress

a 🔊 *11.4* Listen. When we want to correct something we put the stress on the corrected item.
A *Phil's from New York.*
B *No, he isn't. He's from California.*

b 🔊 *11.5* Look at these pairs of statements. Listen to the responses and choose the right statement.
1 ☐ You live at number 25 Brown Street.
  ☐ You live at number 18 Green Street.
2 ☐ Sally's birthday is in July.
  ☐ Cathy's birthday is in August.
3 ☐ The meeting's at 10.30.
  ☐ The meeting's at 11 o'clock.
4 ☐ Karl drives a Ferrari.
  ☐ Colin drives a Porsche.
5 ☐ We went to the movies on Saturday.
  ☐ We went to a disco on Friday.

c 🔊 *11.6* Now listen to the complete dialogues and check your answers.

d Practise the dialogues, using tapescript 11.6. Read the responses with the correct stress to correct the other sentence of each pair.

Extension: Reading and listening
Joe's problem

1 **Read the information and answer the questions.**
1   Who are the people in the photographs?
2   What are their jobs?
3   What do you know about each one's character?
4   What is Joe's problem?
5   What things are contributing to this problem?

Joe's problem

Joe Hill is the marketing manager of Excalibur Holdings. He has two deputies. Samantha Reagan is the sales manager. She's bright and dynamic, but rather volatile and impatient. She's got a good name in the industry and Joe knows that other companies have been showing interest in her. Colin Macgregor is the administrative manager. He joined the company three months ago and has spent most of that time learning the ropes. Colin gets on well with people. He's steady and reliable, but not very imaginative. Joe also has a personal assistant, Mandy Baxter, who is very efficient.

Joe's life at the moment is getting very hectic. In addition to his normal heavy workload, there are a number of other things needing his attention. Next week is the annual meeting of the company directors. Last year the meeting did not go very well. There were some awkward questions asked. So Joe is not looking forward to the meeting. One of the results of the meeting was a decision to keep new appointments to a minimum. People who left could be replaced, but no new posts should be created. In two months' time, Joe's department is moving to a new building. Lately, Joe has been getting some pains in his chest, but he's been putting off going to the doctor, because he can't find the time.

2 **Look at Joe's diary. It's 9.15 and Joe is discussing the day's appointments with Mandy.**
a   🔊 *11.7* Listen and complete Joe's diary for the day.
b   Write down the other things Joe needs to deal with today.
c   Should he change any appointments to accommodate any of these things? Work with a partner and change Joe's diary as you think best.

3 **Read the fax that arrived and answer the questions.**
1   Who is the fax from?
2   What does he want Joe to do? Why?
3   What implications does it have for Joe's diary?
4   What do you think Joe will do?

4 🔊 *11.8* **Listen to Joe's conversation with his wife and answer the questions.**
1   What does he tell her?
2   How does she react? Why?
3   How does the conversation end?

5 **Decide what Joe should do today.**
a   Work in a group and do these tasks.
1   Make a list of all the things that demand his attention.
2   Put the items in order of priority.
3   Decide which items
   • could be postponed.
   • could be delegated (i.e. done by someone else).
   • are unreasonable demands.
4   Write out Joe's diary for the day.
b   Compare your diary with other groups. Justify your decisions.

6 **Joe has to communicate his decisions for the day to other people. Write the dialogue(s) and/ or fax(es) in which he explains his decisions.**

7 🔊 *11.9* **Listen to Joe's decisions and compare them to your own ideas. Do you think he made the right choices?**

October
Thursday
9
282·83   Week 41
▷ First Quarter

9.00 – 9.30	Diary, Correspondence
9.30 – 10.30	
10.30 – 12.00	
12.00 – 1.00	Sheila Gordon
	Re
1.00 – 2.00	with
2.00 –	
	Deadline
5.00	Leave _promptly_

October
M T W T F S S M T W T F S S M T W T
1 2 3 4 5 6 7 8 9 10 11 12 13 14 15 16 17 18 19

1997
Friday
282·82   Week 41
October

EXCALIBUR ◆ HOLDINGS

From: Charles Azil,
Sales Representative Benelux, Brussels

To: Joe Hill, Head Office, London

Subject: Alitrain contract

VERY URGENT

Dear Joe

As you know, Alitrain will be deciding whether to renew our contract at their annual meeting tomorrow. Well, unfortunately, they've got a new chap in their production department and he wants to speak to 'the person at the top', as he put it, before they will sign on the dotted line. I hadn't been expecting this at all, but they've made it clear that if they can't speak to you, they may look elsewhere. And I know that the Americans and the Germans have been pressing hard to get the contract from us. So we need you urgently, Joe. There's a plane from London at 12.30 today that gets here at 2.15. (We're an hour ahead.) So I can set up a meeting for 3.30. Then I would suggest that we take them out to dinner this evening.

Sorry to spring this on you, but there's a lot hanging on this. Please don't let me down, Joe.

Yours,

Charles

Charles

12 News

Grammar
Reported speech

Grammar in use

1 Look at the story and answer the questions.
1 Who are the people?
2 What are they talking about?
3 Why do people like to gossip like this?
4 What other things do people gossip about?

2 Mark these sentences *True* (✓) or *False* (✗).
1 Ken and Pauline had an argument.
2 It was Ken's birthday yesterday.
3 Ken didn't know about the dinner that Pauline had prepared.
4 Ken is now living with Mike.
5 Ken hasn't spoken to Pauline since the row.
6 Isobel doesn't know Ken and Pauline.

Gossip

Mike Are you all right, Ken?

Ken Oh, hello, Mike. No. Well, don't spread it around, but I had a terrible row with Pauline a few days ago and she's kicked me out.

Mike What was the row about?

Ken Well, she'd prepared a special dinner as a surprise for my birthday. But I didn't get in till late, because I went out for a drink with my friends.

Mike Oops! What are you going to do?

Ken Well, I'm staying with my sister at the moment, but I don't know what I'll do after that.

Mike Why don't you just make it up with Pauline?

Ken I've tried, Mike. I phoned her yesterday, but she wouldn't talk to me.

The next day

Mike Hi, Isobel. Have you heard about Ken and Pauline?

Isobel No, I haven't, but it sounds interesting.

Mike Well, don't tell anyone else, but ...

3 📼 *12.1* Read and listen to Mike and Isobel's conversation and answer the questions.
1 What do you think Isobel will do?
2 Who do you have most sympathy for in the story?

Mike Well, don't tell anyone else, but I met Ken yesterday and he didn't look too happy. When I asked him if he was all right, he said that he and Pauline had had a terrible row a few days ago and she'd kicked him out.

Isobel No!

Mike Yes, it's true. Anyway, I asked him what the row had been about.

Isobel Ooh, what did he say?

Mike Well, he said that Pauline had prepared a special dinner as a surprise for his birthday, but he hadn't got in till late, because he'd gone out for a drink with his friends.

Isobel Oh dear! Did he say what he was going to do?

Mike He said he was staying with his sister at the moment, but he didn't know what he would do after that, so I asked him why he didn't just make it up with Pauline. He said he'd tried, but she wouldn't talk to him.

Isobel Oh dear. She must be really mad this time, but I won't breathe a word to anyone about it. Anyway, I must go. Bye.

The next day

Rules

1 When Mike tells Isobel about his conversation with Ken, he uses reported speech. When the reporting verb is in the past tense, e.g. *he/she said,* the tenses in the reported conversation change.

a Look at the chart below. In Mike and Ken's conversation find an example of each of these tenses.

direct speech	reported speech
past perfect	
past simple	
present perfect	
present simple	
present continuous	
the future with *will*	
the conditional with *would*	

b What tenses do they change to in reported speech? Look at Mike and Isobel's conversation. Write the names of the tenses in the reported speech column.

c What happens to pronouns and possessive adjectives in reported speech?

2 Complete these two questions from the story.
What _____ _____ _____ about?
I asked him what _____ _____ _____ _____ about.

a What word order is used in the reported question?

b How does Mike report this question?
Are you all right, Ken?

➤ Check the rules for reported speech in **Grammar References 12.1, 12.2,** and **12.3.**

Practice

1 Here are some of the things that Pauline and Ken said when they were arguing.

a Who do you think said each one?
1 Where have you been?
2 I've been for a drink with my friends.
3 I've been preparing this meal all day and now it's ruined.
4 Why didn't you tell me about the dinner?
5 I wanted it to be a surprise.
6 Did you try to phone?
7 You think more of your friends than you do of me.
8 I'm sorry. It won't happen again.
9 It's all over. If you don't leave, I will.
10 Why are you being so unreasonable?
11 I'll phone you.
12 I never want to speak to you again.

b Ken is telling Mike what was said. What does Ken say? Use these expressions:
I asked/told her …
She asked/told me …
EXAMPLE
She asked me where I had been.

2 **How do you think the story of Ken and Pauline ends?**

a Continue this conversation and decide on an ending for the story.

Have you heard any more about Ken and Pauline?

Oh, yes. Well, I met Pauline the other day and she told me that ...

b 🔲 *12.2* Listen to the conversation and compare it with your own.

3 **Complete these questions to ask your partner.**
Have you ever _____ ?
What kind of _____ do you like best?
Are you doing anything _____ ?
Would you like to be _____ ?
When will you _____ ?
What did you do _____ ?
How long have you been _____ ?
What do you think about _____ ?
How often do you _____ ?

a Ask your partner the questions. Note down his/her answers.

b Find another partner. Report what you found out.
EXAMPLE
I asked him/her whether he/she had ever been to Britain. He/she said that he/she had been there three times.

Vocabulary
Phrasal verbs (2)

1 **Some phrasal verbs have more than two parts. However, they behave in the same way as the two-part verbs.**

a Look back at Unit 6 and revise the rules for using phrasal verbs.

b Look up *run out of* in your dictionary. Is it separable or inseparable?

2 **Each verb in A can take two different parts from B to match the two definitions in C. Choose the correct parts in B to make phrasal verbs which match the definitions. Use your dictionary.**

A	B	C
stand	in on someone down to something	be noticeable take the place of
get	off with something on with someone	start have a good relationship
run	out from something out of something	have none left; finished steal
look	back on something in for someone	make a short visit review the past

3 **Complete these sentences with the phrasal verbs above.**

1 Brenda can't make it to the rehearsal this evening, so can you _____ her?

2 I don't believe it. That cat's just _____ the chicken for dinner again!

3 After a holiday it can be very hard to _____ work again.

4 I'm sorry to hear Tessa's not well. I'll _____ her on my way home.

5 Look at Sarah! She always _____ the crowd in those colourful dresses of hers.

6 Those two can't work together. They just don't _____ each other.

7 Oh no, the photocopier's _____ paper again!

8 When you _____ your life, you'll regret the things you didn't do more than the things you did.

Reading
The soldier's tale

1 **Look at the pictures. When and where did the events take place?**

a Put the pictures in the correct order to make a story.

b Read the story and check your order.

2 **Read the story again and answer these questions.**

1 What are the names of the people in the pictures?
2 Was John Clarke fighting for the North or the South?
3 How old was he when he joined the army?
4 What was in the soldier's pocket?
5 Who were the people in the photograph?
6 Why did John Clarke go to see Ethel Ross?
7 Did Ethel Ross forgive him?

3 **Discuss these questions.**

1 Why does John Clarke say that he grew up very quickly?
2 John Clarke probably killed a lot of people in the war. Why did this incident affect him so much?
3 If you were Ethel Ross, would you forgive him?
4 How do you think the whole incident changed the lives of the people in the story?
5 What message does the story convey?

4 **Write the story from the woman's point of view. Start from when the war began and her husband joined the Confederate army. Use reported speech to tell the story.**

Language focus: Indirect commands/requests

a Look at the sentences in the speech bubbles. How does the soldier report them? Complete these statements.

1 He told _____ .
2 I told _____ .
3 She asked _____ .
4 I asked _____ .
5 She told _____ .

b Complete these rules.

> To report positive commands and requests, we use *asked/told* + person + _____ .
> To report negative commands and requests, we use *asked/told* + person + _____ + _____ .

➤ Check the rules for indirect commands and requests in **Grammar Reference 12.4**.

c We can also use other verbs of reporting. Rewrite the sentences in **a**, using these verbs.

warn	beg	order	advise	invite

THE SOLDIER'S TALE

I can remember that day in June 1861 as if it was yesterday. The Civil War had just started and my sister shouted that the soldiers were coming. The soldiers looked so fine in their smart blue uniforms. I told my sister that I wanted to be a soldier. She said I couldn't because I was only fifteen.

But early next day I ran away to join the army. It was easier than I had thought. At the army camp the sergeant asked me what my name was. I told him proudly that it was John Clarke. When he asked me how old I was, I said that I was seventeen. I don't think he believed me, but he told me to go to the next tent and put on a uniform. Two hours later we marched away. I was a soldier and I was going to win the war for the North.

But nothing had prepared me for the horror of battle. The noise was terrible and all around me men were dying. I grew up very quickly.

One day near the end of the war we were searching some buildings. Suddenly I came face to face with a Confederate soldier. I told him not to move, but he started to take his hand out of his pocket. I thought he was pulling out a gun and I fired.

As he fell, his hand came out of his pocket. He wasn't holding a gun, but a small book. I picked it up. It was a diary and inside was a photograph of a woman and two

young children. On the photograph had been written, 'Darling William. We miss you, Ethel, William junior and Becky.' Sadly I put the diary in my pocket and left the dead soldier.

Eventually the war ended, but I couldn't forget William Ross. I was haunted by the photograph. Finally I made up my mind to look for his family. His address was in the diary and I found the house easily. The woman from the photograph opened the door. I told her that I had known her husband and that I had brought something for her. She invited me to come in and we went into a small sitting room.

I gave her the diary and the photograph and she asked me how I had got them. She listened as I told her my story, and then she asked me why I had come to see her. I asked her to forgive me.

She stood up and turned away from me. Quietly and coldly, she said that she wouldn't forgive me. She told me not to come back.

Outside two children were playing. I recognised them from the photograph. The boy asked me if I was a soldier. He said that his daddy had been a soldier and that one day he was going to be a soldier too. As I turned around, the boy pointed his wooden gun at me and said, "Bang, bang. You're dead!"

Listening and speaking
Here is the news ...

1 **You will hear a news broadcast.**

a What general topics would you expect to hear about? Make a list.

b ▭ *12.3* Listen to the broadcast. What topics are in the news? Compare them with your list.

2 ▭ *12.3* Listen again and match the names and occupations.

Person	Occupation
Mark Lloyd	a prisoner
Dr Sami Rambuka	an opposition spokesperson
Judy Forster	the Managing Director of K. B. Grant
Jack Tinker	the conference president
Sally Walker	a TV personality
Colin Richardson	the Transport Minister
Frank Selwyn	a pigeon owner
Angie Fellows	an actor
Emilio Shaw	the Chancellor of the Exchequer
Eddie Forbes	the governor of Ford Prison

3 **Why is each person in the news?**

a Make notes with a partner.

b ▭ *12.3* Listen again and check your answers.

4 **Look at the photographs of the people in the news.**

a Write the names under the correct pictures. Which people had their words reported in the news?

b Look at tapescript 12.3 and decide what the people actually said.

5

6

7

8

9

10

Pronunciation
Silent letters; word linking (3)

1 Silent letters

a Many words in English have a silent letter. Circle the silent letters in this list.

knee	listen	bomb	ghost
wrist	debt	receipt	unique
walk	climb	when	half
psychology	answer	wrong	
doubt	salmon	building	
what	calm	school	knife
scientist	chemistry	know	
who	wreckage		

b 📼 *12.4* Listen, check, and repeat.

c Can you see any rules for silent letters?

2 Word linking (3)

We have already seen that when a word starts with a vowel, this can affect the pronunciation of the previous word in normal speech. (See Units 5 and 7.) When two consonants come together, they also affect each other.

a 📼 *12.5* Listen to this sentence. What happens to the underlined consonants?
He jus_t_ wanted to spen_d_ more time with his family.

b What kind of sounds come before and after the sounds /t/ and /d/?

c Say these sentences quickly. Which sounds disappear?

1 She phoned me yesterday.
2 I don't know.
3 I saw him the next day.
4 You don't sound very happy.
5 This tastes nice.
6 He resigned today.
7 I've found the money.

d 📼 *12.6* Listen, check, and repeat.

5 Make an interview with someone in the news.

a Work with a partner. Choose one of the stories. Make a list of questions to ask the person.

b Roleplay the interview. Take it in turns to be the interviewer and the person in the news.

6 What is in the news this week?

a Work in a group. Write a news report on one or two of the main stories this week. Try to use reported speech where possible.

b Present your news report to the class, or record it as a radio news programme to play to the class.

Extension: Reading and listening
Monsters

1 Can you identify these monsters? What do you know about them? What other famous monsters do you know of?

2 Look at the newspaper headline. What do you think the *Lizardman* is?

3 Read the newspaper article.

a Match the people and the items.

Christopher Davis	a reward
Two police officers	a skunk ape
A state biologist	a drunk
The local sheriff	blood
A local couple	a bear
A motorist	a scaly monster
A local radio station	enormous footprints
Erik Beckjord	car

b Match the names to the correct pictures.
Lizardman   the Jersey Devil   the Dover Demon

c Report what the people said.

EXAMPLE
Christopher Davis said that a scaly monster had ...

4 Discuss these questions.
1 What do you think the reporter's opinion of the story is?
2 What do you think about the story?

INTERNATIONAL NEWS

Lizardman leaps into US folklore

Sightings of a monster lizard from the swamp have struck terror in a small community in South Carolina, *writes Stephen Milligan.*

The scare began when Christopher Davis, a young driver, claimed he had been attacked by a scaly creature that was green, wet, three-fingered, red-eyed, and 7 ft tall. Davis said the monster chased his car at speeds up to 40 mph and jumped on his roof.

The monster apparently appeared from the nearby Scape Ore swamp. Two police officers found enormous footprints a mile away.

A state biologist suggested that Davis probably saw a drunk who got out of a muddy ditch. And the local sheriff believes the monster was a bear and that the tracks were made by a prankster.

But the story has been widely believed and there have been other sightings. Last week a local couple reported that their car had been 'chewed up' in their garage one night.

Since then, some 70 hunters have been trying to trap the monster, dubbed Lizardman.

On Friday morning, a motorist claimed that he had shot Lizardman but had failed to kill it. He handed police a tissue which he said was stained with the monster's blood.

The sheriff sent two deputies to the scene of the shooting but found no trace of the monster. A local radio station has offered a reward of $1m to anyone who can capture Lizardman alive or dead.

Erik Beckjord, a leading 'monsterologist', says Lizardman may be a 'skunk ape', a creature said to have been sighted in woods and swamps across America for the past 30 years.

Other giant creatures which are said to be stalking the countryside include the Jersey Devil, which has a horse's face and a kangaroo's body and emits a piercing howl, and the Dover Demon, an orange animal with a head shaped like the figure eight, which lives in Massachusetts. They have one common feature: they attract tourists.

---

5 **There are many stories of monsters in different parts of the world.**

a 🔳 *12.7* Listen to a radio news broadcast. Then complete the table about the monster.

Name	
Place	
Evidence	
Explanations	

b 🔳 *12.7* Listen again and check your answers.

c What do you think is the presenter's opinion of the story?

6 **Discuss these questions.**
1 Why do you think stories of strange creatures are so common?
2 What reasons are there to doubt the stories?
3 If a strange creature was found, what do you think would happen to it?
4 What do you think *should* happen to it?

13 Regrets

Grammar

Third conditional; *should/shouldn't have*

Grammar in use

1 Read the story and match the people and actions.

Bill Allen	ordered Mr Allen to pay compensation.
Neville and Greig	broke into Mr Allen's house.
Neville	prosecuted Mr Allen for assault.
The police	have sent Mr Allen money.
The judge	fired a shotgun at two burglars.
Mrs Bleasdale	was injured by the shotgun.
Supporters	said she would have done the same thing.

2 Answer the questions.
   1 How old is Bill Allen?
   2 When did the incident happen?
   3 How badly was Charles Neville injured?
   4 How much compensation must Bill Allen pay?
   5 How do the neighbours feel about the incident?
   6 What happened to Mrs Bleasdale?

3 What do you think about the case?

No regrets

By NICK HOPKINS

THE OLD AGE pensioner who shot two burglars said he had no regrets as he left court yesterday. Six months ago, 67-year-old Bill Allen fired a shotgun at two men, Charles Neville and Philip Greig, who had broken into his house. Neville, 21, was hit several times and needed hospital treatment. Both men were later arrested, but to his amazement, Mr Allen also found himself in court charged with assault. He was ordered to pay Charles Neville £2,000 in compensation for his injuries.
'I couldn't believe it,' said Bill Allen. 'It's his own fault that he was injured. They shouldn't have broken into my house. If they hadn't been there, I wouldn't have fired the gun. It's as simple as that.

The judge says I should have called the police.

The judge says I should have called the police, but if I'd done that, they wouldn't have got there in time. The burglars would have disappeared before the police arrived.'
Bill Allen has received a lot of support from neighbours and from many people around the country. A neighbour, Mrs Bleasdale, said, 'My house was burgled a year ago, and if I'd had a gun, I would have done the same thing.' Several people have already sent Mr Allen money to help him pay the compensation.

Pensioner Bill Allen

Injured Charles Neville

Rules

1 How do we form the third conditional?

a Complete this sentence from the text.
If they _____ there, I _____ the gun.

b Complete the rule with the two correct forms.
- *would have* + past participle
- the present perfect
- the past perfect
- *would* + infinitive without *to*

> In third conditionals we use the _____ tense
> in the *if* clause and _____ in the main clause.

c Which of these situations do third conditionals describe?
- a possible future event
- an unlikely future event
- a past event which didn't happen

d Compare third conditionals with first and second conditionals.

e Find more examples of third conditionals in the story. Explain how each example describes the situation you chose in **c**.

2 Complete these two sentences from the text.

The judge says I _____ _____ called the police.
They _____ _____ broken into my house.

a Translate the sentences into your own language.

b When do we use this structure?

➤ Check the rules for the third conditional and *should/shouldn't have* in **Grammar References 13.1** and **13.2**.

Practice

1 What did the people actually say? Use *should/shouldn't have* **and this information.**

EXAMPLE
You shouldn't have fired a gun at the burglars.
1. fire a gun at the burglars
2. call the police
3. use unnecessary force
4. shout to warn the men
5. take the law into your own hands
6. The police/ prosecute Mr Allen
7. They/ give him a medal
8. Neville and Greig/ be there
9. The judge/ order them to pay compensation
10. Bill/ shoot them both

2 Look at these situations.

a Write what would or wouldn't have happened if …

EXAMPLE
Steven wouldn't have had an accident if he hadn't drunk too much.
1. Steven drank too much, and he had an accident.
2. Susan did no revision at all, and she failed her exam.
3. Mr and Mrs Claude didn't arrive at the airport on time, and they missed the flight.
4. The children ate too much ice-cream, and they were sick.
5. Prem didn't remember his wife's birthday, and they had an argument.
6. Katrina didn't do her homework, and the teacher told her off.
7. Mrs Sewell forgot to set the video recorder, and they didn't see their favourite programme.
8. Jack and Joanne watched a horror movie, and they had bad dreams.

b Now say what the people should or shouldn't have done.

3 Look at this chain of events.

a Describe it using the third conditional.

EXAMPLE
If Ted hadn't had an argument with his boss, he wouldn't have lost his job.

Ted had an argument with his boss.
▽
Ted lost his job.
▽
He went for long walks every day.
▽
He found someone's bag.
▽
He got a reward for returning the bag.
▽
With the reward he bought a lottery ticket.
▽
He won $8 million.
▽
He bought the company where he used to work.
▽
He sacked the boss.

b 🔊 *13.1* Listen and compare your answers.

4 Think about things in your own life that you regret doing/not doing. Tell your partner.
- What should or shouldn't you have done?
- What would have happened if you had acted differently?

EXAMPLE
I should have studied harder at school.
If I'd studied harder at school …

Reading
The frogs

1 Look at the photograph.

a Discuss the questions.
  1 Where do you think this place might be?
  2 What sort of facilities do you think it has?
  3 What do you think life is like there?
  4 How do you think the people make a living?

b Read the first paragraph of the story and check your answers.

2 The paragraphs of the story are in the wrong order. Read and number them in the correct order.

3 Find reasons in the story for these things.
  1 The people weren't unhappy with their life.
  2 The visitors wanted the frogs.
  3 The government supported the scheme.
  4 The villagers agreed to the scheme.
  5 The villagers did not gain any benefits from the scheme.
  6 The plan did not bring any money into the country.

4 What does the text say about
  • the villagers' daily life?
  • the need for a well?
  • the effects that killing the frogs had?
  • the sounds of the night?

5 Look at the train of events and say what would or wouldn't have happened, if …

EXAMPLE
If the visitors hadn't come, the village wouldn't have joined the scheme.
If they hadn't joined the scheme, …
visitors come/ join the scheme/ catch the frogs/ insects breed more rapidly/ diseases increase/ need medicine and pesticides/ spend the development fund/ buy things for the village

6 Discuss these questions.
  1 Did anyone benefit from the events in the story? Who? In what way?
  2 What is the 'deeper meaning' of the sounds of the night?
  3 What is the message of the story?
  4 In this story what were the intended and the actual effects?
  5 Do you know of any other examples from any area of life where the result of a change did not match the intention?

The frogs

☐ Now, there is still no well, health centre, or school in the village. There is no proper road. The people get up early and do their daily work. Then in the evenings they sit in the village square and listen to the buzzing of the insects and the croaking of the frogs. But those sounds of the tropical night now have a much deeper meaning.

☐ The change started gradually at first, and people hardly noticed it, but it seemed as if the crops in the fields were not doing so well. More worrying was that the children of the village seemed to be ill more often, and, perhaps it was just their imagination, but there seemed to be more insects around lately.

☐ Agreement was reached, and the children were sent out into the fields to catch frogs. Every week the lorry arrived and took away its croaking load, and every week the village got a little more money. For the first time, the people were able to dream of a better future. But the dream did not last long.

[ ] What was to be done? The villagers decided that they could not risk the crops and the children's health. They would have to use the money they had earnt to buy pesticides and medicines. Unfortunately these things were very expensive, as they had to be bought from abroad. Soon there was no money left.

[1] It was a village like thousands of others in India. The people were poor. There was no proper road. The village had no running water, so all day the women and girls walked to the river and back with enormous pots of water on their heads. In spite of the poverty, however, the people were not unhappy. After all, their ancestors had lived in the same way for centuries. And so the people got up when the sun rose and did their daily work in the fields. Then, in the evenings, they sat together in the village square. From the fields all around the village came the sounds of the night – the buzzing of the insects, the croaking of the frogs.

[ ] It seemed like money for nothing. There were millions of frogs in the fields and woods around the village, and they weren't of any use to the villagers. All they had to do was catch them. Then, every week a lorry would come to collect the catch and hand over the money. And what could they do with that money – a proper road, a well in the village square, a medical centre, a school, perhaps even electricity?

[ ] Then the people realized what was happening. It was the frogs. They hadn't been useless. They had been doing an important job – eating insects. Now, with so many of the frogs killed, the insects were breeding more rapidly. They were damaging the crops and spreading diseases among the people.

[ ] Then one day, some visitors from the city arrived. They told the people about a plan that would help to bring some money to the village. The plan was very simple. There were some countries, in Europe and elsewhere, where people liked to eat frogs' legs. However, they did not have enough frogs of their own, and so they wanted to buy frogs from other places. Several other villages had so far joined the plan, they said, and it had the support of the national government, because it would bring money into the country.

Vocabulary
Colloquial expressions

1 Match the expressions in A to their meaning in B.

A	B
It cost an arm and a leg.	That's life
I was stunned.	I was shocked.
They weren't much help.	I'm surprised!
quite a bit	watching television
a bit dodgy	a lot
You're telling me!	That's certainly true.
I was not in too good a mood.	not safe
in front of the box	It was expensive.
Goodness me!	You failed.
You blew it.	It's my turn to buy the drinks.
That's a bit rough.	That's unfortunate.
You're joking!	You aren't being serious.
That's miles away.	I wasn't very happy.
That's the way it goes.	It's a long way from here.
It's my round.	They didn't help very much.

2 Find colloquial expressions in the list which mean the same as:
- *You're kidding.*
- *You can say that again.*
- *Blimey!*

3 Complete the conversations, using expressions from 1. More than one may be possible.

1 **A** We went to that new restaurant yesterday. Well, when we got the bill, I _____ .
   B Expensive?
   A You _____ ! It _____ . I _____ when we left the restaurant.

2 **A** You can't spend all evening _____ . You've got _____ of revision to do.
   B I know.
   A Well, remember what happened with your last exam. You didn't revise and you _____ .

3 **A** Oh no! We've run out of petrol, and the nearest garage is in Waterford.
   B You _____ ! That _____ .

4 Listen and compare your answers.
a 🔊 *13.2* Pay attention to the intonation.
b Practise the conversations with a partner.

Listening and speaking
We had a nice time, but …

1 Things often go wrong on holidays.
a Think of possible problems.
   EXAMPLES
   You could miss the flight.
   You might be ill.
b Have you ever had a problem on holiday? Tell your partner.

2 You will hear three conversations about holiday problems.
a Look at the photographs. What do you think the problems were and what happened in the end?
b 🔊 *13.3* Listen and check your ideas. What went wrong with each holiday?

c Complete the table with your partner.

	1	2	3
Problem			
Cause			
Result(s)			
Whose fault?			
Why?			

d 🔊 *13.3* Listen again and check your answers.

Conversation pieces:
Talking about a holiday

a Listen to the conversations again. How do people
- ask about holidays?
- indicate that there was a problem?
- ask what happened?
- show sympathy?
- relate the story to their own experience?

b Look at tapescript 13.3 and check your answers.

3 Make more conversations about holiday disasters.

a Work with a partner and make conversations about the situations below, following the diagram.

A	B
Greet and ask about the holiday
	Indicate a problem
Ask what happened
	Describe what happened
Sympathize
	Express blame or regrets
Ask about results
	Describe results
Compare the problem to your own experience

1 lose passports/ leave bag on beach/ have to get new ones at the embassy/ wife's fault/ didn't leave passports at hotel
2 injured/ walk into glass door/ go to hospital/ hotel's fault/ couldn't see door
3 get lost/ car runs out of petrol/ spend night in car/ own fault/ didn't check the petrol gauge
4 holiday cancelled/ tour company goes bust/ have to go home/ husband's fault/ choose cheap holiday
5 house burgled while away/ door not locked/ TV and video stolen/ neighbour's fault/ came in to feed pets and forgot to lock door
6 arrested/ smuggling money out of the country/ taken to police station/ own fault/ didn't declare it on immigration form

b Think of a similar experience that might have happened to you. Make more conversations with your partner.

Pronunciation
-r-; expressing interest

1 The letter -r-

In British English, the letter -r- sometimes isn't pronounced.

a 🔊 *13.4* Listen to these sentences. Circle the -r-s that are pronounced.
Was your credit card stolen?
Did you break your arm?
The insurance didn't cover us for snowboarding.

b Match the sentence halves to complete the rules.

When -r- comes before a vowel sound	it is pronounced.
When -r- comes after a vowel sound	it is not pronounced.
When -r- comes between two vowel sounds

c 🔊 *13.4* Listen again. What do you notice about the -r on the end of *your*? Why does this happen? Find another example in the sentences.

d Say these sentences.
1 We were on our way to the airport.
2 The traffic was terrible.
3 There were hundreds of cars and lorries.
4 We were stuck for an hour.
5 We arrived at four o'clock.
6 The tour firm arranged a later departure for us.

e 🔊 *13.5* Listen, check, and repeat.

2 Expressing interest

When we respond to what somebody says, our intonation shows whether we are interested or not.

a 🔊 *13.6* Listen to the responses and match them to the correct meaning.
We've bought a new house.
1 Have you?   interested
2 Have you?   not interested

b 🔊 *13.7* Listen and decide if the person is interested or not.
1 A We're getting married.
  B Are you?
2 A Jane's expecting a baby.
  B Is she?
3 A We went to Rio for our holidays.
  B Did you?
4 A I've got a new job.
  B Have you?
5 A They won 3-nil.
  B Did they?
6 A Sally's resigned.
  B Has she?

c Practise saying the responses in an interested voice.

Extension: Reading and listening

Is honesty always the best policy?

1 Look at the newspaper article and answer the questions.
1 Where does it take place?
2 Who was the victim?

2 Read the article and match the subjects and sentence endings to make correct sentences.

	was changing a wheel.
	stopped to help.
	stole a suitcase.
	dropped a lottery ticket.
The robber	found the ticket.
	claimed the prize.
The victim	put adverts in the press.
	recognized the voice.
	returned the suitcase.
	refused a reward.

3 Discuss these questions.
1 What do you think of the story?
2 What reason did the professor give for not keeping the money? Do you agree?
3 What would you have done if you
• had found the ticket?
• were the professor's wife?
• were the robber and had read the advert?
• had been offered a reward?
4 What difference would it have made to his life if the professor had kept the money?
5 Does the story change your views on human nature?

A thief's lucky day

From RONALD SINGLETON in Rome

A THIEF who dropped a winning lottery ticket at the scene of his crime has been given a lesson in honesty. His victim, who picked up the ticket, then claimed the £25,000 prize, managed to trace him, and handed over the cash.

The robbery happened when maths professor Vinicio Sabbatucci, 58, was changing a tyre on an Italian motorway. Another motorist, who stopped 'to help', stole a suitcase from his car and drove off.

The professor found the dropped ticket and stuffed it in his pocket before driving home to Ascoli in eastern Italy.

Next day, he saw the lottery results on TV and, uncrumpling the ticket, realised it was a winner. He claimed the 60 million lire prize.

Then began a battle with his conscience. Eventually, he decided he could not keep the money despite having been robbed.

Victim hands back highway robber's £25,000 lottery ticket.

He advertised in newspapers and on radio, saying: 'I'm trying to find the man who robbed me. I have 60 million lire for him – a lottery win. Please meet me. Anonymity guaranteed.'

Professor Sabbatucci received hundreds of calls from people hoping to trick him into handing them the cash. But there was one voice he recognized – and he arranged to meet the man in a park.

The robber, a 35-year-old unemployed father of two, gave back the suitcase and burst into tears. He could not believe what was happening. 'Why didn't you keep the money?' he asked.

The professor replied: 'I couldn't because it's not mine.'

Then he walked off, spurning the thief's offer of a reward.

4 **Look at these situations and answer the questions.**
1 What do they all have in common?
2 Is there any difference in the situations?
3 Why are they not telling the truth?

5 🔈 *13.8* **Listen to a psychologist talking about honesty and lying. Which of these statements is the best summary of what she says?**
- ☐ Deception is a natural part of life.
- ☐ Everybody tells lies.
- ☐ It's best to always tell the truth.
- ☐ We shouldn't manipulate people's thoughts and feelings.

6 🔈 *13.8* **Listen again and answer the questions.**
1 Which of these are mentioned?
- ☐ marriage
- ☐ bringing up children
- ☐ entertainment
- ☐ courtship
- ☐ advertising
- ☐ sport
- ☐ education
- ☐ politics
2 What examples are given for each?
3 What do they have in common with lying?

7 **Discuss these questions.**
1 How would you answer the psychologist's final question?
2 Work out a definition of lying. Compare your ideas with other members of the class.
3 Think of a situation where not telling the truth
- would be a good thing (a white lie).
- would be all right as long as it was not discovered.
- would be a definite lie.
4 Can you think of situations in your own life where
- you told a white lie? What would have happened if you hadn't?
- you told the truth but then wished you hadn't? Why would it have been better if you hadn't?

'He's at a meeting.'

14 Success

1 **Look at the title and photographs.**

a Where is the woman in each photograph?

b What do you think the connection is between the pictures?

c Read the text and check your ideas.

To follow a dream

Two years ago, Joanna Verkerk had a well-paid and challenging job in London. With an active social life and a boyfriend that she was very fond of, life was comfortable. But it wasn't the life that she had dreamed of as a teenager. At 37 years old, she felt that life was passing her by. Then, while she was lying in a hospital bed after a serious illness, she decided to change things. She had always wanted to travel round the world, so she gave up her job and set off to follow her dream.

2 Write five sentences about what Joanna's life had been like before she left England.

EXAMPLE
She had lived in London.

3 When she decided to leave, some people were surprised.

a Report what they said, using *say, tell,* or *ask*.

EXAMPLE
They said that she was mad.
1 You're mad.
2 It will be dangerous.
3 Please change your mind.
4 Don't give up your job.
5 Most people would be happy with your life.
6 Why do you want to do it?
7 Are you worried?
8 How long will you be away?
9 Don't go.

b What would you have said to her?

4 Complete the next part of the story with the verbs in brackets in the best tense.

The journey _____ (take) Joanna through Europe and Africa, where in a remote corner of Tanzania she _____ (meet) Eric Baldauf, an American who _____ (teach) in a school there. Eric was like no other man that Joanna _____ ever _____ (meet), and she _____ (fall) madly in love with him. After two romantic weeks together, Joanna _____ (continue) her journey to India, but then she _____ (decide) to go back to Africa. As the plane _____ (approach) Nairobi airport in Kenya, she _____ (feel) very nervous. _____ they _____ (feel) the same way about each other? _____ Eric _____ (receive) her letters?
The plane _____ (land). While she _____ (wait) for her luggage, the doubts _____ (increase). Should she _____ (return)? Would it have been better if she _____ just _____ (continue) her journey? Should she have stayed in England in the first place? The luggage _____ (arrive) and Joanna _____ (walk out) into the arrivals hall. She _____ (look around), but Eric _____ (not be) there.

5 What do you think will happen to Joanna?

a Choose some of these possibilities and decide how the story will end.
- Eric dies.
- Eric and Joanna live together in Tanzania.
- They find their feelings have changed.
- Eric returns to America.
- They never see each other again.
- Joanna realizes that she shouldn't have left England.
- Joanna has a baby.
- Eric hasn't received any of Joanna's letters.
- They live in London.
- Joanna continues her journey round the world.
- Joanna marries her former boyfriend.
- Joanna and Eric get married.

b Compare your ideas with other members of the class.

c 🔊 *14.1* Listen and find out what actually happened.

6 How has Joanna's experience changed her life? What do you think would or wouldn't have happened if she had
- not become ill?
- stayed in England?
- married her former boyfriend?
- not returned to Africa?
- not met Eric?

7 Discuss these questions.
1 What do you think of Joanna's story?
2 What would you do if you could follow your dream?

8 Imagine you decided to follow your dream. Write the story, using this format.
- Describe your life before your decision.
- What did you decide and why?
- What actually happened? What problems did you meet?
- How has the experience changed your life? What would your life have been like if you hadn't made your decision?
- How do you feel about your experience now?

Vocabulary
Expressions with prepositions

1 **The reading text on the opposite page contains many expressions with prepositions.**

a Complete these sentences with the correct preposition.

  1 Handy's father was the rector _____ a church in Ireland, but when Handy grew up he didn't go _____ church.

  2 We've got a house _____ the country.

  3 I didn't think much _____ that film we saw. I couldn't see the point _____ it.

  4 Handy felt a little disappointed _____ his father.

  5 _____ the news conference the politician said he would like to spend more time _____ his family. I read about it _____ the newspaper.

  6 The film star was dressed _____ white. She was surrounded _____ hundreds of fans.

  7 The people _____ the funeral had tears _____ their eyes.

  8 We got stuck _____ a traffic jam and _____ the time we arrived the meeting had finished.

b When you read the text, see how many of the expressions with prepositions you can find.

2 **Find examples in the text of**
- compound nouns.
- phrasal verbs.
- abstract nouns.

Reading
What is success?

1 **Answer these questions.**

a What does 'success' mean to you?

b Who would you regard as successful?

c What would make you feel that you had achieved 'success'?

A Personal Preface

My father was a quiet man. He had been rector of the same country parish in Kildare in Southern Ireland for forty years when he retired, aged seventy-two. He was tired by then, understandably. For the last fourteen of those years he had also been Archdeacon of the Diocese. He died two years later.

I was in Paris at a business conference when I heard that he was dying. I flew back to Ireland, but he was unconscious by the time I got there and died the next day. His funeral, like all funerals in Ireland, was arranged for the day after tomorrow, a quiet family affair, back in the country church he had served for so long.

I was very fond of my father, but disappointed in him. He had turned down big city parishes, had settled for a humdrum life in the same little backwater. His life seemed to be a series of boring meetings and visits punctuated with the unchanging rhythm of Sundays, with old Mrs Atkinson and Eddie to lunch in the rectory afterwards. As a teenager I resolved never to go to church again, once I led my own life, and never to be poor again.

And so it was that, much to the amazement of my friends and family, I became an oil executive and was posted to the Far East to be in charge of Marketing in Sarawak – a job and a country both unknown in the rectory. I had a good time in Malaysia, mostly spending money and drinking too much beer. I came back fat and rather sleek, and also engaged, to a beautiful English girl whom I had met in Kuala Lumpur.

She didn't think much of an oil executive's life or of her predestined role as an oil executive's hostess, so I switched to the newly-discovered world of Business Studies, going to the United States to pick up another degree and coming back to the infant London Business School. Soon I was a professor, gallivanting around to conferences, consulting, lunching, dining, on the edge of the big time. A book had been published and articles galore. We had two young children, a flat in town, and a cottage in the country. More than that, I was tremendously busy, with a diary crammed with engagements. Success!

2 This is the preface to a book by Charles Handy. Read the text and answer these questions.

1 Who is Charles Handy?
2 What was his father?
3 What event does Handy describe?
4 Why was Handy surprised?
5 What effect did the event have?

It was with these thoughts in mind that I followed the hearse down the country roads to my father's funeral; a quiet end for a quiet man, I reflected. A pity that he never really understood what I was doing. When I became a professor I remember my mother's reaction to the news was to ask if this meant that I could now spend more time with the children.

Suddenly I noticed that we seemed to have a police escort; the local police had decided unasked to clear our route for the last few miles to church. A nice compliment to a Protestant vicar in rural Catholic Ireland, but just as well because it was hard to thread our way between the queues of cars trying to get to the little country church. The place was packed, overflowing. How had they heard? He had only died the day before yesterday and there had just been the one notice in the paper.

The choir looked odd, too. Dressed in the little-boy surplices that I remembered from long ago but with older faces. I remembered some of them. Choir boys and choir girls reassembled from all the corners of Ireland, or from England, too. They had dropped everything to be there. The Archbishop too, supposed to be in hospital, and still propped on a stick, was there to say to all of us how special my father had been and how he would be missed but remembered forever by so many whose lives he had touched.

As I stood by his grave, surrounded by people he helped to marry and whose children he had later baptized and then seen marry in his church in their turn, as I saw the tears in the eyes of the hundreds of people who had come from everywhere to say farewell to this 'quiet' man, I turned away and began to think.

Who, I wondered, would come to my funeral with tears in their eyes? What is success and who was successful, me or my father? What is one's life for, and what is the point of our existence in this world? They are not exactly new questions. I had studied philosophy. I knew the theories. I had never applied them to myself before. Not seriously.

Vocabulary file: Guessing from context

What do you think these expressions mean?

- a humdrum life
- a backwater
- She didn't think much of …
- gallivanting around
- on the edge of the big time
- a diary crammed with engagements
- unasked
- to thread our way
- They had dropped everything …
- with tears in their eyes

3 Compare Charles Handy's and his father's life. Complete this table with words and expressions that illustrate each man's life.

Charles Handy	his father

4 Answer these questions.
1 How old was Handy's father when he died?
2 Where was Charles Handy at the time?
3 Where had his father lived?
4 Why was Handy disappointed with his father?
5 Why had he resolved never to go to church again?
6 Where did he meet his wife?
7 Why did he switch careers?
8 What was odd about the choir?
9 Who were the people around the grave?

5 Why was Handy surprised by
- the police escort?
- the number of people there?
- the choir?
- the Archbishop?

6 Discuss these questions.
1 How had Handy defined success before his father's funeral?
2 How do you think the event changed his life?
3 In what way do you think his father was successful?

Listening and speaking
Responding

1 📼 *14.2* Listen to the conversations and match them to the correct photographs.

2 🔊 *14.2* **Listen again and for each conversation, answer these questions.**
1 What are the people talking about, exactly?
2 What is the outcome?

3 Look at the expressions.

a Match the two halves to make complete sentences.

A	B
Do you fancy	doing today?
Well, I suppose we'd better	speak to Mrs Wilson, please?
By the way, I'll be	waiting in traffic jams.
Could I possibly	where the post office is, please?
I can't stand	calling in on the Robinsons tomorrow.
Do you think you could	going to a movie this evening?
Could you tell me	if I use your phone?
I wonder if	be going.
Do you need it	give me a hand with these bags?
Do you mind	you could help me?

b Choose appropriate responses for the expressions in **a**.
I'm sorry. I'm afraid I don't know.
Have a safe journey. Drive carefully.
Sure. Here, let me take that one.
That would be nice.
Oh I'm terribly sorry. Are you all right?
Yes please, if you can manage it.
I'm afraid she's out. Can I get her to call you back?
Not at all. Help yourself.
Not so bad. And you?
Please give them my regards.
I'm afraid I have to disagree with you there.
Me, neither.
I'll do my best. What's the problem?
I'll have to get back to you on that.

c 🔊 *14.3* Listen to the complete conversations and check your answers. Pay careful attention to the intonation.

d Practise the conversations with a partner.

e Some of the responses are not appropriate for the sentences in **a**. When would you use them?

4 Choose two of the conversations and continue them.

5 Make conversations for the following situations using expressions in 3 and this format.
A Start the conversation.
B Give an appropriate response.
A Continue or complete the conversation appropriately.

1 Ask someone if you can borrow their pen.
2 Suggest doing something at the weekend.
3 Ask someone to help you fill in a form.
4 Phone Mr Carter. His line's engaged. Leave a message.
5 You need to get to the station. Ask someone.
6 You want to phone for a taxi. Ask someone for the number.
7 You're at an airport. Say goodbye to the person who came to the airport with you.

Pronunciation Revision

1 Rhymes

a Circle the two words in each group that are different. What vowel sound do they have?

1 stay   weigh   late   head   said
2 up   done   gone   fun   top
3 story   push   book   four   door
4 down   although   known   out   found
5 thing   find   rhyme   rhythm   wine
6 through   look   true   would   do
7 was   want   war   wallet   wall
8 bear   peak   people   where   fair

b 🔊 *14.4* Listen, check, and repeat.

2 Stress and intonation

a Mark the stressed syllables and draw the intonation curves.

1 **A** Shall we have a drink?
   B Do you want tea or coffee?

2 **A** There's a police car outside.
   B Is there?

3 **A** Where's Sally?
   B She's gone to buy a car.

4 **A** Is Peter 22 on Friday?
   B No, he's 23 on Friday.

5 **A** Where's my magazine?
   B I don't know. It's in the living room, isn't it?

6 **A** It's warm today, isn't it?
   B Yes, it is.

7 **A** I've been to Paris.
   B Have you? How nice.

b 🔊 *14.5* Listen and check your ideas.

c Practise the dialogues with a partner.

Extension: Reading and listening
How happy are you?

1 **What is your idea of a happy person?**

a Think of someone that you think is happy. Describe him/her and his/her life.

b Compare your ideas with a partner.

2 **Look at the introduction to the quiz and answer the questions.**

    1 What is it about?
    2 What are the questions based on?
    3 What warning do the instructions give?

3 **Do the quiz and compare answers with a partner.**

Vocabulary file: Synonyms

Find words in the quiz which mean the same as

1	succeed	**8**	on time
2	fits	**9**	when I should
3	helping someone	**10**	treated you badly
4	go to sleep	**11**	not forgive
5	I hate	**12**	try not to meet
6	untidy	**13**	getting better
7	not relaxed		

---

4 **Read the answers at the bottom of the page and work out your score.**

5 **Look at the quiz and the scores.**

a Why do you think the correct choices indicate a happy person?

b You will hear an analysis of the answers. Before you listen, check the meanings of these words and expressions. Would you associate each one with happiness or unhappiness?

- satisfaction
- self-sacrificing
- dependent
- self-esteem
- obsessive
- tolerant
- weakness
- negative emotions
- realistic
- optimistic
- improvement

c 🔊 *14.6* Listen to the analysis. Do you agree with it? How far does it correspond to your idea of a happy person in **1**?

6 **Use the analysis and your own ideas. Write a description of a happy person.**

Check your answers to the quiz. Give yourself one point for each answer that matches these letters.

1	b	**3**	a	**5**	c	**7**	a or b	**9**	c
2	b	**4**	c	**6**	b	**8**	d	**10**	b

How happy are you?

Most of us know when we're unhappy, and we've all had times of pleasure and joy. But the question 'How happy are you?' can be difficult to answer. This quiz is based on research into the characteristics of happy, well-adjusted people.

Choose the response to each question which is closest to your own feelings or situation. Don't try to choose the ones that seem happiest. They aren't necessarily what they appear to be.

If you could have any of the following jobs, which would you choose?
a A difficult and challenging job. If you can pull it off, you'll get promoted.
b A job that you can do well, because it suits your abilities.
c A fairly modest job that will give you the chance to work with a very powerful, important person.

Do you enjoy doing favours?
a Yes. I seldom refuse if I am asked.
b Yes, when it's convenient and will really help someone.
c Not really, but I will help if I think I owe it to the person, or there is some other good reason.

Which of these fits your normal sleeping pattern?
a I fall asleep easily and sleep soundly.
b I'm a light sleeper and I'm easily woken up.
c I'm a sound sleeper, but I don't find it very easy to fall asleep.

Are there times when you need to be alone?
a Definitely. My most peaceful and creative moments are when I am alone.
b No. I love having people around.
c I don't mind being alone, but I wouldn't say that I need it.

Do you think it is important to be neat and tidy?
a It's very important. I can't stand untidiness.
b It's important. I wish I were more tidy.
c It's fairly important. I'm generally tidy and I don't like a mess.
d It's not important. I'd rather be in a messy house where people are relaxed than in a tidy house where people are tense.

Which of the following would you least like as a friend? Someone who is:
a snobbish and pretentious.
b a bully, cruel to people who are weaker.
c crude, pushy, and ill-mannered.

In the past six months, how many times has illness kept you at home?
a None.
b Once.
c Twice or more.

How punctual are you?
a Very punctual. I have an exact time sense.
b Very unpunctual. I never arrive on time.
c It varies. I'm punctual for some things and late for others.
d Quite punctual. I usually arrive when I'm supposed to.

How long do you remain angry with someone who has been unfair to you?
a For a long time. I don't easily forgive.
b I don't get angry. Anger is a sign of a troubled mind.
c Not long. I get angry, but I seldom bear a grudge.
d I don't stay angry, but I will usually avoid the person from then on.

How do you feel about your life at the present moment?
a It's wonderful.
b It's all right. It may not be marvellous but it's improving steadily.
c Fair. I'm working hard for a better future.
d It depends. Sometimes I feel good about it and sometimes I don't.

1.1 The present simple tense
Form
Positive and negative

I We You They	live don't live (do not live)	in Manchester.
He She It	plays doesn't play (does not play)	tennis.

In the third person singular we add *-s* to the infinitive.
Exceptions: When the verb ends in *-ss, -sh, -ch, -z* or *-o*, we add *-es*.

kiss	kiss**es**
wish	wish**es**
watch	watch**es**
buzz	buzz**es**
do	do**es**

When the verb ends in consonant + *y*, we change the *-y* to *-ies*.

worry	worr**ies**
study	stud**ies**

Questions — **Short answers**

Do	you	live in London?	Yes, I do.
Does	he	play golf?	No, he doesn't.

Note: In negatives and questions we use the infinitive (*live*, *work*) of the verb. There is no *-s* in the third person singular.
*He doesn't **live** here.* NOT ~~He doesn't lives here.~~
*Does she **work** here?* NOT ~~Does she works here?~~

Use
We use the present simple tense to
- describe states.
  I live with my parents.
  Water boils at 100 degrees.
- describe regular events.
  I usually work late on Mondays.
  They go on holiday to Ireland every year.

1.2 The present continuous tense
Form
Positive and negative

I	'm (am) 'm not (am not)	reading.
He She It	's (is) isn't 's not (is not)	watching TV.
We You They	're (are) aren't 're not (are not)	working at home.

Questions — **Short answers**

Am	I	meeting Mike at 12.00?	Yes, you are.
Is	she	coming to the meeting?	No, she isn't.
Are	they	driving or coming by train?	

- **Spelling**
  To make *-ing* forms we add *-ing* to the infinitive.

eat	eat**ing**
fly	fly**ing**

  For verbs that end in *-e*, we remove the *-e* and add *-ing*.

drive	driv**ing**
come	com**ing**

  When the verb ends consonant–vowel–consonant and the stress is on the final syllable, we double the final consonant and add *-ing*.

run	run**ning**
admit	admit**ting**

Use
We use the present continuous tense to
- say what is happening at the moment.
  We're having dinner just now.
  'Where's Sue?' 'She's watching TV.'
- describe a temporary state.
  I can't find a flat, so I'm living with my parents.
  I'm doing French evening classes this year.
- describe a future arrangement.
  I'm playing tennis tomorrow evening.
  They're arriving next Monday at 10.00.

Sometimes the use of the present simple or the present continuous depends on whether we see a situation as permanent or temporary.
I live in a flat in George Road. (I see the situation as permanent.)
I'm living with my parents until I find a place of my own. (I think the situation is temporary.)

Where do you work? (I think you have a permanent job.)
Where are you working? (I think you are doing something temporary.)

1.3 Stative verbs
Some verbs are not normally used in the continuous form even when they refer to the present moment. They refer to *states* and not to actions. The most important ones are
- *like, love, prefer, hate, want, wish, need*
  *I **need** a new pen.* NOT ~~I'm needing a new pen.~~
- *think, imagine, believe, know, realize, mean, understand, remember, forget, suppose, hope, see*
  *I **don't understand**.* NOT ~~I'm not understanding.~~
- *be, seem, appear, sound, taste, smell*
  *This **tastes** delicious.* NOT ~~This is tasting delicious.~~
- *belong, contain, include, matter, owe, own*
  *Who **does** the car **belong** to?* NOT ~~Who is the car belonging to?~~

Some of these verbs can be used in the continuous form when they describe actions and not states. Compare these sentences.
*This ice cream **tastes** disgusting.* (state)
*He's **tasting** the soup to see if it needs more salt.* (action)

*I **think** it's important.* (state)
*'What are you doing?' 'I'm **thinking**.'* (action)

Present simple and present continuous
Look at these sentences. In each pair one is right and one is wrong.

1 I'm going to the cinema tomorrow evening. ✓
   I'm going to the cinema every day. ✗
2 She's working here until Christmas. ✓
   She works here until Christmas. ✗
3 He seems very tired. ✓
   He's seeming very tired. ✗
4 **A** Where's Graham? **B** He's cleaning the car. ✓
   A Where's Graham? **B** He cleans the car. ✗
5 Vegetarians don't eat meat. ✓
   Vegetarians aren't eating meat. ✗
6 I want to go out for dinner. ✓
   I'm wanting to go out for dinner. ✗

Look at sections 1.1, 1.2, and 1.3 again and check the rules for the use of the present simple and the present continuous.

1.4 The present perfect tense

Form
We make the present perfect tense with *have/has* and the past participle.

Positive and negative

I We	've (have)	
You They	haven't (have not)	lived abroad.
He She It	's (has)	cooked dinner.
	hasn't (has not)	

Questions   Short answers

Have	you	been to Paris before?	Yes, I have.
Has	she	broken her leg?	No, she hasn't.

To make regular past participles, we add *-ed* to the infinitive.
play   *play**ed***
open   *open**ed***
This is the same as the regular past tense. (See section 2.1 for spelling and pronunciation rules.)

A lot of common verbs have an irregular past participle.
go   *gone*
write   *written*
see   *seen*

➤ See the list of irregular verbs on the inside back cover.

Use
The present perfect links the past with the present.

We use the present perfect tense
● when we are interested in the present result of a past action.
   She's gone home. (She isn't here now.)
   I've bought a new car. (I've got a new car now.)

● when an activity or situation started in the past and still continues in the present.
   He's worked in the same office for twenty years. (He still works there now.)
   I've lived here for three years. (I still live here now.)

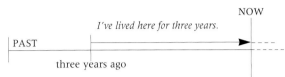

● when we are referring to a time frame that comes up to the present.
   Have you ever been to Brazil? (In your life until now.)
   I've been to Brazil three times. (Until now I've been there three times.)
   Have you seen John today? (We are still in the time frame of 'today'.)

Present perfect, present simple, and present continuous

Look at these sentences. Some are right and some are wrong.

1 How long have you lived in this house? ✓
   How long do you live in this house? ✗
   How long are you living in this house? ✗
2 I've worked here since October. ✓
   I'm working here since October. ✗
   I work here since October. ✗
3 How many times have you been to New York? ✓
   How many times do you go to New York? ✗

Look at sections 1.1, 1.2, and 1.4 again and check the rules for the use of the present simple, present continuous, and present perfect.

(See section 2.1 for the difference between the present perfect tense and the past simple tense.)

1.5 Adverbs of frequency

never   hardly ever   sometimes   often   normally   always
                                           frequently usually

We put the adverb of frequency
● after the verb *to be*.
   *The train **is always** on time.*
   *He's **never** here at 9.00.*
● in front of the main verb.
   *We **often go** to the park.*
   *I don't **usually get up** late.*

Sometimes, normally, and *usually* can also go at the beginning or end of the sentence, but they **usually go** before the main verb.

1.6 Comparatives and superlatives
Form

	adjective	comparative	superlative
one syllable	tall cold	taller colder	the tallest the coldest
one syllable: short vowel + one consonant	hot thin big	hotter thinner bigger	the hottest the thinnest the biggest
two syllables: consonant + *y*	heavy pretty	heavier prettier	the heaviest the prettiest

two or more
syllables
	modern
	
	interesting
		more modern
		
		more interesting
			the most
			  modern
			the most
			  interesting

irregular	good bad far	better worse further	the best the worst the furthest

A comparative adjective is often followed by *than*.
*Russia is **bigger than** Canada.*
*The film was much **better than** I expected.*

as … as … can be used to make comparisons.
*Her house is **as big as** mine.*
*Silver isn't **as expensive as** gold.*

In the negative *so … as …* is also possible.
*Silver isn't **so expensive as** gold.*

Comparatives and superlatives

Look at these sentences. In each pair one is right and one is wrong.

1 The elephant is the heaviest land animal in the world. ✓
   The elephant is the most heavy land animal in the world. ✗
2 He's as tall as his brother. ✓
   He's so tall as his brother. ✗
3 The film was better than the book. ✓
   The film was better that the book. ✗
4 My exam results were worse than Andy's. ✓
   My exam results were more bad than Andy's. ✗

Check the rules for the form of comparatives and superlatives again.

Use
The comparative is used to compare two separate items or groups.

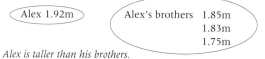

Alex is taller than his brothers.

The superlative is used to compare one member of a group with the rest of the group.

all the mountains in the world
Mount Everest

Mount Everest is the highest mountain in the world.

2.1 The past simple tense
Form
The verb *to be*
Positive and negative

I He She It	was wasn't (was not)	at home last week.
We You They	were weren't (were not)	here yesterday.

Questions

Was	he	at home	last week?
Were	they	here	yesterday?

Short answers

Yes, he was.
No, they weren't.

Regular verbs

● **Spelling**
To make the past simple tense we add *-ed* to the infinitive. The past simple is the same for all persons.

verb	past simple
watch	*We watch**ed** a film last night.*
happen	*It happen**ed** in Rome.*

When the verbs ends in *-e*, we add *-d*.
use	*us**ed***
decide	*decid**ed***

When the verb ends consonant–vowel–consonant, and the stress is on the final syllable, we double the final consonant and add *-ed*.
stop	*sto**pped***
prefer	*prefe**rred***

But we do not double *-y* or *-w* as final letters.
delay	*dela**yed***
show	*sho**wed***

When the verb ends in consonant + *y*, we change the *-y* to *-ied*.
hurry	*hurr**ied***
study	*stud**ied***

● **Pronunciation**
After /p/, /k/, /tʃ/, /ʃ/, and /s/ we pronounce the final *-d* as /t/.
When the verb ends in *-t* or *-d* we pronounce the final syllable /ɪd/.
Otherwise we pronounce the final *-d* as /d/.

/d/	/t/	/ɪd/
pulled lived seemed	watched liked missed	wanted ended decided

Irregular verbs
Many common verbs have an irregular past form. The irregular form is the same for all persons.

verb	past simple
see	*I **saw** her yesterday.*
buy	*They **bought** a new car last week.*

➤ See the list of irregular verbs on the inside back cover.

Negative

He	didn't	go to the theatre.
	(did not)	

Questions

Did	you	see the film last night?
Did	she	visit her parents?

Short answers

Yes, I did.
No, she didn't.

Negatives, questions, and short answers are the same for all persons and for all verbs except the verb *to be*.

Note: In negatives and questions we use the infinitive of the verb.
*Did you **go** out?*   NOT *Did you went out?*
*Did they **buy** a car?*   NOT *Did they bought a car?*

Use
We use the past simple tense to describe
● a completed action in the past.

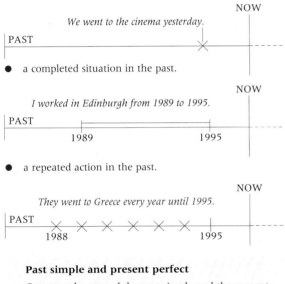

We went to the cinema yesterday.

● a completed situation in the past.

I worked in Edinburgh from 1989 to 1995.

● a repeated action in the past.

They went to Greece every year until 1995.

Past simple and present perfect

Compare the uses of the past simple and the present perfect. We use the past simple
● when we are interested in the action or the time of the action, not the effect.
She's gone home. (She isn't here now.)
*She **went** at four o'clock.* (We're interested in when the action took place.)
● when we are talking about a finished time in the past.
I've lived here for five years. (I still live here.)
*Before that I **lived** in Madrid.* (But I don't live there now.)

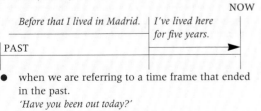

Before that I lived in Madrid. | *I've lived here for five years.*

● when we are referring to a time frame that ended in the past.
'Have you been out today?'
*'Yes, I **went** out this morning.'*

Note: When there is a past time reference (e.g. *in 1993, two days ago, last week*), you must use the past simple tense, not the present perfect.
*I **went** there four years ago.* ✓
I've been there four years ago. ✗
*I **saw** Hamlet last Tuesday.* ✓
I've seen Hamlet last Tuesday. ✗

Look at sections 1.4 and 2.1 again and check the rules for the use of the present perfect and the past simple.

2.2 The past continuous tense
Form
Positive and negative

I He She It	was / wasn't (was not)	going to work.
You We They	were / weren't (were not)	standing at the bus stop.

Questions

Was	he	having a bath?
Were	they	driving to Scotland?

Short answers

Yes, he was.
No, they weren't.

Use
The past continuous tense describes a continuous or unfinished activity in the past.

We use the past continuous tense to
● describe an action that started before a particular moment, and probably continued after it.
At 8.00 I was having breakfast.
This time last week I was lying on a beach in Greece.

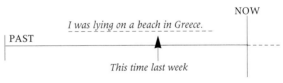

I was lying on a beach in Greece.

This time last week

● describe a temporary situation in the past.
I was living in Bristol last year.

Past continuous and past simple

We often use the past continuous tense with the past simple tense. The past continuous describes the situation – it is background information. The past simple describes the main event. The clauses are usually joined by *while, as,* or *when*.
***While** I was waiting for a bus, it started to rain.*
***As** I was going to bed, the doorbell rang.*

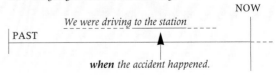

We were driving to the station

***when** the accident happened.*

Compare these two sentences.
While I was waiting for a bus, it started to rain.
When it started to rain, I decided to take a taxi.

The first sentence uses the past continuous tense to describe the background situation and the past simple tense to say what happened.
The second sentence has two past simple tenses. One action happened after the other.

2.3 The past perfect tense

Form

We make the past perfect tense with *had/hadn't* and the past participle.

Positive and negative

I He She It We You They	'd (had)	been there for 2 hours.
	hadn't (had not)	finished the project.

Questions   **Short answers**

Had	you	seen him before?	Yes, I had.
Had	he	eaten breakfast?	No, he hadn't.

Use

We use the past perfect tense to look back on an event that occurred before another event in the past.
We had dinner. We weren't hungry.
We weren't hungry because we'd had dinner.

```
                                        NOW
           dinner      not hungry        |
PAST          1            2             |
           --X----------X--------------------
      We weren't hungry because we'd had dinner.
```

The past perfect is often used with *when, after, before, as soon as.*
I was sure I'd seen him before.
After we'd finished dinner, we went for a walk.

The past perfect is necessary when we need to make it clear that one thing happened before another. Compare these sentences.
Sheila got up, got dressed, had some breakfast, and went out.
When Sheila got to the party, Amanda had gone home.

In the first sentence we do not use the past perfect, because the order of events is clear. In the second sentence we need to use the past perfect to make it clear that Amanda went home *before* Sheila got to the party.

Past perfect and past simple

Look at these sentences. In each pair one is right and one is wrong.

1 I was sure I had never heard the song before. ✓
   I was sure I never heard the song before. ✗
2 I met him yesterday and I told him the news. ✓
   I had met him yesterday and I told him the news. ✗

3 How long had you worked for the company when it closed? ✓
   How long did you work for the company when it closed? ✗

Look at sections 2.1 and 2.3 again and check the rules for the use of the past simple and the past perfect.

2.4 *used to*

Form

Positive and negative

I He She It We You They	used to	smoke.
	didn't use to	live in London.

Questions   **Short answers**

Did	you	use to	smoke?	Yes, I did.
Did	she	use to	play squash?	No, she didn't.

Use

We use *used to* to
* describe a state in the past which is not true now.
  *She **used to be** a teacher.*

```
                                              NOW
She used to be a teacher  | but now she works in
                          | publishing.
  PAST                    |----------------------->  - - -
                          |
```

* describe a habit in the past which is not true now.
  *He **used to smoke**, but he gave up five years ago.*

Note: The past simple tense can also be used to describe states and habits in the past. For individual past actions, or past actions which were not habits, only the past simple can be used.
*We **went** to the cinema twice last week.*
*Last year he **went** on five foreign holidays.*

Used to can only be used to talk about the past. It has no present form. To describe present states and habits we use the present simple tense.

3.1 Talking about the future

There are several ways of talking about the future in English. It can be difficult for learners of English to choose between them, and in some cases more than one form is possible. The form used does not depend on how certain a future event is, but on how the speaker sees the future.

3.2 The future with *will*

Form

Positive and negative

I He She It	'll (will)	see you tomorrow.
We You They	won't (will not)	get the job.

Questions			Short answers
Will	you	be at the meeting?	Yes, I will.
Will	he	lend you his car?	No, he won't.

Use

We use the future with *will* to

- make predictions or general statements about the future.
  We'll need some more money soon.
  In the year 2050 the world's population will reach 10 billion.
- describe a decision made at the moment of speaking, often to make an offer.
  'Have you got that report?' 'Yes, I'll fax you a copy.'
  'I can't hear the TV very well.' 'I'll turn it up.'

3.3 *going to*

Form

Positive and negative

I	'm (am)		do the shopping.
	'm not (am not)		
He She It	's (is)	going to	have a shower.
	isn't 's not (is not)		
We You They	're (are)		clean the windows.
	aren't 're not (are not)		

Questions			Short answers
Are you	going to	play football?	Yes, I am.
Is he	going to	buy the wine?	No, he isn't.

Use

We use *going to* to

- describe plans, intentions, and things we have decided to do.
  I'm going to look for a new job.
  I'm going to sell my car.
- describe things we can see or feel will definitely happen in the future.
  She's going to have a baby.
  3–0 up with five minutes to play, Manchester City are going to win.

3.4 The present continuous with future meaning

Form

See section 1.2 for the form of the present continuous tense.

Use

We can use the present continuous to describe personal arrangements in the future. There is normally a future time expression.
She's going to the doctor's next week.
We're meeting at four o'clock this afternoon.

It is often possible to use either the present continuous or *going to* to talk about the future. Sometimes there is a difference between an arrangement and something we have decided to do.
I'm seeing my grandmother on Saturday.
(I've arranged it. She knows I'm coming.)
I'm going to see my grandmother on Saturday.
(I've decided to go, but possibly it isn't arranged yet.)

> **Will, going to, and the present continuous**
>
> Look at these sentences. Some are right and some are wrong.
>
> 1 A I've got a terrible headache.
>   B I'll get you some aspirin. ✓
>   B I'm going to get you some aspirin. ✗
>   B I'm getting you some aspirin. ✗
> 2 A What are you doing this evening?
>   B I'm going to go to a party. ✓
>   B I'm going to a party. ✓
>   B I'll go to a party. ✗
> 3 The weather forecast says it'll rain tomorrow. ✓
>   The weather forecast says it's going to rain tomorrow. ✓
>   The weather forecast says it's raining tomorrow. ✗
> 4 You'll feel better after a good night's sleep. ✓
>   You're feeling better after a good night's sleep. ✗
> 5 He's lost control! He's going to crash! ✓
>   He's lost control! He'll crash! ✗
>
> Look at sections 3.2, 3.3, and 3.4 again and check the rules for the use of *will, going to,* and the present continuous.

3.5 Expressing probability

Here are some ways of making statements about possible or probable future events.
- The modal verbs *may, might,* and *could*
  Might can be less definite than *may.*
  *The train **may** be late.* (It is probable.)
  *We **might not** survive the 21st century.* (It is possible.)

Could can only be used to describe future possibility in the positive form.
*The train **could** be late.*   NOT ~~We could not survive the 21st century.~~

Note: *Can* is not used to describe possible or future events.
It may/might/could rain tomorrow.   NOT ~~It can rain tomorrow.~~

- The adverbs *possibly* and *probably* + future verb form
  *We **will possibly see** some rain in the morning.*
  *It **probably won't be** very warm tomorrow.*
  *I'm **probably going to** play tennis this afternoon.*
  *She's **probably coming** this weekend.*

Note: *Possibly* and *probably* are placed after *will* but before *won't.*

● Adjectival clauses

I'm	likely	to come to the party.
You're		
It's	unlikely	to rain this afternoon.
It is	likely	that the Prime Minister will resign.
	unlikely	that there will be wars about water.

Expressing probability

Look at these sentences.

It'll probably rain today.   most likely
It's likely to rain today.

It may (not) rain today.
It might (not) rain today.
It could rain today.

It's unlikely to rain today.
It probably won't rain today.   least likely

3.6 would

Form

Positive and negative

I	'd	like to live alone.
He	(would)	
She		
It		
We	wouldn't	steal from a friend.
You	(would not)	
They		

Questions			**Short answers**
Would	you	buy a car?	Yes, I would.
Would	she	like to come?	No, she wouldn't.

Use

Would has many uses. Two of the most common uses are to
● describe improbable, impossible, or imaginary situations.
   If I had the money, I'd buy a house. (But I haven't got the money.)
   She'd be a good politician. (But she works in a bank.)
● make polite offers.
   Would *you like a cup of coffee?*
   Would *you like to go to the cinema?*

4.1 Relative clauses

A relative clause gives more information about a noun in a sentence.
I saw the man.
I saw the man **who lives next door**.

A relative clause starts with a relative pronoun. We use
● *who* with people.
   He's the man **who** *lives next door.*
● *which* with things.
   Where's the disk **which** *was on my desk?*
● *that* with people and things.
   He's the man **that** *lives next door.*
   Where's the disk **that** *was on my desk?*

4.2 Reduced relative clauses

In a relative clause we can sometimes leave out the relative pronoun *who*, *which*, or *that*.

We can only do this if the relative pronoun is the object of the clause. Look at these sentences.
He's the man. She married him.
                              object
He's the man (who/that) she married.

In this sentence the man is the object of the relative clause, so we can leave out the relative pronoun.

He's the man. He lives next door.
                    subject
He's the man who/that lives next door.

In this sentence the man is the subject of the relative clause, so we can't leave out the relative pronoun.

4.3 Question tags

Form

When the statement is positive the tag is negative.

| You're | Italian, | **aren't you?** |
| He's | from Bristol, | **isn't he?** |

When the statement is negative the tag is positive.

| They aren't | coming to the party, | **are they?** |
| She isn't | here yet, | **is she?** |

With the verb *to be* we make the tag with the verb and the subject.
It **isn't** *very warm,* **is it?**

When there is a modal verb or an auxiliary verb we make the tag from the modal or auxiliary and the subject.

You can	swim,	**can't you?**
She won't	be here tomorrow,	**will she?**
It doesn't	matter,	**does it?**
You've	finished,	**haven't you?**
It was	raining,	**wasn't it?**

When the verb in the sentence hasn't got an auxiliary, we make the tag from the auxiliary that we would normally use for making questions in that tense.
She arrived yesterday, **didn't** *she?   You like fish,* **don't** *you?*

Note: Negative tag questions are contracted.
You knew about this yesterday, **didn't** *you?*   NOT … ~~did not you?~~
She can speak Russian, **can't** *she?*   NOT … ~~can not she?~~

When the subject of the statement is a noun, we replace it with a pronoun in the tag.
This chair's French, isn't **it?**
Bob and Betty live near here, don't **they?**

The question tag for a sentence with *Let's* is *shall we?*
Let's get a pizza, **shall we?**

The question tag for a sentence with *I am* is *aren't I?*
I'm going to Helsinki next week, **aren't I?**

When we write a question tag it is separated from the statement by a comma (,) and is followed by a question mark (?).

Use

A question tag turns a statement into a question. It is less direct than an ordinary question.

We can use falling intonation or rising intonation on a question tag. We use falling intonation when we think the statement is true and we expect the other person to agree. We use rising intonation when we are less certain and we want to check something.

5.1 The passive

Form

We make the passive with the verb *to be* and a past participle.

These computers	are	made	in Japan.
This wine	is	produced	in Portugal.

We can use the passive in any tense. To make different tenses we change the verb *to be*.

Past	The car	was	stolen.
Present perfect	Someone	has been	arrested.
Present	Thousands of cars	are	stolen.
will	The crime	will be	solved.
would	Fewer crimes	would be	committed.

To make the negative of the passive, we use the negative of the verb *to be*.

*The man **wasn't** sent to prison.*
*The weapon **hasn't been** found.*

To make questions we use the normal question form of the verb *to be* in each tense.

***Was** the man sent to prison?*
***Has** the weapon **been** found?*

We can use the passive with a modal verb. We use a modal verb + *be* + past participle.

*Cars **shouldn't be parked** there.*
*It **can't be done**.*
*She **must be told**.*

Use

We use the passive when

● the action is more important than the agent (who or what did the action).
● we don't know the agent.
    The car has been found.
    The suspect was identified.
    These houses were built in the 1930s.

    If we want to show the agent, we use *by*.
    *The car has been found **by some children**.*
    *The suspect was identified **by a witness**.*

6.1 First conditional

Form

We use the present simple tense in the *if* clause and the future with *will* in the main clause. We usually use a comma (,) when the *if* clause is first, but not when the main clause is first.

If	she	eats	all that ice cream,	she	'll feel	terrible.
If	I	have	time,		'll phone	you later.

You	'll be	hungry	if	you	don't have	some dinner.
They	won't arrive	on time	if	they	miss	the bus.

Note: We do not use *will* in the *if* clause.
If it rains, we'll go to the cinema.
NOT ~~If it will rain, we'll go to the cinema.~~

Use

First conditionals predict the results of a real or probable action or event.

If you get up late, you'll miss the appointment.
(There is a real chance that you'll get up late.)
We won't go if it rains.
(There is a real chance that it will rain.)

6.2 Second conditional

Form

We use the past simple form in the *if* clause and *would* + infinitive without *to* in the main clause. We usually use a comma (,) when the *if* clause is first, but not when the main clause is first.

If	I	had	enough money,	I	'd buy	that house.
If	you	didn't eat	so much,	you	'd lose	weight.

He	'd feel		better	if	he	didn't smoke	so much.
They	wouldn't play	tennis		if	it	was	raining.

Note: We do not use *would* in the *if* clause.
If I had enough money …
NOT ~~If I would have enough money …~~

Use

Second conditionals describe unreal, unlikely, or imaginary situations.

If we had more money, we'd travel business class.
What would you do if you saw a ghost?

> **First and second conditionals**
>
> First and second conditionals both refer to the present or the future. The difference between them is how probable the action or situation is.
>
> *If I get the job I'll earn more money.* (I think there is a real chance that I'll get the job.)
> *If I got the job I'd earn more money.* (I don't think I'll get the job.)
>
> Look at sections 6.1 and 6.2 again and check the rules for the use of first and second conditionals.

6.3 Time clauses

As in clauses with *if*, we do not use *will* or *would* in time clauses with the conjunctions *when, as soon as, until, before,* and *after*.

*I'll phone you **when she arrives**.*
NOT ~~… when she will arrive.~~
*I won't know the situation **until Phil gets back**.*
NOT ~~… until Phil will get back.~~
*We'd have dinner **before we went** to the cinema.*
NOT ~~… before we would go to the cinema.~~

6.4 Phrasal verbs

Phrasal verbs consist of a verb + a particle, e.g. *up, on, in, away*.

Literal/idiomatic phrasal verbs

Some phrasal verbs have *literal* meanings – you can work out what they mean from the meaning of the verb and the meaning of the particle.
*He heard a helicopter and **looked up**.*

Some phrasal verbs have *idiomatic* meanings – the meaning is not obviously connected to the meanings of the two parts.
*She **takes after** her mother.*

Many phrasal verbs have a literal and an idiomatic meaning.
*He saw the mouse and **ran out**.*
*Oil will **run out** in the next century.*

Transitive/intransitive phrasal verbs

Like other verbs, phrasal verbs can be transitive (they have an object) or intransitive (they do not have an object).
*He took off **his jacket**.* (transitive)
The plane took off. (intransitive)

Separable/inseparable phrasal verbs

Some transitive phrasal verbs are separable – the object can go between the verb and the particle.

verb particle object   verb object particle
*She **switched on** the TV.*   or   *She **switched** the TV **on**.*

When the object is a pronoun we must separate the two parts.
*She **switched** it **on**.*   NOT ~~She switched on it.~~

Other transitive phrasal verbs are inseparable – the verb and the particle cannot be separated.

verb particle   object
*Could you **look after** the children this evening?*
NOT ~~Could you look the children after this evening?~~

You can tell if a phrasal verb is separable or inseparable by looking in a dictionary. If the object is shown between the verb and the particle, the verb is separable.
look** something **up
*I **looked up** the word in a dictionary.*
or *I **looked** the word **up** in a dictionary.*

If the object is shown after the verb and the particle, the verb is inseparable.
***come across** something*
*I **came across** some old photographs the other day.*
NOT ~~I came some old photographs across the other day.~~

7.1 The present perfect continuous tense

Form

Positive and negative

I We	've (have)		playing football.
You They	haven't (have not)	been	having a rest.
He She It	's (has)		
	hasn't (has not)		waiting for an hour.

Questions   Short answers

Has	he	been	reading?	Yes, he has.
Have	you	been	waiting long?	No, I haven't.

Use

We use the present perfect continuous tense to
- describe an activity that is still incomplete.
  I've been writing a letter. (I haven't finished it yet.)
  How long have you been reading that book? (You haven't finished it yet.)
- focus on the process of an activity.
  'What have you been doing?' 'I've been running.'
- emphasize the duration of an activity.
  You're late. I've been waiting for an hour.

Present perfect simple and present perfect continuous

The present perfect continuous and the present perfect simple can both be used to describe situations which started in the past and are still going on, or about past actions which have present results. The important difference is that the present perfect continuous focuses on the action itself, but the present perfect simple focuses on the completion or result of the action.
I've been playing a lot of football this week. (focus on activity)
I've played two matches. (focus on completion)

We always use the present perfect simple when we say *how much* or *how many*.
*How many letters **have you written** this week?*
*How much rice **have you cooked**?*

With the verbs *live* and *work* we can normally use either the present perfect simple or the present perfect continuous.
Have you lived here long?
Have you been living here long?

Sometimes the present perfect simple can describe a more permanent state and the present perfect continuous can describe a temporary activity.
I've lived here for ten years. (permanent)
I've been living with my sister for the last few months. (temporary)

The present perfect continuous, like other continuous forms, is not normally used with stative verbs (see section 1.3).

8.1 Question forms

If the sentence contains the verb *to be*, a modal verb, or an auxiliary verb, we invert this verb and the subject to make a question.

We're going to be late.
Are we going to be late?

She can swim.
Can she swim?

They've arrived.
Have they arrived?

In the present simple and the past simple tenses there is no auxiliary verb, so we must provide one, using *do/does* in the present or *did* in the past.

They live here.   ***Do** they live here?*
You saw her.   ***Did** you see her?*

In *Wh-* questions, if the question word is the subject of the sentence we use the positive form of the verb to make a question. Compare these questions.

object   subject   object
*Who did you tell? (I told **my parents**.)*

subject   object   subject
*Who **told you**? (**My wife** told me.)*

object   subject   object
*Who did they invite? (They invited **all their friends**.)*

subject   object   subject
*Who **invited them**? (**Barbara** invited them.)*

Prepositions go at the end of questions.

*Who did you talk **to**?*
*What were you looking **at**?*
*Who are you going **with**?*

8.2 Indirect questions

An indirect question is a question that is in a statement or another question.

*Where does he live? I can't remember **where he lives**.*
NOT *~~I can't remember where does he live?~~*
*What's the time? Do you know **what the time is**?*
NOT *~~Do you know what's the time?~~*

Indirect questions use the statement form of the verb. We do not use a question mark (?) in statements.

We use indirect questions after verbs like *know, remember, decide, imagine, see, ask, know, have no idea, wonder*.

	question word(s)	subject	verb
I don't know	where	he	lives.
I can't remember	what	his name	is.
I'll ask	what time	the bus	arrives.
I have no idea	why	she	left.
I wonder	how much money	they	've got.

With *Wh-* questions we use the question word in the indirect question. In *Yes/No* questions we use *whether* or *if*.

Should I buy the computer?   *I can't decide **whether/if** I should buy the computer.*
Has the parcel arrived?   *I'll see **if/whether** the parcel has arrived.*

Indirect questions are often used to make polite requests with expressions like *Could you (possibly) tell me … ?* or *Do you think you could tell me … ?*

*Could you tell me **where the post office is**, please?*
*Do you think you could tell me **how much this costs**?*

Indirect questions

Look at these sentences. In each pair one is right and one is wrong.

1   I've decided how much money I need. ✓
    I've decided how much money do I need. ✗
2   I don't know if he's coming. ✓
    I don't know is he coming? ✗

3   Could you tell me where the post office is? ✓
    Could you tell me where is the post office? ✗
4   I wonder why he did that. ✓
    I wonder why did he do that? ✗

Check the rules for indirect questions again.

8.3 Compound nouns

Form

Compound nouns are very common in English. We make a compound noun by putting two or more separate nouns together to make a new noun.

football boots
a telephone box
a car seat
a computer software shop

In a compound noun there is a headword and one or more words that define the headword. The headword always goes at the end.

football boots
These are boots. What kind of boots? Boots for playing football.

a computer software shop
This is a shop. What kind of shop? A shop that sells software. What kind of software? Software for computers.

A defining noun in a compound noun is normally singular.
*A shop that sells records is a **record** shop.*
*A shop that sells books is a **bookshop**.*

Note: However, we say *clothes shop* and *sports shop*.

A compound noun sometimes has a different meaning from a noun phrase with *of*. Compare these sentences.
*How many **bottles of wine** do we need for the party? (How much wine?)*
*They threw the **wine bottles** away. (Empty bottles.)*

*He bought three **packets of cigarettes**. (New packets.)*
*The floor was covered with **cigarette packets**. (Empty packets.)*

Some compound nouns are written as one word. Others are written as two words, or are hyphenated. Unfortunately there are no rules.
a teacup, a bathroom
a coffee cup, a tennis racket
a living-room, stomach ache

● **Pronunciation**
In compound nouns the stress is usually on the first noun.

   ●   ●   ●
football boots   a coffee cup   a wine bottle

There are exceptions, so it is a good idea to check in a dictionary.

9.1 *-ing* forms

Form

See section 1.2 for the spelling rules for *-ing* forms.

Use

-ing forms are used
● in continuous tenses.
    *He was **driving** at 120mph.*
    *She's **playing** tennis.*
    *I've been **working** since 7.00.*

- as gerunds (a verb used as a noun). Gerunds can be subjects or objects.

subject
|
Swimming *is my favourite sport.*

object
|
I don't enjoy **cooking**.

- with *there is/are* to describe what is or was happening.
  There's someone **coming**.
  There were two people **waiting** *for you.*
- to describe what someone can sense (with *see, hear, feel, watch, smell, notice,* etc.).
  I can hear someone **coming**.
  We saw them **leaving** *the house.*
  I could smell **burning**.
- as adjectives.
  This is a really **boring** *film.*
  I read a **fascinating** *book the other week.*
- with *after, before,* and *while* to replace a clause, when the subject of both clauses is the same.

┌─── subject ───┐
After *I'd had a shower, I got dressed.*

After *having a shower, I got dressed.*

┌─── subject ───┐
I had the idea **while** *I was driving home.*

I had the idea **while** *driving home.*

9.2 -*ing* form or infinitive

a   Some verbs can take an *-ing* form or an infinitive and the meaning is more or less the same.
- *like, love, hate, prefer*
  I **prefer watching** *horror films to action films.*
  I **prefer to watch** *horror films to action films.*

In British English, *like + -ing* is usually used to talk about enjoyment, whereas in American English *like +* infinitive is usually used.
I **like lying** *in bed late.* (British)
I **like to lie** *in bed late.* (American)

Note: *would + like/love/hate/prefer* always takes the infinitive.
I'd **like to live** *abroad.*
I'd **prefer to go** *to the cinema.*

- *begin, start, continue*
  It's just **started raining**.
  It's just **started to rain**.

Note: We normally use infinitives after continuous tenses and with verbs which are not used in the continuous form (see section 1.3 for a list of these verbs).
I'm beginning **to learn** *the piano.*
I began **to realize** *how he felt.*

b   Some verbs can take an *-ing* form or an infinitive but the meaning is different.
- *remember, forget*
  I **remembered meeting** *her.* (I had met her before and I remembered it.)
  I'll never **forget dancing** *with him that night.* (I danced with him and I won't forget it.)
  I **remembered to meet** *her.* (I had to meet her and I did.)
  I **forgot to dance** *with him at the party.* (I was supposed to dance with him, but I didn't.)

- *try*
  I **tried to speak** *to her about it, but she wasn't there.*
  (I wanted to speak to her, but I couldn't.)
  I **tried speaking** *to her about it, but she still wouldn't listen.*
  (I spoke to her, but it didn't work.)
- *stop*
  He has **stopped smoking**. (He used to smoke but he doesn't now.)
  He **stopped to have** *a cigarette.* (He was doing something, then he stopped in order to smoke.)

c   Some verbs can only be followed by an *-ing* form. Some of the most common are *finish, enjoy, consider, give up, imagine, feel like, suggest,* and *can't stand.*
I **enjoy doing** *the gardening.*
NOT *I enjoy to do the gardening.*
She's **considering emigrating** *to Australia.*
NOT *She's considering to emigrate to Australia.*

-*ing* forms

Look at these sentences. In each pair one is right and one is wrong.

1   Smoking is bad for your health. ✓
    To smoke is bad for your health. ✗
2   There's someone coming up the stairs. ✓
    There's someone that comes up the stairs. ✗
3   Before leaving the office, I made a phone call. ✓
    Before to leave the office, I made a phone call. ✗
4   I'd love to go to New Zealand. ✓
    I'd love going to New Zealand. ✗
5   I began to understand the problem. ✓
    I began understanding the problem. ✗
6   I must remember to post this letter. ✓
    I must remember posting this letter. ✗
7   Stop making so much noise! ✓
    Stop to make so much noise! ✗

Look at sections 9.1 and 9.2 again and check the rules for the use of *-ing* forms.

9.3 Agreeing and disagreeing

To agree with a positive statement we use
So + auxiliary verb + subject.
A   *I really love pizza.*
B   *So do I.*

To agree with a negative statement we use
Nor/Neither + auxiliary verb + subject.
A   *I've never been to Ireland.*
B   *Nor/Neither have I.*

To disagree with a positive statement we use
(*Oh,*) *I* + negative auxiliary verb.
A   *I'd like to live abroad.*
B   *Oh, I wouldn't.*

To disagree with a negative statement we use
(*Oh,*) *I* + positive auxiliary verb.
A   *I couldn't read until I was seven.*
B   *Oh, I could.*

Note: In informal speech we can use *Me, too* to agree with a positive statement, and *Me, neither* to agree with a negative statement.
A   *I'd love to go to New Zealand.*
B   *Me, too.*
A   *I can't stand people talking in the cinema.*
B   *Me, neither.*

10.1 Modal verbs

These are the modal verbs in English: *can, could, may, might, must, need, ought to, shall, should, will, would.*

Form

Modal verbs have these features.
- They are the same for all persons.
- They are followed by an infinitive without *to* (except *ought to*).

I	can	swim.	
You	might	go	to London.
She	should	see	a doctor.
They	ought to	be	more careful.

- They have no infinitive or participle form.
  ~~to must~~ ~~to should~~ ~~to can~~
- To make questions the modal verb and subject are inverted.
  What **should we** do?
  Can you speak Japanese?
  Shall we go out for dinner?
- We make negatives with *not.*
  You **shouldn't** do that.
  They might **not** come to the party.
  I **couldn't** believe what he told me.
- Modal verbs have no tense forms.

Note: *Need* can behave as a modal verb or as a normal verb.
Need I go? or *Do I need to go?*
You needn't come or *You don't need to come.*

Modal verbs – form

Look at these sentences. In each pair one is right and one is wrong.

1   I must remember to post this letter. ✔
     I must to remember to post this letter. ✗
2   Can you swim? ✔
     Do you can swim? ✗
3   You shouldn't leave your car there. ✔
     You don't should leave your car there. ✗
4   He might come later. ✔
     He mights come later. ✗

Check the rules for the form of modal verbs again.

Use

Each modal verb can have different meanings. For example, we can use *could* to talk about *ability, possibility,* and *permission.*
I couldn't read until I was eight years old. (ability)
If the traffic's bad I could be late. (possibility)
Could I borrow your pen? (permission)

Ability

Can and *could* are used to describe ability.
Present: *He can speak four languages.*
Past: *He could speak French when he was four.*

Can and *could* become *be able to* in other tenses.
Past: *I could play the piano when I was six.* (or *I was able to play the piano when I was six.*)
Present perfect: *I haven't been able to find a new job.*
will: *I'll be able to find a new job.*
would: *I'd be able to find a new job.* (or *I could find a new job.*)

Could, was/were able to, and managed to

Could and *was/were able to* can both be used to describe general ability in the past, though *could* is more common.
I could drive when I was sixteen. ✔
I was able to drive when I was sixteen. ✔

To describe the ability to do something successfully on one occasion in the past, we use *was/were able to* or *managed to.*
The firemen managed to save everyone. ✔
The firemen were able to save everyone. ✔
The firemen could save everyone. ✗

Obligation

Must and *need* are used to describe obligation and necessity. *Have to* is also used.
Passengers **must** *show their boarding cards.*
You **need** *to be at the station by 8.30.*
I **have to** *work on Saturday this week.*

Must and have to

Have to is not a modal verb, but it is also used to describe strong obligation. *Must* is used to describe obligation that comes 'from the speaker'. *Have to* is used to describe general obligation, which comes from 'outside' the speaker.
I must start taking more exercise. (I want to, it is 'my' obligation.)
My doctor says I have to start taking more exercise. (It is an 'outside' obligation, from my doctor.)

You must drive more slowly if you want to pass your test. (The obligation comes 'from the speaker', a driving instructor.)
In Britain you have to drive on the left. (It is a general obligation.)

We use *mustn't* to describe *strong obligation not to do something.*
You **mustn't** *park on double yellow lines.*
You **mustn't** *do that – it's very dangerous.*

If there is no obligation or necessity to do something, we use *don't/doesn't have to* or *needn't/don't need to.*
You **don't have to** *come if you don't want to.*
The party's informal. You **needn't** *wear a suit./You* **don't need to** *wear a suit.*

Note: *Must* has no tense forms. We use *have to* to describe obligation in other tenses.
Past: *I had to find a new job.*
Present perfect: *I've had to find a new job.*
will: *I'll have to find a new job.*
would: *I'd have to find a new job.*

Advice

Should and *ought to* are used to give advice, or to say what we think is the best thing to do.
If you feel ill you **should** *go to the doctor.*
You **shouldn't** *work so hard.*
You drive much too fast – you **ought to** *be more careful.*
You **ought not to** *carry so much cash.*

Probability

May, might, and *could* are used to describe probability and possibility. See section 3.5.

Permission

Can, *could*, and *may* are used are used to ask for permission. *Could* is more polite than *can*, and *may* is the most polite and formal.

Can *I open the window?*
Could *I borrow the car this evening?*
May *I use your phone?*

Shall/will/would

In modern English *shall* is usually only used in suggestions and offers, with *we* and *I*.

Where **shall we** *go for our holidays this year?*
Shall we *go to the cinema?*
Shall I *open the window?*

For the use of *will*, see section 3.2.
For the use of *would*, see section 3.6.

Modal verbs – use

Look at these sentences. Some are right and some are wrong.

1 The bus driver managed to avoid hitting the dog. ✓
  The bus driver was able to avoid hitting the dog. ✓
  The bus driver could avoid hitting the dog. ✗
2 Yesterday I had to get the bus to work. ✓
  Yesterday I must get the bus to work. ✗
3 I'll be able to go swimming every day next week. ✓
  I will can go swimming every day next week. ✗
4 She might not be here tomorrow. ✓
  She could not be here tomorrow. ✗
5 Don't worry about the report – you needn't do it today. ✓
  Don't worry about the report – you don't have to do it today. ✓
  Don't worry about the report – you mustn't do it today. ✗

Check the rules for the use of modal verbs again.

11.1 causative *have* (*have something done*)

We use *have* + object + past participle to describe a job that is done for us by someone else. Compare these sentences.
I had my room painted.
This means that the room was painted but I didn't do it myself. I arranged for a decorator to do it for me.
I painted my room.
This means that I painted the room myself.

We often use *have* + object + past participle to describe services that we pay someone else to do.
I had the car fixed.
He had his jacket dry-cleaned.
I had my hair cut.

11.2 *make/let someone do something* *get someone to do something*

Make someone do something means that one person forces or compels another person to do something that they probably don't want to do.
The judge **made the man apologize**.
My parents **made me practise the piano** *for two hours every day.*

Let someone do something means that one person allows another person to do something.
David's father **lets him use** *the car.*
My boss **let me leave** *work an hour early yesterday.*

Get someone to do something means that one person asks or persuades another person to do something.
I'll **get my secretary to type** *the letter.*
I **got the garage to service** *my car.*

Make and *let* are followed by the infinitive without *to*.
Get is followed by the infinitive with *to*.

11.3 *need + -ing*

We can also use *need + -ing*.
The car's really dirty. **It needs cleaning**.

We can also use *need* with *to be* + past participle.
The car's really dirty. **It needs to be cleaned**.

Need + -ing is more informal.

12.1 Reported speech

When we report what somebody says we make the following changes.

● The pronouns and possessive adjectives change, because a different person is now speaking.
  Direct speech: *I like cooking.*
  Reported speech: *Sally says that she likes cooking.*
● When we report something with a past tense verb (e.g. *said* or *told*), some of the tenses of the verbs also change.

Direct speech	→	Reported speech
present perfect	→	past perfect
past simple	→	past perfect/past simple
present simple	→	past simple
present continuous	→	past continuous
will	→	would

Note: The past perfect tense, *would*, and modal verbs do not change.

Direct speech	Reported speech
Walter: *I've read that book.*	*Walter said (that) he'd read that book.*
Zoe: *We saw a great film last week.*	*Zoe said (that) they had seen a great film the week before.*
Tom: *I don't want to stay here.*	*Tom said (that) he didn't want to stay there.*
Andrea: *I'm going out.*	*Andrea said (that) she was going out.*
Luke: *I'll be away till March.*	*Luke said (that) he'd be away till March.*
Zoran: *I had never been there before.*	*Zoran said (that) he had never been there before.*
Helen: *I'd like a coffee.*	*Helen said (that) she'd like a coffee.*
Monica: *I might phone you later.*	*Monica said (that) she might phone us later.*

Note: In everyday speech the rules are not always followed, particularly when the direct speech is still true at the time of reporting.
Zoe said that they saw a great film.
Tom said that he doesn't want to go.

12.2 *say* and *tell*

We *say* something. We *tell* somebody something.
*Andrea **said** (that) she was going out.*   NOT ~~Andrea said me …~~
*Andrea **told me** (that) she was going out.*   NOT ~~Andrea told (that) …~~

Tell is almost always followed by a personal object, but there are some expressions where it is not necessary to use one.
*You have to tell (me) **the truth**!*
*He's always telling (her) **lies**.*
*They told (us) **a story**.*
*She told (them) **jokes** all night.*

12.3 Reported speech: Questions

Reported questions are a form of indirect question (see section 8.2). When we report questions, we make the following changes.
- The tenses and pronouns change as for statements.
- The word order changes to a statement word order, and verbs have a statement form.
- There is no question mark at the end of a reported question.
  'Where does John work?'
  *A man asked me **where John worked**.*

  'How many times have you seen this film?'
  *She asked me **how many times I'd seen the film**.*
- With Yes/No questions, the reported question starts with *whether* or *if*.
  'Have you seen them today?'
  *He asked me **whether/if I had seen them today**.*

12.4 Reported speech: Commands and requests

We normally use *tell* for commands and *ask* for requests, but other verbs can also be used, such as *advise, warn, persuade, beg, order*, and *command*. To report a command or a request we use the following structure: *told/asked* + person + (*not*) *to* + verb.
'Don't worry.'
He told me not to worry.

'Please sit down.'
The doctor asked me to sit down.

Reported speech

Look at these sentences. Some are right and some are wrong.
1   Mary said that she didn't enjoy the film. ✓
    Mary said that she doesn't enjoy the film. ✗
2   They told me that the exam was very hard. ✓
    They said me that the exam was very hard. ✗
3   She asked me where I lived. ✓
    She asked me where did I live? ✗
4   The instructor told me not to do that. ✓
    The instructor told me don't do that. ✗
    The instructor told me that I don't do that. ✗

Look at sections 12.1, 12.2, 12.3, and 12.4 again and check the rules for reported speech.

13.1 Third conditional
Form
We use the past perfect (continuous) form in the *if* clause and *would have* + past participle in the main clause. We usually use a comma (,) when the *if* clause is first, but not when the main clause is first.

| If | I | had told | the truth, | she | wouldn't have | left. |
| If | you | hadn't studied | so hard, | you | would have | failed. |

| I | would have | passed | if | I | 'd worked | harder. |
| They | wouldn't have | come | if | they | hadn't wanted | to see you. |

Use
We use third conditionals to describe something that didn't happen, an imaginary situation in the past.
If I'd worked harder I would have passed the exam.
(I didn't work hard, and I didn't pass the exam.)

You wouldn't have crashed if you hadn't been driving so fast.
(You were driving too fast, and you crashed.)

Conditionals

Look at these sentences. In each pair one is right and one is wrong.
1   If it doesn't rain this evening we'll play tennis. ✓
    If it won't rain this evening we'll play tennis. ✗
2   I'd lend you some money if I had any. ✓
    I'd lend you some money if I would have any. ✗
3   If I knew the answer I'd tell you. ✓
    If I knew the answer I'll tell you. ✗
4   I'd have got lost if I hadn't had a map. ✓
    I'd have got lost if I wouldn't have had a map. ✗

Look at sections 6.1, 6.2, and 13.1 again and check the rules for conditionals.

13.2 *should/shouldn't have*
Form
Positive and negative

I He She It We You They	should have	gone.
	shouldn't have (should not)	said anything.
		stayed in bed.

We can also use this structure in the continuous form.
should/shouldn't + *have been* + present participle
*You **shouldn't have been driving** so fast.*
*She **should have been wearing** a seatbelt.*

Use
We use *should/shouldn't* + *have* + past participle to express regret and criticism.
*I **shouldn't have left** at ten o'clock.*
(I regret leaving at ten o'clock.)
*They **should have bought** the house.*
(They didn't buy the house – I think it was a bad decision.)

Tapescripts

Unit 1

📷 0.1

Marie Hi, everyone. Welcome to *Thrillseekers*. I'm Marie Gregg and this is Jack Roberts. We're going to be your guides on our expedition from London to South Africa.

Jack Hi! As you heard, my name's Jack and, as you can probably tell from my accent, I'm from South Africa. And this is Bessie, our trusty vehicle. She's going to take us all the way down through Europe and Africa to Cape Town. Now we're going to be together on the road for the next five weeks, so we need to get to know each other. Can I ask you all to introduce yourselves briefly to the group? Now, who would like to start? Yes?

Lulu Hello, everybody. My name's Lulu McNulty and I'm from Sydney, Australia. I'm a fashion designer. My father was born in South Africa. I've always wanted to go there, because he's told me so much about the place. So I'm really looking forward to the trip.

Jack Thanks, Lulu. And now the person next to Lulu.

Paola Hi. I'm Paola, Paola Rossi. I'm an accountant. I work for a big chemical company. Oh, and I'm from Argentina – from Buenos Aires. At the moment I'm working in London. I've been here for about a year now. I like travelling but I like a bit of adventure, too. So that's why I wanted to go on this trip.

Jack Thank you, Paola and … ?

Istvàn Hi. I'm Istvàn Tisza. I'm from Hungary and I'm a student.

Marie What are you studying, Istvàn?

Istvàn I'm studying psychology at the University of Budapest. I wanted to come on this trip because I'd like to do something unusual. And also I'll have a chance to practise my English.

Jack Thanks a lot, Istvàn, and …

📷 1.2

Sandra Hi, my name's Sandra.

Colin Colin. Pleased to meet you.

Sandra Where do you work, Colin? Around here?

Colin No, I work for an insurance company in London.

Sandra Oh, yes? What do you do?

Colin I'm a computer programmer.

Sandra Really? That sounds very technical. Do you enjoy it?

Colin Yes, it's all right. It isn't the most interesting job in the world, I suppose, but it's quite well paid, so …

Sandra Well, that's important.

Colin Yes, I suppose so. Anyway, what about you? What do you do?

Sandra Oh, I'm a student.

Colin Oh, really? Where?

Sandra At Manchester University.

Colin Manchester, eh? I've never been there. What's it like? It rains all the time, doesn't it?

Sandra Well, yes. It's a bit wet, but it's a great city. There's lots to do there. You know, theatres, cinemas, clubs.

Colin Oh, right. I've never thought of Manchester like that. What are you studying?

Sandra I'm doing an MA in Management.

Colin That sounds interesting. Are you enjoying it?

Sandra Yes, it's great, but it's hard work. We have a lot to read.

Colin Yes, I bet. Are you living on the university campus?

Sandra No. I'm sharing a flat in the city. I really like living in the city centre. Do you live in London, then?

Colin No, I live near Oxford. I find London a bit too crowded these days. I've lived in Oxford for about two years now, I suppose.

Sandra Do you actually live in Oxford itself?

Colin No, in a village about ten miles outside. I've got a cottage down by the river.

Sandra Mmm, that sounds lovely. So, do you commute every day?

Colin Yes, I go by train.

Sandra That must be a bit of a drag.

Colin Well, no, not really. It only takes about an hour and a half, and I read on the train, so it's not too bad.

Sandra What time do you usually get to work in the morning, then?

Colin Well, we've got a flexitime system, so we can choose our time. I always start at 8, so that I miss the rush.

Sandra Good idea. But so early in the morning! Do you finish early, too?

Colin Yes, around 4, if I can. What about you? Do you have lectures every day, then?

Sandra No, but I usually go into the university every day, because I like to work in the library. It's warmer than my flat and I don't have to pay for the electricity. It's hard being a poor student!

Colin I bet it is. What time do you have to start in the morning?

Sandra Well, it depends. I don't usually get in till about 10 o'clock, but then I often stay till 9 or 10 at night.

Colin That's a long day. How do you get there? Do you drive?

Sandra No, I cycle, or get the bus if it's raining. I prefer cycling, though. It keeps me fit.

Colin I'm sure it does. Look, would you like a drink?

Sandra Yes, please. Shall we … ?

📷 1.5

So how did you score?
Here's the scoring key. Complete the grid.

For statements 1 to 3 in each section score 5 for A (agree), 3 for a question mark (not sure), and 1 for D (disagree).

For statements 4 and 5 in each section score 1 for A (agree), 3 for a question mark (not sure), and 5 for D (disagree).

Add up your scores for each section. There is a maximum score of 25 and a minimum score of 5 for each section.

📷 1.6

This psychometric test is used to decide what kinds of jobs would suit people best.

Section A is about whether you're an introvert or an extrovert. Extroverts do well in service industries such as tourism, travel, sales, and shop work. Introverts, on the other hand, make good researchers and librarians. They also do well in farming.

Section B is about whether you're a calm, stable person or a nervous worrier. Stable people can take a lot of stress and stay calm in difficult situations. They do well in challenging jobs, such as a police officer or a pilot. Worriers often have problems, because almost any job creates stress. They like either very repetitive jobs in factories and offices, or very creative jobs in the theatre, the arts, or advertising.

Section C tests whether you are conservative or an experimenter. Experimenters do well in marketing, advertising, and the media, where they can constantly develop new ideas. Non-experimenters, however, prefer a stable and predictable life in, for example, the civil service

or local government. They make good lawyers, bank managers, and accountants.

Section D is about whether you're a competitive or a co-operative type. Co-operative people like to help other people. They make good doctors, nurses, teachers, and social workers. Competitive people enjoy the fast and risky world of the financial markets.

Unit 2

📷 2.3

Bill Well, well, well. I don't believe it. It's Kathy, isn't it? Kathy Wallis?

Kathy Bill Jordan. How lovely to see you. I haven't seen you since – oh, when was it? – Sam and Laura's wedding.

Bill Yes, that's right. That must be nearly fifteen years now. Good heavens! Doesn't time fly?

Kathy You've put on weight!

Bill Yes, well, you know how it is. Too much easy living. Anyway, what are you up to these days? Are you still working for that bank?

Kathy Bank?

Bill Didn't you use to work for a bank?

Kathy Oh, yes, the bank. Well, it was a building society actually. No. I left there ages ago. I wanted to see the world.

Bill And did you? See the world, I mean.

Kathy Well, some parts of it. I went to Italy first and then Egypt.

Bill Very nice. What were you doing there?

Kathy I was teaching English. But then I came back to England and I worked in a shop for a while and then did a few other jobs.

Bill So what are you doing now?

Kathy I'm a singer.

Bill Wow, that sounds exciting.

Kathy Well, I had all those jobs but I just got bored and well, I'd always wanted to be a singer so I finally decided I'm going to go for it. So I got a job on a cruise ship and I'm really enjoying it. I'm doing what I enjoy and I see the world, too.

Bill Good for you!

Kathy What about you? You used to talk about becoming a teacher, as I recall.

Bill Well, yes, I thought about it for a long time, but while I was still thinking, I got married and we bought a house and then the kids came along and I was promoted. So I'm still there at the glass factory. Still, that's the way it goes.

Kathy How many children have you got?

Bill Two – John's five and Clara's three, and there's another one on the way.

Kathy Oh, how lovely!

Bill Are you married?

Kathy No. … I was, but, well, things didn't work out and we split up.

Bill I'm sorry to hear that.

Kathy Oh, these things happen, but, well, it was very unpleasant at the time, the divorce, and it took me a long time to get over it, but I suppose it was just one of those things. You know.

Bill Yes, I see. So where are you living now? Are you still in Birmingham?

Kathy No, we sold that house. I've got a flat in London now – Docklands with a view over the river.

Bill Sounds great.

Kathy Yes, it's not bad. I've been there about two years now, though I don't spend a lot of time there, because I'm away with my job.

Bill Yes, I suppose you must be. Hey, do you remember old Harry Clarkson?

Kathy Yes, of course. I used to work with him.

Bill Oh yes, I remember. Well, I saw him a few months ago. It's amazing. He's …

2.6

Presenter On that fateful day in 1981 Jim hadn't gone to the coast. He had gone to the local golf course and dived into one of the lakes on the course.

Jim Yeah, well, I just wanted to see what was down there and it was really amazing. I had never expected it, but the bottom of the lake was completely white with golf balls – thousands and thousands of them. I had never seen so many golf balls in my life. I brought a few up and looked at them carefully. They looked fine to me – just like new ones. Well, I showed them to the manager of the golf course and he offered me ten cents a ball, so I dived back in.

Presenter That day Jim brought up more than 2,000 balls, making almost as much money as he would normally earn in a week. When he got home that day he was very excited.

Jim That evening I talked things over with my wife, Beverley. We discussed it for hours and we finally decided to go for it. So the next day I gave up my job and started to dive for golf balls full-time.

Presenter Every day Jim brought home a car full of balls. At first he used to put them in the washing machine to clean them, but Beverley objected. So he bought his own machine.

Jim Have you ever heard a washing machine full of golf balls? Well, believe me, it's pretty noisy and the neighbours soon objected to all the noise, but that wasn't a problem. I just offered them all a job and then they didn't mind the noise!

Presenter Word spread and soon other divers were bringing lorryloads of balls to his house. The business just grew and grew. Jim decided to set up a company called Second Chance and he bought a factory on an industrial estate.

Jim When I gave up my job, I thought I would need to find 2,500 balls a week to break even. Now between 80,000 and 100,000 balls arrive at the company every day. They come from golf courses all over the country, some from as far away as Hawaii.

Presenter When the balls are unloaded, they are counted and cleaned. The ones that are in a bad condition are taken out. They aren't thrown away, but are stored until, as Jim says, 'someone can think of a use for them'. The good balls are put into a special whitener. After they have been dried, they are sprayed with an acrylic, then packed into boxes and sent out to golf courses all over the world. They're sold for half the price of new balls. After selling Second Chance, Jim Reid now relaxes on his yacht. What's he going to do now?

Jim Well, I may take up golf. You know, I've never played it.

Unit 3

3.3

Good evening. Well, it's been another fine day over most of the country with temperatures up to 23 degrees in southern areas. But it isn't going to last, I'm afraid. By tomorrow evening most of us will see some rain.

Tomorrow morning will start off dry with a good deal of sunshine in most places. There will be a bit of fog in the south-east at first, but this will soon disappear. Along the north-east coast, however, it will be cloudier and light winds from the north-east will keep this coast cooler. In the north-west it will stay dull and cloudy with some heavy showers. Temperatures in these parts will be a cool 16 degrees.

As the day goes on, we're going to see a big change, as warm, humid weather pushes in from the south. This will bring rain to most of the southern half of the country by the evening. And there will be some thunderstorms, but only in the south-west, where temperatures will reach 26 or possibly 27 degrees. In the northern half of the country the weather will be brighter and fresher. It will stay dry, but it will be quite windy and that east wind will keep temperatures down to about 19 degrees.

That's it. Have a good day tomorrow.

3.4

1 A Do you fancy having a game of tennis tomorrow?
  B The forecast said it might rain.
  A Oh, well, shall we see how it is in the morning and then decide?
  B OK. I'll give you a ring about 9.30.
  A Right.

2 A Would you like to go out for a walk?
  B Yes, OK. I could do with a bit of fresh air. What's the weather like?
  A It's nice and sunny but you'd better put a jumper on. I think it might be a bit chilly.
  B OK. I'll just go and get one.
  A OK. I'll see you outside.

3 A Hey, look. It's snowing.
  B Great. Let's go sledging.
  A What, now?
  B Yes, it might be gone by this afternoon.
  A That's true. I'll get the sledges out.

4 A Shall we go to the park?
  B Mmm. That would be nice. What's it like out?
  A Well, it's a bit dull, but it may brighten up. You never know.
  B OK. I'll get my coat.

5 A Well. We'd better be going home, I suppose.
  B Oh, well. Thank you very much for coming. It's been lovely.
  A Yes. We've really enjoyed it.
  B Bye. Drive safely. It might be foggy on the motorway.
  A Don't worry. We'll be careful. Bye now.

6 A What about going for a bike ride?
  B Is it still raining?
  A No. It stopped about an hour ago.
  B Yes, but the roads might still be wet. Let's hang on for half an hour or so.
  A OK.

7 A How about going to the beach this weekend?
  B What's the forecast?
  A I don't know, but it's fine at the moment.
  B Yes, but it may change before the weekend.
  A Yes, I suppose so. Well, why don't we see how it looks on Friday?
  B OK.

3.7

DJ Hello. A lot of you have probably just got your A-levels and you're looking forward to going to university. But more and more young people are deciding to take a year out before they start their degrees. Today I'm talking to a group of young people who've all decided to spend a year at the university of life. What are they going to do? Rosie? What are your plans?

Rosie I'm going to work in a department store.

DJ Why do you want to do that?

Rosie Two reasons really. I'm going to study Management at university and this will give me the chance to find out what it's like to work in a big organization. And I'll also be able to earn some money.

DJ What about you, Christopher?

Christopher I'm going to do community work with a conservation group. I think it will be good to do something really useful. And I'll meet a lot of interesting people, I'm sure.

DJ Will you get paid for it?

Christopher Well, we won't get rich doing it, but we'll be all right. We'll get about £20 a week plus food and accommodation.

DJ Helen, what are you going to do?

Helen I'm going to travel around Europe.

DJ Are you going to work there?

Helen I hope so, or I'll have to come home again. I might try and get a job – you know – in a hotel or something like that.

DJ Why do you want to do it?

Helen Well, mainly because it will be a change. After all, I've been at school for 13 years. I just want to do something different. It will give me new experiences and I'll need to be more independent.

DJ Are you going to travel, too, Martin?

Martin Yes, I am. I'm going to join an expedition to Alaska.

DJ That sounds exciting.

Martin Yes, I'm really looking forward to it. It'll be a real challenge. But we aren't leaving till next January, so I'll have to get a job first to pay for it. It's going to cost about £3,000.

DJ Wow! What are you going to do to get the money?

Martin I don't know yet, but I'm sure I'll find something.

DJ Well, good luck to all of you and I hope you enjoy your year out.

Unit 4

4.2

1 **Man 1** Come on. Let's go.
  Man 2 But the match hasn't finished yet.
  Man 1 Well, they aren't going to win now, are they? – Two-nil down with five minutes to play.
  Man 2 No, I suppose not. It was a pretty awful match anyway, wasn't it?
  Man 1 You can say that again. I'm going. Come on.
  Man 2 No, just a minute. Yes. You beauty! What a goal!
  Man 1 What? They haven't scored, have they?
  Man 2 They have. Shackley's just put it in the net. We can't leave now, can we? Come on, lads. Let's get another one.

2 **Woman** The bride looks lovely, doesn't she?
  Man Yes, she does.
  Woman That's the bridegroom's mother over there, isn't it?
  Man The lady with the big, white hat? Yes. Sandra her name is.
  Woman But that isn't her husband with her, is it?
  Man No, it's her brother-in-law. You know, the one who lives in Australia.
  Woman Oh, yes. I've heard of him. He works in television, doesn't he?
  Man Yes. I don't know what he does exactly, but it's something important. Sandra never stops talking about him.
  Woman Oh, I see. And who's that woman over there …

3 **Ellen** Hello, James. How nice to see you.
  James Ellen. I didn't expect to see you here. You're working on a new film, aren't you?
  Ellen Yes, I was, but we finished this weekend.
  James Oh, I see. It's a lovely day, isn't it?

Ellen Well, Paula always picks the right day for a party, doesn't she?

James That's true. Do you know any of these people?

Ellen Not really. I'm a bit out of touch these days. What about you?

James Well, yes, I know most of them.

Ellen Can you see that chap over there in the pink jacket? Isn't that Brad Conran, the actor?

James Oh, yes, I see him. Well, it can't be Brad Conran, can it? He's making a film in Hollywood.

Ellen Well, I told you I was out of touch, didn't I?

James No that's Paula's new boyfriend. He …

4 **Man 1** Right, well, I think it's my round, isn't it?

Woman 1 Why don't we go somewhere different?

Man 1 Yes, all right. Where?

Man 2 Let's go to that new club, shall we? You know, the one in the square.

Man 1 That's a good idea. John said it was good, didn't he?

Woman 2 You don't mean the Top Hat Club, do you?

Man 2 Yes, that's right.

Woman 2 Well, it won't be open tonight, will it? John said it was closed on Mondays and Tuesdays.

Man 2 Oh yes, he did, didn't he?

Man 1 Right, well in that case we might as well get another round. Same again?

All Yes.

📼 **4.7**

1 **Researcher** Excuse me, we're doing some research on how people spend Christmas. Can I ask what you do?

Young male adult Well, eat, drink, and watch telly mostly. On Christmas Eve I usually go to a party with some friends. On Christmas Day I get up late and then we go down the pub, come home, watch the Queen on the telly – my Mum and Dad always like to see the Queen's Speech. Then we have dinner and well, watch telly – or go to sleep.

Researcher And what about Boxing Day?

Young male adult We always go and watch a football match.

Researcher Do you like Christmas?

Young male adult Yeah, it's great.

2 **Researcher** Excuse me, can I ask you how you celebrate Christmas?

Youngish woman Well, we don't really celebrate it, because we're not Christians. We're Hindus and it isn't a Hindu festival.

Researcher So is Christmas Day just a normal day for you, then?

Woman No, not really, because we don't go to work. And we still give the children presents. You see, when they go to school all their friends are talking about the presents that they got. And so we give the children presents, but we don't really celebrate it.

Researcher Do you put up decorations or have a Christmas tree?

Woman Yes, we do, actually, but some families don't. And we do enjoy all the films and things on the telly.

3 **Researcher** Excuse me, we're doing some research on how people spend Christmas. Can I ask how you celebrate it?

Woman Certainly. Christmas is a family thing for us. We usually have my parents-in-law and my brother.

Researcher And what sorts of things do you do?

Woman On Christmas Eve we go to church for the midnight carol service. Then on Christmas Day the children open their presents from Father Christmas. We have lunch at about 3 o'clock – turkey and Christmas pudding, of course. Then after that we open the family presents and then usually play games or watch a film on TV.

Researcher And what about Boxing Day?

Woman We normally go out for a walk, if the weather's fine. Or we sometimes go to see a pantomime.

Researcher Do you like Christmas?

Woman Yes, it's very nice for the children, but I think it's getting too materialistic nowadays what with all the presents and the decorations that people buy. I think we've forgotten what it's really for.

4 **Researcher** Excuse me, we're doing some research on how people spend Christmas. Can I ask how you celebrate it?

Man We don't.

Researcher Oh, why's that?

Man We always go on holiday over Christmas. We usually go somewhere where's there's sunshine – Egypt, India, places like that.

Researcher Do you like Christmas?

Man No, I can't stand it. I mean, I don't mind having a party on Christmas Day, but all the rest of it – eating and drinking too much, sending cards to people that you haven't seen for years. And the weather in Britain's awful at that time of year. No, you can keep it.

Unit 5

📼 **5.2**

Man Constable, Constable!

Police officer Yes, sir. What seems to be the problem?

Man I'd like to report a robbery. It's my car. It's been stolen!

Police officer I see. And where was the vehicle parked at the time?

Man Just round the corner here in Samwell Street. I left it there about an hour ago and now it's gone!

Police officer Samwell Street, you say? Are you sure?

Man Of course, I'm sure. What …

Police officer And you parked it there at about … ten o'clock?

Man Yes, that's right. I bet some young thug has stolen it. These young people, they have no respect for the law these days. I …

Police officer Yes, sir. Well you'd better just give me a few details so that we can see about tracing the vehicle. What kind of car is it?

Man It's a BMW 540i.

Police officer Colour?

Man It's red.

Police officer Red? And the registration number?

Man P67 HKL.

Police officer HKL. Right. Just a minute, sir. We've got a report here of a vehicle that has been removed from Samwell Street. It's a red BMW 540i, registration number P67 HKL. Yes, that's right.

Man Well…?

Police officer Just a moment, sir. They're checking whether anything has been reported about the vehicle.

Man Well, I hope it's not going to take too long. I'm a busy man. If I get my hands on the young hooligans that have taken it, I'll …

Police officer Excuse me, sir. You've got it? Fine, thank you …

Man Great! Has it already been found?

Police officer Not exactly, no …

Man It hasn't been damaged, has it? If it has, I'll …

Police officer No, sir, I don't suppose it's been damaged, because it was never stolen.

Man What do you mean?

Police officer It was towed away at 10.45 this morning.

Man Towed away? Towed away? But, but it was only parked there for an hour!

Police officer Yes, sir, but cars shouldn't be parked there at all. It's a very narrow street.

Man But, they can't just tow away my car!

Police officer It seems that a lorry couldn't get past your car and I'm afraid that any vehicle which is blocking the road can be towed away.

Man But there was nowhere else to park!

Police officer There's a car park a hundred yards or so down the road, sir.

Man Well, where has my car been taken to?

Police officer All vehicles that have been towed away are taken to the car pound in Hilton Road.

Man What? Hilton Road? But that's miles away.

Police officer Yes, sir.

Man This is ridiculous. I haven't got time to go to the other side of town now.

Police officer Well, sir, perhaps you'll be more careful about where you park in future. There's a bus stop over there. You'll need the number 26. Good day.

📼 **5.8**

Detective Did you shoot your brother-in-law, Mr Ewers?

Craig Ewers No, I didn't.

Detective Why were you holding the gun?

Craig Ewers I found it in the garden. I heard the shots and then I heard a noise in the bushes outside the sitting room. I thought there was someone in the bushes, so I went to have a look and I found the gun. So I picked it up. I know it was a silly thing to do, but I … well I just didn't think.

Detective Mrs Ewers. Where were you when you heard the shots?

Belinda Ewers I was in bed.

Detective Were you asleep?

Belinda Ewers No, no I wasn't. I was just … just … sitting on the bed.

Detective Did you like your brother?

Belinda Ewers No, he deserved to die.

Detective Why?

Belinda Ewers He killed our younger brother. There was an accident, you see. Harry was driving too fast. He was drunk. The car crashed and poor Tim was killed.

Detective What were your brother and Mr Clayton arguing about?

Belinda Ewers Harry wanted to get rid of Julian. He wanted the whole company for himself.

Detective Mrs Squires. You were in the library, but the light was not on.

Martina Squires Yes, I was sitting in the dark.

Detective So you weren't reading?

Martina Squires No, I was just thinking I …

Detective What about?

Martina Squires I … I had asked Harry for a divorce, but he had said no.

Detective You're lying, Mrs Squires. You weren't in the library at all. The door was locked. You were in the garden with Mr Ewers.

Martina Squires No … I … it's not true.

Detective You and Mr Ewers are lovers. Is that not true, Mrs Squires?

Martina Squires No … No.

Detective This is a big room, Mr Clayton. Where

exactly were you when the shots were fired?

Julian Clayton I was standing here.

Detective About the middle of the room, next to Mr Squires?

Julian Clayton Yes.

Detective Do you often come to the house, Mr Clayton?

Julian Clayton Yes.

Detective Were you here on June 6?

Julian Clayton June 6? Yes, I was here for dinner the day that the Ewers arrived.

5.9

Detective Everybody hated Harry Squires. You all had a motive, but did you have the opportunity? What about you, Mrs Squires? You weren't in the library, as you said. You were in the garden with your lover, Mr Ewers.

Belinda No. I don't believe it.

Detective Don't look so shocked, Mrs Ewers. You knew about it. That's why you weren't in bed. You were going out into the garden to catch them. You were on your way to the garden when the shots were fired.

Belinda So did those two murder Harry?

Detective Well, they had a motive – Martina needed a divorce – but no, they aren't the murderers.

Belinda Then who did kill him?

Detective It was you, Mr Clayton.

Julian Don't be ridiculous. I was wounded myself.

Detective No, Mr Clayton, you were shot *by yourself*. Three days ago you were here for dinner. You stole the gun. Harry wanted to get rid of you. So you decided to get rid of him first.

Martina But how did he do it?

Detective Well, Mrs Squires, it was quite simple, wasn't it, Mr Clayton? You held the gun with the handkerchief so that there would be no fingerprints. You shot Harry Squires. Then you shot yourself in the hand – a very good alibi. Then you threw the gun through the open window into the bushes.

Julian A very good story, but where's your evidence?

Detective It's simple, Mr Clayton. The forensic scientists have examined your hand and the bullet hole in Mr Squires' chest. You see, both shots were fired from less than one metre away.

Unit 6

6.1

Bill So we're agreed on where to go. Now how do we get there? There won't be any point in going to the travel agent until we know exactly what we want.

Marie OK, then. Well, we can fly, or we can go by coach.

Bill Hmm. If we go by coach, it will be a lot cheaper.

Marie Yes, but the plane's much quicker and it's more comfortable.

Bill What time's the flight?

Marie Just a minute. It's 7.30 in the morning or … No, that's the only one that day.

Bill 7.30! That means we'll have to check in by 5.30 if we want decent seats. And we'll need to leave the house two hours before we check in! If I get up that early, I'll be in a bad mood for the rest of the holiday.

Marie You'll be able to sleep when we're on the plane.

Bill What time's the coach?

Marie Eleven o'clock from the local bus station.

Bill Well, that settles it. If the flight was later, I'd pay extra to fly, but not if it means getting up at 3 o'clock.

Marie I can see that, but the coach journey takes nearly a day and a half. As soon as we got there, we'd have to think about coming back.

Bill Oh, you're exaggerating. Flying won't be much faster, if you include the time for checking in and getting to and from the airport.

Marie Well, I don't agree. If we had two weeks for the holiday, the coach would be all right. But we've only got one week, so I'd rather fly.

6.4

1 **Passenger** Is this the Manchester check-in?

Check-in clerk Yes, it is. Can I see your ticket, please?

Passenger Er, oh, yes, here you are.

Check-in clerk Thank you. Do you have luggage to check in?

Passenger No, just hand baggage. Could I have a seat in the smoking section, please?

Check-in clerk I'm sorry. This is a non-smoking flight. Would you prefer a window or an aisle seat?

Passenger Oh, er, aisle, please.

Check-in clerk Here's a label for your hand baggage.

Passenger Thank you.

Check-in clerk And here's your boarding pass. You're in seat number 23C. Boarding will be at 15.20 at gate number 39. Have a nice flight.

Passenger Thank you.

2 **Passenger** Is this right for Barcelona?

Check-in clerk Yes, it is.

Passenger Oh, good. Here's my ticket.

Check-in clerk Thank you. Could I see your passport, too, please?

Passenger Passport? Oh, yes. Here you are.

Check-in clerk Thank you. How many pieces of baggage are you checking in?

Passenger These two suitcases.

Check-in clerk I see. What about those two bags?

Passenger They're hand baggage.

Check-in clerk I'm sorry. You can only take one piece of hand baggage on board.

Passenger Oh, I see. Well I'll check in this one as well, then.

Check-in clerk Would you like smoking or non-smoking?

Passenger Non-smoking, please, and I'd prefer a window seat, if you've got one.

Check-in clerk Let me see. Yes. So here's your boarding pass. Boarding is at 11.10 at gate number 5. Have a nice flight.

Passenger Thank you.

3 **Passenger** Do we check in here for the flight to Rome?

Check-in clerk Yes. May I see your tickets and passports, please?

Passenger Yes, here you are.

Check-in clerk There are four of you travelling. Is that correct?

Passenger Yes, that's right; two adults and two children.

Check-in clerk And how many pieces of baggage are you checking in?

Passenger These four.

Check-in clerk Did you pack the suitcases yourself?

Passenger Yes, we did.

Check-in clerk And do they contain any electrical items?

Passenger Oh, er, a hairdryer, I think and er, I think that's all.

Check-in clerk Thank you. Would you like smoking or non-smoking?

Passenger Oh, non, please.

Check-in clerk Here are your boarding passes. I've put you in row 19 A and B and row 20 A and B.

Passenger Fine, thank you.

Check-in clerk Boarding will be at 18.35. The gate number will be announced.

Passenger Thank you very much.

Check-in clerk Thank you. Have a nice flight.

6.8

Mr Wilson What shall we do today, then?

Mrs Wilson There's a few things in this leaflet. Why don't we try one of these places? The Plymouth Dome looks interesting.

Mr Wilson Hmm. Yes.

Sasha I'd rather go to the beach. It's a nice day and we haven't been to the beach yet.

Robert Hey, but look at this Woodlands place. It's got a Commando Course and an Astroglide and a Triple Drop Slide. Great.

Sasha Oh wow. Don't you ever get fed up with things like that? We went to a theme park on Monday.

Mrs Wilson But it's got animals, too.

Sasha And we went to a zoo yesterday.

Mr Wilson That's true. What about this Morwellham Quay place with the copper mine? There's a lot to do there. There's an old farm and life aboard a ship. It's very educational.

Robert Thanks, Dad. We get enough education at school. We don't want it on holiday, too.

Mr Wilson Just because it's educational, it doesn't mean it's boring. And look, it's got this AA award for Leading Day Out.

Sasha But I want to go to the beach, and there's a nice one here.

Mrs Wilson But not all day. It gets boring being on a beach all day.

Sasha There are things to do there – look, there's sailing and windsurfing and a boating pond.

Mrs Wilson Well. I tell you what. Why don't we go to the copper mine place in the morning and then go to the beach in the afternoon?

Mr Wilson Possibly, but it's rather a long drive from Tavistock to Dartmouth.

Robert Yes, and according to this you need 5–6 hours for the Morwellham place.

Mrs Wilson Well, what about the Dome, then? I'd like to see that and that only takes two hours.

Sasha At least two hours, it says.

Mrs Wilson OK, but we could still do that in a morning and then go to the beach in the afternoon.

Sasha and Robert Oh, all right.

Mr Wilson Right. That's it then. Let's get ready.

Mrs Wilson OK. You kids get your swimming things and …

Unit 7

7.1

Last year they didn't go out, but this year they've been out a lot.

Last year Mark only read comics and magazines, but this year he's read lots of books.

Last year they didn't go to the theatre once, but this year they've seen a lot of plays.

Last year Emily didn't play any musical instruments, but this year she has been learning to play the piano.

Last year Mr Benson didn't play any sport, but this year he has taken up tennis.

Last year they watched a lot of TV, but this year they haven't watched much TV at all.

Last year they didn't have much free time, but this year they've all started new hobbies.

Tapescripts

📟 **7.3**

Presenter And here's our first caller. What would you like to say?

Middle-aged woman Well, I just can't believe it when people say that children aren't affected by TV violence. Of course they are. We all know that children love to act out things that they have seen in films and so on. Now that's all right if they're acting out a scene from *Cinderella*, but if they can act out things like that, they can act out violent things, too, can't they? It's obvious.

Presenter Thank you for that and now our next caller.

Middle-aged man I agree with what the last speaker said, but any TV has got a switch on it. If you don't want your children to watch something, switch it off. Programmes that contain sex, bad language, or violence can't be shown before 9 p.m., and after that the kids should be in bed. In my opinion it's the parents' responsibility to make sure that the kids haven't been watching unsuitable things. I should be able to watch what I want. It's not my problem.

Presenter What does our next speaker think about that?

Young mother I'm sorry, but I can't agree. I mean, he says it's not his problem, but it is his problem if he gets attacked by a teenager who's been watching violent movies. If we breed a violent society, we all suffer. I try to control what my children watch but it isn't easy. They can always go round to their friends' houses and watch videos.

Presenter Thank you. Now what does our next caller want to say?

Woman Well, personally, I don't like all the sex and bad language that there is on TV. I know that these things happen in life, of course, but that doesn't mean that I want them happening in my living room. I mean I'm sure that my husband swears when he's out with his mates, but I wouldn't stand for it at home in front of the children. So why should it be all right for two strangers on the telly to swear in front of them?

Presenter An interesting point. Now our next speaker.

Young man I simply don't agree with the results of the research. How can we prove that when somebody acts violently it's because they've been watching violent TV programmes? You know, millions of people watch violent films but they don't all become murderers, do they? We can't blame television for everything that's wrong with society. I maintain that it's just an excuse for censorship.

Presenter Thank you. Now another point of view.

Young man I'd like to support what the last caller said. I mean what is violence anyway? Look at any cartoon. The characters are blown up and hit by trains – all sorts of things. Should we stop children watching Tom and Jerry or Mickey Mouse? As I see it, children know what's fantasy and what's reality.

Presenter Now our next caller. What would you like to say?

Young woman Real life isn't always pleasant and I think television should show that. In real life people do swear and they aren't nice to each other all the time. I don't just want to see some cosy middle-class view of the world where everything's sweet and nice.

Presenter And now our last caller.

Older man I'm afraid I have to disagree with the last speaker. It's very easy to talk about real life, but whose real life do you mean? Four hundred murders in one week certainly isn't my real life. I would say that most people's real lives are quiet and rather boring. I wouldn't agree with the 'real life' argument. All this sex, violence, and bad language is quite unnecessary.

Presenter Well, we've certainly got a wide range of views there. Let's take a break for some music now. Then we'll put those views to our experts in the studio …

📟 **7.7**

Interviewer Alan, you've been involved in pop music for a long time now. How did you first get interested in it?

Alan Well, like a lot of teenagers in the fifties I wanted to be like Elvis Presley. The trouble was I couldn't sing or play a guitar, but I loved rock and roll, so I got a job with a record company and eventually became a record producer.

Interviewer Now when rock and roll first came out people said it wouldn't last, didn't they?

Alan Oh yes. And by 1961 it looked as if they were right. All the heroes had disappeared. Elvis was in the army, Buddy Holly had been killed in a plane crash, Chuck Berry was in jail, Little Richard had decided to become a preacher and nobody wanted to know Jerry Lee Lewis after they found out he had married his fourteen-year-old cousin.

Interviewer So how did rock and roll survive?

Alan The funny thing was it was rescued on this side of the Atlantic by British groups like the Beatles and the Rolling Stones. They brought rock and roll back from the dead and gave it new life. They opened up all sorts of new possibilities for it. Before the Beatles and the Stones only teenagers had really listened to rock and roll, but afterwards it became everybody's music.

Interviewer So do you think pop music hasn't changed much since then?

Alan Oh no, far from it, there have been some great bands and singers, like Abba, for example. They were great. Queen, Michael Jackson, Madonna … . They've all added something new to pop music. In fact, it's very difficult to talk about pop music now, because there are so many different types. There's mainstream pop, soul, heavy metal, and so on.

Interviewer What about the future?

Alan Well, there are new young bands coming along all the time, of course, but personally I don't think we'll ever see anything really new. I mean, take songs for example. I don't know, but the modern songs don't seem as fresh and exciting as they did in the sixties and seventies.

Interviewer What do you mean?

Alan I think it's interesting that so many of the old songs are re-released or re-recorded. My teenage kids are often surprised when I start singing one of the latest hits. They think it's a new song, but it was actually first recorded before they were even born. Perhaps all the good songs have already been written – or maybe I'm just getting old.

Interviewer If you had to choose just one song that sums up rock and roll for you what would it be?

Alan Oh, now there's a question. Well, there are thousands of songs that you could choose and I suppose everyone would have their own opinion, but for me there's one that's got everything – the rhythm, the good melody, the great guitar, and most of all, it's fun. It makes you feel happy. You just can't sit still when you hear it. And that for me is what rock and roll is all about.

Interviewer So what is it?

Alan It's *Johnny B Goode* written by Chuck Berry.

Interviewer OK. Let's hear it.

Unit 8

📟 **8.1**

OK. Here are the answers to the quiz.

1 Where is Mount Fujiyama? It's in Japan.
2 Who wrote *Sense and Sensibility*? The answer is Jane Austen, of course. That's spelt A-U-S-T-E-N.
3 Which country won the football World Cup in 1994? No, it wasn't Italy. It was Brazil.
4 What language did Jesus speak? He spoke a language called Aramaic. That's spelt A-R-A-M-A-I-C, Aramaic.
5 How many strings has a mandolin got? Eight.
6 Where does the film star, Arnold Schwarzenegger, come from? He comes from Austria.
7 How fast can a cheetah run? You can have this if you're 10 kilometres either side. The answer is 100 kilometres an hour. So anything between 90 and 110 will be OK.

📟 **8.2**

Team member 1 OK. So, number one. Do you know where Mount Fujiyama is?

Team member 2 Yes, it's in Japan, isn't it?

Team member 1 OK. Now what about *Sense and Sensibility*? I don't know who wrote it. What about you?

Team member 3 No. I've no idea.

Team member 4 Hang on. I'll remember in a minute.

Team member 1 Right, let's leave that one. What about the World Cup? Was it Brazil?

Team member 3 No. I think it was a European team, but I can't remember whether it was Italy. Or maybe Germany.

Team member 1 Well, what shall we say? Germany?

Team member 3 Yes, OK.

Team member 1 Now, what language did Jesus speak?

Team member 2 I've no idea what language he spoke.

Team member 4 Was it Hebrew?

Team member 1 I'm not sure. …

📟 **8.3**

1 Could you tell me where I can park my car, please?
2 I wonder if you could tell me what time you start serving breakfast, please?
3 We've just checked into room 245 and I'm afraid there are no towels in the bathroom.
4 Could you tell me whether you have a restaurant here, please?
5 Do you think you could send someone to collect some laundry, please?
6 We want to use the swimming pool. Could you tell me whether we need to take the towels from our room?
7 Could you possibly tell me whether there have been any calls for me, please?
8 Could I order something from the room service menu, please?
9 I'd like to make an international call. Could you tell me what I need to dial, please?

📟 **8.4**

1 A Could you tell me where I can park my car, please?
  B If you give me the keys, I'll get one of the porters to see to it for you.
  A Oh, thanks very much.
2 A I wonder if you could tell me what time you start serving breakfast, please?

B At seven in the dining room, but you can get it earlier in your room, if you wish.
A Thank you.
3 A We've just checked into room 245 and I'm afraid there are no towels in the bathroom.
B Oh, I'm very sorry about that. I'll get some sent up straight away.
A OK. Thank you.
4 A Could you possibly tell me whether you have a restaurant here, please?
B Yes, it's on the second floor. Turn left when you come out of the lift.
A Thank you.
5 A Do you think you could send someone to collect some laundry, please?
B Certainly, which room is it, please?
A Room 503. Thanks a lot.
6 A We want to use the swimming pool. Could you tell me whether we need to take the towels from our room?
B No, they're provided at the poolside.
A Oh good, thanks.
7 A Could you possibly tell me whether there have been any calls for me, please?
B Let me see. Ah yes, there's a fax and a phone message. Here they are.
A Oh, thank you.
8 A Could I order something from the room service menu, please?
B Certainly. What would you like?
A A club sandwich and a pot of coffee, please.
B Certainly.
9 A I'd like to make an international call. Could you tell me what I need to dial, please?
B You need to dial 9 for an outside line, then 00 and the code for the country you want.
A All right. Thanks.

8.5
1 A Could you tell me what time the film starts, please?
B At 3.15.
A Thank you.
2 A Excuse me, but I haven't got my glasses. I wonder whether you could tell me what that sign says, please?
B It says, 'The museum is open every day from 10 till 6'.
A Thank you very much.
3 A Do you think you could tell me whether the 10.20 flight from Madrid has arrived, please?
B No, I'm afraid it will be half an hour late.
A Oh dear. Thank you.
4 A Could you tell me how much these shorts are, please?
B They're £15.99.
A Thanks.
5 A Could you possibly tell me whether we need a visa for Singapore, please?
B No, you don't.
A Thank you.
6 A Could you tell me how far it is to the station from here, please?
B It's about ten minutes' walk.
A Thanks a lot.

8.9
Presenter So now it's time for our phone-in. Our guest today is Greg Mortimer. Just to remind you, Greg is a regular competitor in the *Ironman* triathlon race, which involves swimming four kilometres, cycling 180 kilometres, and running 42 kilometres. Our first caller is Christine Goodyear. What's your question, Christine?
Christine I'd like to know how long the race takes.
Greg Well that depends on how good you are. The top athletes take about nine hours, but for

the people at the back it might take 12 hours or longer. Of course, some people don't finish.
Presenter Thank you, and now Ben Clough.
Ben How do you train for the race?
Greg I train for about 10 or 12 hours every day, but I don't do the same thing each day. In a normal week I go to the swimming pool about four times and each time I swim six or seven kilometres. I do three or four 100-kilometre bike rides and two long runs – maybe 50 kilometres each. And I usually go to the gym to exercise with weights about twice a week.
Presenter I feel exhausted just listening to that. And now Jamie Watts. What's your question?
Jamie I'd like to ask Greg what kind of diet he eats.
Greg I eat most things, meat, fish, cheese, eggs, vegetables, but the most important thing for me is to eat a lot of carbohydrates – bread, pasta, potatoes, fruit, and things like that. I need about 9,000 calories a day. A normal person would probably eat about 2,000. During the race the most important thing is water. We have to drink every ten to fifteen minutes during the race. Dehydration could kill you very easily if you didn't.
Presenter And our last question for now comes from Betty Lamb.
Betty Like a lot of people I think, I'd like to know why you do it!
Greg Yes, that's the question that most people ask me! Well, it may sound strange but I actually enjoy it. But most of all it's a challenge. I suppose it's like climbing a mountain. It's hard work, but it's a wonderful feeling to stand on the top. So I do it because at the end of the race I can look back and say I did it.

Unit 9

9.2
1 A I saw an interesting programme on TV last night about ghosts.
B Oh, yes, so did I.
C Oh, I didn't. I missed it. Was it any good?
B Well, I didn't believe any of it, to be honest.
A Nor did I at first, but some of the stories were difficult to explain, weren't they, especially that one about the woman who fell out of the train.
B Well, yes, I suppose so, but I just don't believe in ghosts.
A Oh, I do, I think.
C Yeah, so do I. I'm sure there are lots of things that we don't really understand and there are just so many people who say that they've seen one.
B Well, people can say anything. It doesn't mean that it's true.
2 A Have you seen this article in this magazine about UFOs? It says that thousands of people have seen them and that they really exist.
B Hah, well, I've never seen one.
A No, neither have I. I'm sure it's a lot of rubbish.
C Oh, but I have.
B You're joking.
C No, it was about four years ago now. I was out in the garden and this big bright light appeared in the sky.
B Well, it was probably an aeroplane.
A Yes, that's what I reckon, too.
C No, it wasn't. It was too low down for that. Anyway, it just stayed there in the sky for about thirty seconds, I suppose, then it just disappeared.
A Yes, but you don't know that it was, you know, little green men invading the Earth.
C No, but you don't know that it wasn't either, do you?

3 A I had a really strange dream last night. I dreamt that we bought a house, but when we moved in there were two dogs living there, but we couldn't get rid of them, because they liked living there. And they liked watching all the kinds of TV programmes that I don't like. Funny, eh?
B Weird. I can never remember my dreams.
C No, nor can I.
A Oh, I can. I always remember mine and if I wake up in the middle of a dream I can go back to the same dream again.
B Really? That's amazing. So what do you think this dream about the dogs means, then?
A Oh, I've no idea.
C I don't think that dreams have any special meaning, anyway.
B Don't you? Oh, I do. But dogs and televisions! Who knows what that means.

9.3
1 A I like learning English.
B So do I.
C I don't.
2 A I can't swim very well.
B Nor can I.
C Oh, I can.
3 A I won't be at work tomorrow.
B Nor will I.
C I will.
4 A I've never been in hospital.
B Nor have I.
C Oh, I have.
5 A I went to the cinema last week.
B So did I.
C I didn't.
6 A I didn't like the story about the haunted house.
B Nor did I.
C Oh, I did.
7 A I'm going to watch TV tonight.
B So am I.
C Oh, I'm not.
8 A I've got a very interesting job.
B So have I.
C I haven't.
9 A I'm not married.
B Nor am I.
C I am.
10 A I'll be rich one day.
B So will I.
C I won't.

9.7
1 Compere So can you tell everyone your name and where you are from and your job?
Contestant 1 Hello, I'm Tom. I'm from Sydney, Australia and I'm a student.
Compere Thank you, Tom.
Contestant 2 Hi. I'm Sarah and I'm from London, England. I'm a teacher.
Compere Nice to see you, Sarah.
Contestant 3 And my name's John. I'm from New York in the United States and I'm a scientist.
Compere Thank you, John.
Contestant 4 And my name's Ann. I'm from Dublin in Ireland and I'm an artist.
Compere Thank you, everyone.
2 The number you require is 01724 364964. I repeat 01724 364964.
3 A Excuse me, can you tell me where the station is?
B Yes, go down here. Take the second turning on the left, go past the supermarket and the cinema and turn right. The station is in front of you.

A So that's second on the left, past the supermarket.
B Yes, and the cinema.
A Then turn right and the station's in front of me.
B That's it.
A Thank you.

📼 **9.8**

We all have problems remembering things, but there are some techniques that you can use to help you remember. Let's take the activities that you have just done.

First of all, remembering the names and jobs of the people and where they come from. Here, the best thing is to imagine images of the people and the names that you want to remember. And you should try to think of funny images as they are easier to remember. For example, we have Tom the student from Australia. Well, for Tom you might imagine a tomato. Then Australia has a shape a bit like a dog. Now let's imagine it's a very clever dog and is studying. So imagine Tom's face as a tomato and he's with a dog and the dog is reading a book. So now we have a picture of Tom the student from Australia.

Now let's take the numbers. The best thing to do here is to break the larger number up into smaller numbers and then think of things that the numbers remind you of, such as a birthday, a particular year, the number of a house. Or with a number like 747 you might think of a jumbo jet – a Boeing 747.

With the directions the best thing is to imagine yourself following the directions. Create a picture in your mind of yourself going down the street. Count the turnings 1, 2. Then turn left. Now imagine going past a supermarket and a cinema and so on.

When you have to remember lists of words try to build them into a story. So with our words we might start with, 'The sun was shining, so I went for a walk. I saw a horse wearing trousers. It was kicking some bananas over a television. The bananas landed in a bag'. And so on. Again the funnier the story the better.

Try some of these techniques and you'll be amazed at what you can remember.

Unit 10

📼 **10.3**

1 Patient Good morning, Doctor.
Doctor Good morning. What can I do for you?
Patient I've hurt my wrist.
Doctor How did it happen?
Patient I fell downstairs and I bent my wrist back.
Doctor When was that?
Patient Three days ago now, I think, but it hasn't got any better.
Doctor Well, let me just take a look at it. Hmm. Yes, it is rather swollen. Can you move it?
Patient A bit, but it's very painful.
Doctor Well, I think you've only sprained it, but it could be a fracture, so we'd better get it X-rayed. You'll have to go to the hospital for that. Take this letter with you, and you ought to go as soon as possible.
Patient Right. Thank you. Goodbye.
Doctor Goodbye now. And don't drive there, either!
Patient No, of course not, Doctor. Thanks. Bye.
2 Doctor Ah, Mr Scales. Do come in and sit down.
Mr Scales Thank you.
Doctor How are you? Are you still feeling very tired all the time?
Mr Scales Yes, I am.

Doctor Well, I've got your test results back now and they confirm what I thought. Your blood pressure and your cholesterol level are very high, and well, to put it bluntly, if you don't change your lifestyle, you're going to have a heart attack sooner or later.
Mr Scales Oh, I see. Oh, dear. What do I have to do?
Doctor Well, there are three things that you ought to do. First, stop smoking. Secondly, you really must lose weight. Your cholesterol level is very high so you must reduce the amount of fat that you eat. And lastly, you must take more exercise. You mustn't do too much exercise at first, but build up gradually.
Mr Scales I see. But what sort of exercise should I do?
Doctor Walking is best. You needn't exercise every day, but you should walk about three miles four or five times a week.
Mr Scales But I don't have time. I'm just so busy at work.
Doctor That's another thing. You mustn't work so hard. Look, take this information and read it through. Then make an appointment to see our lifestyle consultant. She will work out a full diet and exercise programme for you. And don't worry. That's the last thing you should do! I'll see you again next month.
Mr Scales OK. Thank you, Doctor. Goodbye for now.
Doctor Goodbye.
3 Receptionist Julia Carson to see Doctor Bates.
Patient Hello, Doctor.
Doctor Good afternoon. Do take a seat. Now what seems to be the problem?
Patient My ear hurts. My left ear.
Doctor I see. Could you just turn your head to the side a bit? That's it.
Doctor Hmm. Yes. When did you first notice it?
Patient A couple of days ago. It started Tuesday evening and it's been getting steadily worse.
Doctor Could I just take a look at the other ear? Thank you. ... Well, you've got a bit of an infection in your left ear. I'll give you a prescription for some medicine. Now, you aren't allergic to penicillin, are you?
Patient No.
Doctor Fine. I'm prescribing some drops and some tablets. Put the drops into your left ear every six hours and take one tablet twice a day.
Patient Drops every six hours and tablets twice a day?
Doctor Yes, that's right. It should clear up in about three days, but don't stop taking the medicine. Make another appointment for a week's time.
Patient I will. Thank you, Doctor. Goodbye.
Doctor Goodbye.
4 Patient Good morning, Doctor.
Doctor Good morning. How can I help?
Patient Well, I don't feel very well. I've got a headache and I've got this rash all over my neck and chest.
Doctor Could you just slip your shirt off a minute? How long have you been feeling unwell?
Patient Since yesterday afternoon.
Doctor Just pop this thermometer under your arm for me, will you? Do you feel feverish?
Patient Yes, I do.
Doctor Hmm. Yes. You've got a bit of a temperature. You can put your shirt back on now. Have you got a sore throat?

Patient No.
Doctor Well, I think it's just a virus. There's nothing you can do, really. But you must stay in bed and keep warm for a few days. Take some painkillers for the headache, if necessary.
Patient When should I go back to work?
Doctor Well, you should feel better in two or three days, but it would be best to stay off work till next week. Come back and see me if you don't feel any better after three days.
Patient All right. Thank you. Goodbye.
Doctor Goodbye.

📼 **10.6**

Newsreader Good evening. Here is the news for Wednesday 25 October. Child B – the girl who was refused treatment for leukaemia by her local health authority – has been named as eleven-year-old Jaymee Bowen. The court today lifted the ban on using her name.
The case first hit the headlines in March, when the local health authority refused to pay the £75,000 that was needed for her treatment. They believed that it would be a waste of money, because she had very little chance of surviving. Jaymee eventually received the treatment after an anonymous donor provided the money.
Today smiling and happy, Jaymee faced the cameras for the first time. She was asked what she would say, if she was sitting next to the chief executive of the health authority, who had made the decision about her treatment.
Jaymee I wouldn't say anything to him. I'd just go over there and whack him one. Then I'd say 'Thank you for nothing, because now look at me. I'm fine. You could have paid for it. You had the chance and you blew it.'
Newsreader Jaymee is not yet completely cured. When she started her treatment, doctors put her chances of survival at 10 per cent. Now they're 20 to 30 per cent. But Jaymee had this message for everyone.
Jaymee I say never give up hope unless you are on the last little drop of life you have in you. Never give up, because if you give up, you will just end up with nothing left.

Unit 11

📼 **11.2**

1 Customer Hello. I wonder if you can help me? I bought these trousers here the other day, but they're faulty.
Sales assistant Oh, what's the problem?
Customer Well, I've only worn them once and the zip's broken.
Sales assistant I see. Do you have the receipt?
Customer Yes, here you are.
Sales assistant Thank you. Do you wish to take another pair or would you like a refund?
Customer I'd prefer a refund, if that's all right.
Sales assistant Yes. Would you mind coming over to the cash till, and I'll see to it for you.
2 Customer Excuse me, I'm afraid this soup is too salty.
Waiter Oh, I'm sorry about that. I'll take it away.
Customer Thank you.
Waiter Would you care to choose something else, madam?
Customer Could you just get me the menu again, please?
Waiter Certainly. Here you are.
Customer Yes, I'll have the smoked salmon, please.
Waiter Thank you, madam.

3 Receptionist Hello, Lancaster Hotel. How may I help?

Mr Curtis Oh, hello. My name's Curtis. I'm sorry to trouble you, but we stayed at your hotel last week and I think I may have left something in the room.

Receptionist Can you remember the room number?

Mr Curtis I think it was number 14, but I can't be certain.

Receptionist And what was it that you think you left there?

Mr Curtis A pair of black leather gloves.

Receptionist Just a minute. I'll check whether anything's been found.

Mr Curtis Thank you.

Receptionist Hello, Mr Curtis. Yes, the chambermaid did find a pair of gloves in room 14.

Mr Curtis Oh, good.

Receptionist Would you like us to keep them for you or send them on?

Mr Curtis Could I possibly ask you to send them on, please?

Receptionist Yes, of course.

Mr Curtis Thank you very much. Can I just give you my address?

4 Shop assistant Good afternoon. Can I help you?

Customer Yes, could you just take a look at my watch? It's stopped.

Shop assistant Hmm. Yes. The battery's probably dead. How old is the watch?

Customer I've had it for a couple of years, I suppose.

Shop assistant Oh well, the battery needs replacing, then. Do you want a new one putting in?

Customer Yes, please.

Shop assistant OK. It won't take a minute.

5 Garage mechanic Good morning. What can I do for you?

Mr Morris Hello. I wonder if you could take a look at my car? I've had a bit of a bump and dented the back of it.

Garage mechanic Oh dear. How did that happen?

Mr Morris I backed into a wall. Very silly. I wasn't concentrating.

Garage mechanic Hmm. Yes. Well, it happens to us all. It'll need repairing and repainting. Do you want it doing today?

Mr Morris Yes, if possible.

Garage mechanic OK, but it won't be ready till tomorrow.

Mr Morris That's OK.

🔊 **11.6**

1 You live at number 18 Green Street.
No, we live at number 25 Green Street.
2 Sally's birthday is in July.
No, Sally's birthday is in August.
3 The meeting's at 10.30.
No, the meeting's at 11.30.
4 Colin drives a Porsche.
No, Colin drives a Ferrari.
5 We went to a disco on Friday.
No, we went to the movies on Friday.

🔊 **11.7**

Mandy Are you ready to go through the diary for today?

Joe Yes. OK.

Mandy Well, first there are several letters on your desk that need signing. Then from 9.30 to 10.30 you've got a meeting with John Clark from KRP. He's already arrived.

Joe Uh-huh.

Mandy At 10.30 there's the regular monthly meeting of the finance committee.

Joe When does that finish?

Mandy At 12.00. Then Sheila Gordon is coming over about the new offices. She wants to discuss the new designs with you.

Joe Does that have to be today?

Mandy Well, it seems so. We're the only department that hasn't chosen the colours and furniture and so on. So we've been holding everything up.

Joe All right.

Mandy That will probably take till 1.00. And we were supposed to be going over to see the building some time today, too. Then at 1.00 you'll be having lunch with the Managing Director.

Joe Oh, yes. He wants to discuss next week's meeting. 'We don't want a repeat of last year, do we, Joe?' Oh dear.

Mandy Then we've set aside this afternoon for writing the annual report. The deadline is 5 o'clock, if we're to get it out in time for the Directors' meeting next week.

Joe I hate that job. It always takes at least three hours.

Mandy And you're leaving at 5.00 promptly today.

Joe Yes, it's my son's birthday party.

Mandy Well, you can't miss that. It's … is something wrong, Joe?

Joe No, I've just been getting some pains in my chest lately, that's all. It's probably nothing.

Mandy You should see a doctor.

Joe When do I get the chance? The surgery is only open till 1.00.

Mandy Well, you shouldn't take chances with your health. Oh, I'm afraid we need to fit something else in today. Samantha phoned just now. She wants to see you today about getting a new assistant.

Joe But she knows the policy on new posts.

Mandy Well, yes, but she says she's got too much work for one person and …

Joe Yes?

Mandy And if you don't see her today, she'll resign. And I think she means it this time, Joe.

Joe Oh dear! Well, when …

Male voice Sorry to disturb you, but we've just had this urgent fax for Mr Hill.

🔊 **11.8**

Marcia Hello 87549.

Joe Hello, Marcia.

Marcia Hello, darling. This is a nice surprise.

Joe Well, actually I've got a problem. I've had this urgent fax from Brussels. They want me to go out there this afternoon.

Marcia But it's Donald's birthday party and you promised you'd be there this year. You remember how upset he was when you missed it last year.

Joe I know, but we may lose an important contract if I don't go.

Marcia Well, what time will you be back?

Joe Tomorrow morning, I imagine.

Marcia What? Oh, this is the limit, Joe. You know I'm going to the BCI Conference tomorrow and you said that you'd take Donald and Sarah to school and pick them up.

Joe Oh no. I'd forgotten about that. Can't you get someone else to take them?

Marcia It doesn't matter. I should have known better than to rely on you in the first place.

Joe Marcia. … Marcia! Oh damn.

🔊 **11.9**

Presenter Joe has one main problem. He has too much to do. It's a common problem that we all have at some time in our lives. How should you deal with this problem? Well, there are three things that you must decide:
1 What are my priorities?
2 What can I delegate? What can or should be done by someone else?
3 Are other people making unreasonable demands?
So let's see how Joe deals with the situation in the light of these questions.

Joe Right then, Mandy. I've had a think about today. This is what we're going to do.

Mandy OK. I'll get the diary.

Joe Now. I've got to see John Clark, because he's already here. But the finance meeting and the meeting with Sheila Gordon … Colin can deal with those. He's learning the ropes and the best way to do that is to take responsibility.

Mandy Right. I'll phone him.

Joe So I'm now free after 10.30?

Mandy That's right.

Joe Now my first priority is to stay alive. So I want you to make an appointment at the doctor's about these pains in my chest, please.

Mandy Very sensible.

Joe Then after that, could you ask Samantha to come and see me? We can't lose her so I must see her.

Mandy But what are you going to say to her about the new post?

Joe I'll promise to put her request for a new post to the Directors' meeting next week. I hope that will keep her happy.

Mandy What about Belgium?

Joe Well, I've promised my wife and children that I will be there this evening, so I'm going to keep that promise and I need to keep the Directors happy. So it's very important that I have lunch with the Managing Director and that I write the annual report. But I think Colin can help me with that.

Mandy So what about the Alitrain contract?

Joe Well, I think Alitrain are being unreasonable. If their new chap wants to speak to me, he shouldn't leave it to the last minute. You can't do business like that. So I think that's it. Could you get me the Belgium office on the phone, please?

Mandy Yes, of course. Oh, what about going over to see the new building?

Joe Oh, that can wait. I'll go and see it tomorrow.

Unit 12

🔊 **12.2**

Mike Have you heard any more about Ken and Pauline?

Isobel Oh, yes. Well, I met Pauline the other day and she told me that they were back together again.

Mike Did she tell you how it happened?

Isobel Well, it seems it was Pauline's mother that did it.

Mike Pauline's mother?

Isobel Yes, well, Pauline went over to see her parents, because she was feeling upset about it all. She told her mother all about it and she thought that her mum would understand.

Mike But she didn't.

Isobel No, apparently she told Pauline not to be so silly. It wasn't worth splitting up with him over that.

Mike So did Pauline go and make it up with Ken?

Isobel Oh, no. She didn't tell Ken that she had been to her parents. She just waited till he phoned again and then she said that he could come back, if he promised not to do it again.

Mike   And did he promise?

Isobel   Oh yes, and he bought her loads of flowers and asked her if she wanted to go on holiday!

Mike   But he still doesn't know what Pauline's mum told her?

Isobel   No, so don't tell him, will you?

Mike   No, of course not. I wouldn't do a thing like that.

🖭 12.3

Good evening. Here is the news at 6.00 p.m.

The Transport Minister, Mark Lloyd, has resigned. In a brief statement from his family home this morning he said that he was resigning for personal reasons. The resignation comes after reports in several newspapers that Mr Lloyd had had an affair with his secretary. Mr Lloyd has denied the reports. This morning he said that he just wanted to spend more time with his family.

The Prime Minister is attending the World Conference on the Environment. The conference president, Dr Sami Rambuka, told the conference that the world was running out of time to solve the problems of the environment. He asked countries to put the interests of the Earth before their own national interests.

The computer company, K. B. Grant, plans to open a new factory in Wales. The Managing Director, Judy Forster, said that the new factory would create up to 300 new jobs. She added that if the business software market continued to expand, even more jobs could be expected.

Figures released today show that inflation fell slightly last month from 3.8% to 3.6%. The Chancellor of the Exchequer, Jack Tinker, said that the government was continuing to keep inflation under control. For the opposition, however, Sally Walker said that inflation was still too high and the government was not doing enough to get it down.

A prisoner has escaped from Ford prison. The prison governor, Colin Richardson, said that Frank Selwyn, who is serving 12 years for armed robbery, had escaped at about 2 o'clock this afternoon by hiding in a builder's lorry. He said that Selwyn was dangerous and anyone seeing him should call the police immediately.

American TV star, Angie Fellows, is getting married for the second time. Miss Fellows announced the news at lunchtime today. She said that she and her fiancé, up-and-coming actor Emilio Shaw, were very happy, and they were both looking forward to the wedding, which would be on June 8.

And finally a story of an extraordinary journey. A racing pigeon from Scotland turned up recently in Canada, over 3,000 miles away. The pigeon is now back home with its owner, Eddie Forbes. Mr Forbes said he didn't think that the bird had actually flown across the Atlantic. He thought it had probably landed on a ship.

That's it. Now here's Carla Green with the weather forecast.

🖭 12.7

Presenter   Mountaineer Chris Fordam has visited the Himalayas several times, but on his next expedition, to the peak of Menlungtse, he plans to do more than just climb a mountain. He's going to look for the Yeti.

Fordam   Yes, I firmly believe that the Yeti exists, and I'm not the only one. Several people have seen it. In 1948 two geologists said that they had been chased by two huge ape-like creatures. They said that they had shot and

wounded one and that the other one had attacked them. There have been reports of Yeti sightings throughout the Himalayan mountains. It is a huge area with few people and many parts are virtually impossible for people to get to. So there are many isolated valleys and forests where the Yeti could live and hunt for food.

Presenter   But where's the evidence? Well, there isn't much. In 1951 a climber, Eric Shipton, took photographs of some enormous footprints in the snow. He claimed that they were the footprints of the Yeti. Mike Wooldridge took a photograph of something that he claimed was the Yeti, but the picture is very unclear. It could just be a rock. Fordam himself took photographs of some footprints on a previous expedition.

Fordam   I've seen footprints and taken photos of them. When I asked the local people in Tibet what the footprints were, they immediately said it was the Yeti. They all believe that the Yeti exists.

Presenter   But when he asked whether any of the people had actually seen the creature, they said they hadn't. It was always a cousin's friend's brother who said he had seen it. Sceptics say that the stories are just superstition. The footprints are made by falling rocks and the creatures that people say they have seen are just bears. But Chris Fordam is determined to try and find the creature. If he succeeds, then we will know that the stories were correct. Of course if he doesn't find it it won't mean that the Yeti *doesn't* exist. That's the whole point of these mysteries. You can never prove that they are wrong.

Unit 13

🖭 13.1

If Ted hadn't had an argument with his boss, he wouldn't have lost his job.

If he hadn't lost his job, he wouldn't have gone for long walks every day.

If he hadn't gone for long walks every day, he wouldn't have found someone's bag.

If he hadn't found the bag, he wouldn't have got a reward for returning it.

If he hadn't got a reward, he wouldn't have bought a lottery ticket.

If he hadn't bought a lottery ticket, he wouldn't have won $8 million.

If he hadn't won $8 million, he wouldn't have bought the company where he used to work.

If he hadn't bought the company, he couldn't have sacked the boss!

🖭 13.3

1 A   Hello. Did you have a good holiday?

B   Well, yes and no.

A   Why? What was the problem?

B   My wallet was stolen.

A   No! That's a bit rough. How did that happen?

B   Oh, we stopped at this market and I was just sitting in the car when some people – a man and a woman, it was – came up. I thought they were selling things. Well, like a fool, I'd put my wallet on the dashboard. Anyway, these people came up to the car, and while I was talking to the man, the woman put her hand in and grabbed the wallet.

A   Goodness me! What did you do?

B   There wasn't much I could do. I was stunned. They just ran off into the crowd. Well, I reported it to the police, but they weren't much help.

A   Was there much money in it?

B   Yes, quite a bit, and my credit cards. But it was my own fault. I shouldn't have put it on the dashboard where people could see it. If

I'd left it in my pocket, as I usually do, it wouldn't have happened.

A   Well, I hope it didn't spoil your holiday too much. Actually it reminds me of when we were on holiday a couple of years ago and …

2 A   Hello. I haven't seen you around for a while. Have you been away?

B   Yes, we've been skiing in the States.

A   Oh yes, I remember you telling me you were going. Was it good?

B   Well, it was until the last few days.

A   Why? What happened?

B   Well, Tina decided that she wanted to have a go at snowboarding. You know this thing where you stand on, like a board.

A   Yes, I know.

B   Well, I thought it was a bit dodgy, but she wanted to do it. You know what kids are like. So she did. Well, anyway, she fell off and broke her arm.

A   Oh no. Poor Tina. Was she all right?

B   Yes, she was OK. The ambulance took her to the hospital and they dealt with it. But then when I came to pay, I found that our insurance didn't cover us for snowboarding – only for skiing.

A   Blimey! So what did you do?

B   Well, what could I do? I had to pay for everything myself. It cost me an arm and a leg! You know what medical costs are like in the States.

A   I hear they're rather expensive.

B   You're telling me! Well, I suppose I should have checked the insurance policy before she went snowboarding, but I blame the insurance company. I mean lots of people go snowboarding these days.

A   Well, funnily enough, something similar happened to a friend of mine. His son wanted to go snowboarding and …

3 A   Hi. Welcome back. Have you had a good time?

B   Well, we did when we finally got there.

A   What do you mean?

B   Well, we only missed the flight, didn't we?

A   No! How did you manage that?

B   We got stuck in a traffic jam on the way to the airport and by the time we got there the flight had already left.

A   Oh dear.

B   It was all John's fault. We should have set off earlier. But you know what he's like – everything at the last minute. I mean, it would have been all right if the road had been clear, but it wasn't, so …

A   So what happened?

B   Well, the tour company got us on another flight later in the day. So we had to wait for 12 hours at the airport and then when we arrived it was too late to get to our hotel. So we had to book into another hotel at the airport for the night.

A   But you got there in the end?

B   Yes, but I was not in too good a mood by then, I can tell you.

A   I'm not surprised. We missed a flight once, but it wasn't because of the traffic. We …

🖭 13.8

Happy Birthday, dear. I've knitted this for you.
(*Thinks*) Oh no! Not another ghastly jumper.
Oh, thank you. It's lovely, and just what I wanted.

Where is the money?
(*Thinks*) I stole the money, but I know you can't prove it.
Look. I'm telling you. I didn't steal that money.

Two very different situations, but they have something in common. Neither person is telling the truth. But are they both lying? What is a lie? Why do we tell them? Wouldn't life be easier if everyone told the truth all the time? Well, as our examples show, no. It may sound strange, but lying, or rather the ability to deceive other people, is an essential part of life.

When we tell a lie, we are trying to deceive someone. We are trying to make someone think or feel something that they would not otherwise think or feel. In other words, lying is about manipulating someone else's thoughts or feelings. However, so are many other parts of life. If we couldn't manipulate other people's thoughts and feelings, life as we know it would be impossible.

Most sport, for example, is based on deception. The footballer who is taking a penalty kick wants to make the goalkeeper think that he's going to shoot into the right hand side of the net, when in fact he intends to put it into the left hand corner. Entertainment, too, depends on deception. We know that the people on the stage aren't really Julius Caesar and Cleopatra. We know that vampires don't really exist. We let ourselves be deceived. Indeed, in many cases we want to be deceived. The conjuror's tricks, the comedian's jokes, the film-maker's special effects are all forms of deception.

Think about everyday life. What would it really be like, if we had to tell the absolute truth every time? What would that do to courtship, family life, advertising? Could we still tell children about Father Christmas? If your partner cooked an awful dinner, would it really be best to actually say that it was awful? Deception is a natural part of life. We need to get other people to do things all the time, and so we naturally manipulate their thoughts and feelings by not telling the truth, or by telling only part of the truth. The question is, when does not telling the whole truth become a lie?

Unit 14
🔊 14.1
The luggage arrived and I walked out into the arrivals hall. When I looked around I couldn't see Eric anywhere. I started to panic. Then I saw him walking towards me. We kissed and hugged and it was as if I had never been away.

Eric had six months of his contract in Tanzania left. Though we were living in one of the poorest parts of one of the poorest countries in the world, they were the happiest six months of my life. At night we would sometimes sleep on the roof. You could almost touch the stars.

At the end of the six months Eric had to return to the United States, and we flew to Texas where I met his family. One morning, we got up very early and walked to the top of a place called Enchanted Rock. At the top, while I was looking at the view, Eric asked me to marry him.

We now live in London, so I'm back where I started, but I don't regret anything. The trip was the best thing I have ever done. If I hadn't taken the chance I wouldn't have met so many wonderful people, or seen so many fascinating places. Most of all, I wouldn't have met the man of my dreams.

And now we know that we probably won't be travelling again, because I'm expecting our first child. My life is complete, and it wasn't before. I am happy now.

🔊 14.2
1 Mechanic Hello. What can I do for you?
Customer Oh, hello. I wonder if you could just take a look at the tyres on my car. I think one of the ones at the front needs replacing.

Mechanic Driver's side or passenger's side?
Customer Driver's side.
Mechanic Mmm. Yes, it definitely needs replacing. It's illegal like that.
Customer Oh dear.
Mechanic And the passenger one, too, looks a bit dodgy. If I were you, I'd have that one done, as well.
Customer Oh, I see, well, if you think they both need changing, then you'd better change them, I suppose.
Mechanic Right. Do you want them doing now? You shouldn't really use the car with them like that.
Customer Yes, all right. How long will it take?
Mechanic Oh, only about half an hour. Would you like to wait in the office, while I …

2 Receptionist Hello, Reception.
Guest Hello. This is room 234. Could I book a wake-up call for tomorrow morning, please?
Receptionist Certainly, what time would you like that for?
Guest Half past six, please.
Receptionist So that's a wake-up call for 6.30 in room 234.
Guest Yes, thank you. Could you tell me what time you start serving breakfast?
Receptionist We serve breakfast from 7 o'clock in the restaurant, but you can order breakfast in your room before 7 o'clock.
Guest Oh, I see. Seven o'clock in the restaurant, you say?
Receptionist Yes, that's right.
Guest Oh well, in that case could I possibly have the wake-up call at quarter to seven, then?
Receptionist Certainly. Six forty-five. Anything else?
Guest No thank you. Goodnight.
Receptionist Goodnight.

3 Patient Good morning.
Doctor Good morning. Do take a seat. Now, what can I do for you?
Patient Well, I've been getting a lot of headaches recently.
Doctor I see. And do you normally suffer from headaches?
Patient No, not normally.
Doctor And are there any other symptoms? I mean, do you feel sick, or anything like that?
Patient No, just a headache.
Doctor When do you get these headaches?
Patient It's usually when I've been reading or watching the telly.
Doctor Mmm. Do you wear glasses?
Patient No, I don't.
Doctor Well. Cover your left eye. Now, can you read the letters on the chart over there? Try the third line from the bottom.
Patient Erm … . H, T, P … er, or is it R … and then it's E, isn't it? That's all I can read.
Doctor Hmm. Well, I think that's probably the problem. So as a first step, I'd like you to have your eyes tested. I'll give you a letter, and you need to take this to the optician's for an appointment.
Patient Oh, right. OK.
Doctor I'm sure glasses will clear up the headaches, but if they don't, then come back and see me again.
Patient Thank you, Doctor. Goodbye.
Doctor Goodbye.

🔊 14.3
1 A Do you fancy going to a movie this evening?
  B That would be nice.
2 A Well, I suppose we'd better be going.

  B Have a safe journey. Drive carefully.
3 A By the way, I'll be calling in on the Robinsons tomorrow.
  B Please give them my regards.
4 A Could I possibly speak to Mrs Wilson, please?
  B I'm afraid she's out. Can I get her to call you back?
5 A I can't stand waiting in traffic jams.
  B Me, neither.
6 A Do you think you could give me a hand with these bags?
  B Sure. Here, let me take that one.
7 A Could you tell me where the post office is, please?
  B I'm sorry. I'm afraid I don't know.
8 A I wonder if you could help me?
  B I'll do my best. What's the problem?
9 A Do you need it doing today?
  B Yes please, if you can manage it.
10 A Do you mind if I use your phone?
  B Not at all. Help yourself.

🔊 14.6
What do the scores mean?
  According to this quiz, if you got two points or less, there is not much happiness in your life. A score of three to five shows that you have some happy moments. Six or more means that you are a happy person.
  What do your answers to the quiz mean? As the introduction to the quiz says, happy people appear to show similar characteristics. So let's look at what those characteristics are.
Question 1 Happy people like to do jobs that use their talents. This means that they get the satisfaction of doing a job well but with little stress.
Question 2 Happy people enjoy helping other people, but they are not self-sacrificing. So they will help when it is convenient and useful. People who choose **a** for this question help people because they want other people to like them. This shows a basically unhappy person.
Question 3 Happy people find it easy to go to sleep and they sleep soundly.
Question 4 Happy people generally get on well with other people, but they are not dependent on them, so they can enjoy being on their own but don't have a need for it.
Questions 5 and 8 Happy people are generally tidy and punctual, but they are not obsessive about it. Untidiness or obsessive tidiness indicate low self-esteem.
Question 6 Happy people accept their own weaknesses and are normally tolerant of other people's weaknesses, too, but they don't like cruelty, especially towards people who can't defend themselves.
Questions 7 and 9 Happy people are normally healthy and they don't hold on to negative emotions. So it's perfectly all right to get angry, but not to stay angry for a long time.
Question 10 Finally, happy people are realistic but optimistic. They accept that their life is neither perfect nor totally bad, but they also have a general feeling of progress and improvement.

143

ACKNOWLEDGEMENTS

The author would especially like to record his gratitude to his wife, Eunice,
and his children, without whose support and patience *Lifelines* would not
have been written. The author would also like to thank all those at Oxford
University Press who have contributed their skills and ideas to producing
this course.

*The publishers and author are very grateful to all the teachers and institutions
involved in reading and/or piloting Lifelines for providing invaluable comment and
feedback on the course. We would especially like to thank*: Edward Martin (CLM Bell
School, Bolzano, Italy), David Massey (Teach-in, Rome, Italy), Lindsay
McLellan (British Institute, Valencia, Spain), Juan Marcel Sánchez Martínez
(E.O.I. Alzira, Valencia, Spain), Alex Boulton (Liverdun, France), Debbie
Derrick (Scanbrit School of English, Bournemouth, UK), Amanda Jeffries
(Regent Oxford, UK), Jacek Rysiewicz (Poznan, Poland), Erika Áipli (Coventry
House, Kecskemét, Hungary).

*The publishers and author are grateful to the following for permission to use extracts
and adaptations of copyright material*: BBC *Wildlife Magazine*, for extract
from article by Sarah Cunliffe. For more information contact Friends of
Di-Di, Balikpapan Orangutan Society, c/o POB 319, Balikpapan 76103,
E. Kalimantan, Indonesia; *Focus* magazine, for extracts from articles by Ian
Nicolson: 'Ultramen' in *Focus*, May 1994, and by Robert Matthews: 'The Laws
of Freak Chance' from *Focus*, July 1996; Charles Handy, for extract from 'A
Personal Preface' in *Waiting for the Mountain to Move* (Arrow Books, 1991); IPC
Magazines, for article from *Eva*, 22 March 1995; Oxford University Press, for
extract from *The Oxford Wordpower Dictionary* (1993); The Reader's Digest
Association Limited, for material from *Marvels and Mysteries of the Human
Mind*, © 1992 The Reader's Digest; Solo Syndication/*Daily Mail*, for extracts
and adaptations of articles from the *Daily Mail* by Sean Poulter: 'What job
will suit?', 14.10.93, Sinclair McKay: 'Coincidence: Is it more than chance?',
3.11.90, Vikki Orvice: 'What's good for the heart may not be good for the
mind', 24.6.95, Tony Burton: 'A Life of Misery will not be the death of you',
11.11.93, and Ronald Singleton: 'A Thief's Lucky Day', 17.1.94; South Devon
Association of Tourist Attractions, for advertisements from the 1995
brochure; Times Newspapers Ltd, for article by Stephen Milligan:
'Lizardman leaps into US folklore' from *The Sunday Times* 7.8.88, © Times
Newspapers Ltd, 1988.

Illustrations by: Paul Dickinson, Gay Galsworthy, Lynda Gray, Ian Jackson,
Joanna Kerr, Claire Littlejohn, Henning Löhlein, Mark Oldroyd, Raymond
Turvey, Technical Graphics Dept., OUP

Location photography by: Emily Andersen, Gareth Boden, Rob Judges, Maggy
Milner

Studio photography by: Stephen Oliver

*The publishers would like to thank the following for permission to reproduce
photographs*: Allsport: Gary Newkirk; Ancient Art and Architecture; Heather
Angel; Blackpool Sands; Colorific!; Colorsport: Benjamin Sanson, Simon
Lessing; Cunliffe & Franklyn Productions Ltd; Mary Evans Picture Library;
Fortean Picture Library; Ronald Grant Archive; Sally and Richard Greenhill;
The Hutchison Library; The Image Bank; Impact: Bruce Stephens, Michael
George, Eliza Armstrong, Piers Cavendish, Colin Jones; Life File: Jeremy
Hoare, Oleg Svytoslavsky, Tony Abbot, Dave Thompson, Barry Mayes; The
Morwellham and Tamar Valley Trust; Oxford Scientific Films; Pictor
Uniphoto; Rex Features; Frank Spooner: Alain Benainous; Superstock; Sally
Ann Thompson: Animal Photography; Telegraph Colour Library; Tony
Stone: Peter Correz, Darryl Torckler, Tony Latham, Nigel Press, Tim Davis,
Jon Riley, Warren Jacobs, Gary Holscher, Lori Adamski Peek, Gary
Brettnacher, Tom Bean, Dale Durfee, Aldo Torelli, Paul Webster, Michael
Harris, Dennis O'Clair, G Brad Lewis, Stuart McClymont, Howard Grey,
Chris Windsor, Terry Vine, Bob Thomas, David Joel, Bruce Ayres, Mark
Junak; Joanna Verkerk; Woodlands Leisure Park; Zefa Pictures

Song: Johnny B Goode © 1958 Chuck Berry Arc Music Corp By kind permission
of Jewel Music Publishing Company Ltd.

The publishers would like to thank the following for permission to reproduce cartoons:
Exley Publications Ltd, the *Spectator* and Deirdre McDonald Books.

The publishers would like to thank the following for their time and assistance: Ardi,
Oxford; The Jericho Café, Oxford; Café Rouge, Oxford; Oxford United
Football Club; Thame Police Station; Thames Trains